D0856887

AMERICA IN THE SIXTIES

AMERICA IN THE TWENTIETH CENTURY

John Robert Greene, *Series Editor*

Other titles in America in the Twentieth Century

AMERICA
IN THE
SIXTIES

John Robert Greene

SYRACUSE UNIVERSITY PRESS

BAKER COLLEGE OF CLINTON TWP

Copyright © 2010 by Syracuse University Press
Syracuse, New York 13244-5290

All Rights Reserved

First Edition 2010
10 11 12 13 14 15   6 5 4 3 2 1

∞ The paper used in this publication meets the minimum requirements of the
American National Standard for Information Sciences—Permanence of Paper
for Printed Library Materials, ANSI Z39.48-1992.

For a listing of books published and distributed by Syracuse University Press,
visit our Web site at SyracuseUniversityPress.syr.edu.

ISBN (cloth): 978-0-8156-3276-4
ISBN (pbk.): 978-0-8156-3221-4

Library of Congress Cataloging-in-Publication Data
Greene, John Robert, 1955–
America in the sixties / John Robert Greene. — 1st ed.
p. cm. — (America in the twentieth century)
Includes bibliographical references and index.
ISBN 978-0-8156-3276-4 (cloth : alk. paper) —
ISBN 978-0-8156-3221-4 (pbk. : alk. paper)
1. United States—History—1961–1969. 2. United States—Social conditions—
1960–1980. 3. Social movements—United States—History—20th century.
4. Kennedy, John F. (John Fitzgerald), 1917–1963—Influence. 5. Civil rights
movements—United States—History—20th century. 6. Feminism—United States—
History—20th century. 7. Vietnam War, 1961–1975—Social aspects—United States.
8. Counterculture—United States—History—20th century. 9. Nineteen sixties. I. Title.
E841.G65 2010
973.92—dc22   2010027770

Manufactured in the United States of America

For Patty, T. J., Chris, and Mary Rose

and for Julia K. Ruse, Dorothy Harrington,
John P. Gensler, Frank Sacco, Myron Kotch,
Peter Marron, Nicholas Amato, Louis Leotta,
Edward Eckert, and Patrick O'Dea . . .
who showed me where I belonged.

John Robert Greene is the Paul J. Schupf Professor of History and Humanities at Cazenovia College, where he has taught for the past thirty years. Dr. Greene's teaching and writing specialty lies in American political history, particularly the American presidency. He has written or edited seventeen books, including one on the election of Dwight Eisenhower, one on the Nixon presidency, three on the Ford presidency, a biography of Betty Ford, and a critically acclaimed study, *The Presidency of George H. W. Bush*. He serves as an associate editor for the journal *Congress and the Presidency* and edits the America in the Twentieth Century Series for Syracuse University Press, of which this book is a part. He is a regular commentator in the national media, having appeared on such forums as MSNBC, National Public Radio, C-SPAN, the History Channel, and the Public Broadcasting System. In other lives, he was a radio disc jockey and played in a very bad small rock band.

Contents

Foreword

JOHN ROBERT GREENE

"THERE JUST NEVER SEEMS TO BE ENOUGH TIME"—"The textbook is so bland, the students won't read it"—"Don't *teachers* ever write?"—"If I could only find more than one book that I feel good about assigning."

These are several of the complaints endemic to those of us who teach survey American history courses. The book series America in the Twentieth Century was designed to address these issues in a novel fashion that attempts to meet the needs of both student and instructor alike. Using decades for its organizational schema (admittedly a debatable choice, but it is our experience that chronology, not theme, makes for a better survey course), each book tackles the main issues of its time in a fashion at once readable and scholarly in nature. Authors are chosen by the editor of this series primarily for their teaching skills—indeed, each book proposal was accompanied by syllabi that showed the prospective author's course pedagogy. In fact, contributors have been urged to write these books from their lecture notes and limit footnote references that can often distract or intimidate the student-reader. In a departure from virtually every textbook series of note, one member of our editorial board is a presently sitting college student, whose comments on the manuscript may well be the most helpful of all. Each chapter ends with a recommended reading list, representing the author's favorite books as they would recommend them to their students. It is, admittedly, not an exhaustive list, but no list of our favorite works *is*.

The result is a readable, concise, and scholarly series of books from master teachers who know what works in the college classroom. We offer it to college instructors and their students in hopes that they will, in the words of the Latin maxim, do the one thing that we all hope in the academy that professor and student will do together; *Tolle et Lege*—"Take and Read."

Preface

THERE ARE FEW EVENTS more boring than an academic conference. To be sure, professional historians get to travel on their college's dime, meet other historians from around the country, and, at the book exhibits, get to scarf up dozens of free books. But the sessions—academics droning their dense, over-footnoted paper to a virtually empty room—remind one of an 8:00 A.M. class with the proverbial professor who talks to himself. Truth in advertising—early in my career, I read many such papers to many such conferences; my vita grew, but as I reflect on it, few of those conference performances were any good. I stopped going to them.

However, the 2008 meeting of the Organization of American Historians was held in my backyard—in New York City. I could not resist. Early in the conference, there were no surprises—at my first session, a teacher repeatedly referred to himself as a "genius" for guiding high school students through a History Day assignment. I got up and left, and went to the book fair. But, ever hopeful, I circled a session on my program—the last one for the day, and a plenary session—"Storm Warnings: Rethinking 1968, The Year That Shook the World." There was hope—one of the presenters, Michael Kazin of Georgetown University, is one of the most thoughtful analysts of America in the 1960s, and his panel would be speaking to an overflow crowd in the largest ballroom in the New York Hilton Hotel.

The beginning of the session was uninspiring; I began to plan my exit. But then, things picked up. The second presenter referred in an excited voice to recent scholarship on America in the 1960s as representing a "revolution in modern American historiography." To him, scholars were only now, in the first decade of the twenty-first century, taking the 1960s seriously as subject matter. He was excited, and so was the rest of the panel. So was the audience.

They applauded, laughed, and in general gave nonverbal testimony in favor of the panel's overall thesis—that the sixties were now worth our time.

This was worth thinking about. After all, I have written on and taught about the 1960s for almost thirty years. The subject matter always energized me. To me, it was the last time things *mattered,* the last time debates were *real* and not scripted for cable, and the last time the country *cared.* As I listened to the panelists, I began to think about my students. Even in my class on the 1960s, when I have egotistically considered myself to be at my best with great material (as the great comedian Jack Benny said, anyone can be funny if he has a good writer), I had to admit to myself that my students in the 1980s and 1990s approached five months of reading on the 1960s with the same glazed-over attitude that they did their survey courses. To them, the sixties were nothing special. But then it occurred to me that in the week preceding my attendance at this convention, a rather sizable cohort of my upperclassmen had been in my office, asking me when I was going to run my sixties class again. They seemed sincere and said they wanted to read about Kennedy and civil rights (the two subjects they mentioned without prodding). They seemed energized by the prospect of studying the sixties—maybe the convention panel was on to something. I began to think and jot down some notes—if there was in 2008 a new desire on the part of professional historians to *write* about the 1960s and, more important, if there is a new desire on the part of bright young minds to *study* the 1960s, why *is* that?

I begin to answer that question with an observation that may be interpreted as an insult by students who have taken my courses in the past, but it is one I am prepared to defend with three decades of classroom experience— the college students of the 1980s and 1990s were the dramatic opposite of the students of the 1960s. The more modern students largely disassociated themselves from social causes, concentrated on immediate financial reward rather than intellectual gain as a reason for going to college, and in short found the experiences of students in the 1960s to be completely irrelevant to their experience. Many things conspired to lead to this result: the return of conservative thought in the 1980s; the general disenchantment with civic life; the rise of a Clintonian "Third Way" that was completely uninspiring; the rise of the Yuppie as the gold standard of American society; the dumbing-down of high school "history" (read, "Social Studies" courses); the decline of reading in general. All this led to those glazed-over looks when I would argue that there was, indeed, a time, in postwar America, when public and private life was exciting.

Since the turn of the century, however, college students have come into the history classroom with a decided, and noticeable, gleam in their eye. The attacks of September 11, 2001, and the subsequent Wars on Terror played key roles in this change—students are now exposed to an America at war in ways that their immediate predecessors, who experienced only a handful of quick and painless surgical strikes—were not. Perhaps as a result of this awareness, they have become *political* again. They represent *both* the Right and the Left with a passion that the students of the eighties and the nineties simply did not have—even those students who found themselves enamored of Reaganism. They are, once again, critical of what they are told. Brought up on a media that savages the establishment, and Internet blogs that offer hourly opinions on everything, they are questioning, often thoughtful consumers of ideas. Today's students are also demanding a post-Clinton morality in politics and, as evidenced in the presidential contest of 2008, are beginning to vote in larger numbers. Most important, a large number of today's students are social activists. They build houses on their spring breaks, accrue credits for community experience, take the campus newspaper seriously, and articulate themselves better. They are organizers, planners, and doers; they join more social action clubs than their predecessors and that stay the course in those organizations. The students once again *care;* no *wonder* they are drawn to the 1960s. They are, in many respects, the "New, *New* Left."

I have been energized about the 1960s for my entire career. I knew I would enjoy writing about an electric era that I loved to speak about. I hope that I have accomplished part of that goal. If I have not, blame me, not the material. But after some reflection about students past and present, I have a new hope for this book—that twenty-first-century students will look at this book's title and want to read it.

It is impossible to thank everyone who helps a writer to write. We try to do so, however, because writers know (as nonwriters don't seem to) that writing is not a solitary effort; few of us write under our bedcovers by flashlight and then have our manuscripts whisked off to Pulitzer-land. Our work is very largely, to borrow a phrase that helped define a substantial portion of the sixties, a communal effort.

Thanks goes to Indiana University Press and to Syracuse University Press for their gracious permission to reprint selections from several of my previous books in this one (specific credit is given in the text).

Professor Melvin Small of Wayne State University was kind enough to read the manuscript and give me the benefit of his knowledge of the period.

Students in my classes on the 1960s, as well as several advanced undergraduates, have read chapters from this volume over the years, and offered salient criticisms and additions. I thank Eric Bird, Kari Cadrette, Whitney Evans, Jessica Hanley, Mara Hogan, Katrina Iaconis, Jenna Lipiska, Adam Lonkey, Andrea Medici, Shannon O'Leary, Melissa Ozimek Purcell, Christine Parry, Jessica Robillard, Abby Rose, Shannon Skavis, Kaleb Wilson, and Mara Yuzwak. Allison Hoffman served as an excellent research assistant, particularly on the chapter on the culture of the decade. Shannon Torgersen served in many areas of this project—as a research assistant, a typist, and an editor. She read the entire manuscript and offered many excellent observations.

The faculty and staff of All Saints Elementary School (Syracuse, N.Y.) deserve a special note of thanks and praise as colleagues who do extraordinary work every day in an educational labor of love. They—and especially Principal Rosalie Pollman—inspire me.

I have great friends and colleagues at Cazenovia College; they contribute to my ability to write—and help me create the time to do so—in myriad ways.

This is the fifth manuscript of mine that has been edited by D. J. Whyte. Each time, she has made the manuscript into a vastly improved book.

Yet without the efforts of three people, this project would not have been completed. Mary Selden Evans of Syracuse University Press has been a nurturing colleague. She has believed not just in this volume, but in the entire series, from the beginning—and she continues to believe. Andrea Mintonye of Cazenovia College is not just a superb typist with the skills of a critical reader, although she is, indeed, that. She is also a good friend whose inspired humor and balance kept me writing. And Professor Andrew Dunar of the University of Alabama at Huntsville deserves a special note of gratitude. He read every word, commented on every line, pointed out every logical lapse, and helped me turn my manuscript into a book. He is a good writer, and his efforts made me a better writer.

My entire family lets me write; moreover, they think my writing is important.

Recommended Reading

There are simply too many general books, articles, and other writings on American in the 1960s to list usefully here. Rather, let me credit, and recommend, the four general treatments of the decade that were always within arm's reach while I was writing this book: Terry H. Anderson, *The Sixties,* 3d ed. (New York: Pearson Longman, 2007); Alexander Bloom and Wini Breines, ed. *Takin' It to the Streets: A Sixties Reader* (New York: Oxford Univ. Press, 1995); Maurice Isserman and Michael Kazin, *America Divided: The Civil War of the 1960's,* 2d ed. (New York: Oxford Univ. Press, 2004); and Douglas T. Miller, *On Our Own: Americans in the Sixties* (Lexington, Mass.: D. C. Heath, 1996). Each succeeding chapter will be followed by brief recommendations for further reading—or, in some cases, viewing or listening.

AMERICA IN THE SIXTIES

1

Comfort and Crisis

The 1950s

WILLIAM MCGUIRE "BILL" BRYSON was born in Des Moines, Iowa, in 1951.
He would go on to become a prolific author, writing travel books, books on
the English language, and the prize-winning *Short History of Nearly Everything*.[1] But in the 1950s he was a charter member of the post–World War II
baby-boom generation, when an estimated seventy-eight million babies were
born between 1946 and 1960. Like most baby boomers, Bryson looks back
on growing up in the fifties with a sentimental fondness. In his hilarious and
prescient memoir *The Life and Times of the Thunderbolt Kid* (named after the
alter-ego Bryson took for himself after watching a few too many space-action
shows on that brand new gadget, the television), Bryson waxed nostalgic for
what he felt was a simpler, safer, and gentler time—what a later television
show based on the 1950s would call "Happy Days":

> I can't imagine there has ever been a more gratifying time or place to be
> alive than America in the 1950s. . . . By 1951 . . . almost 90 percent of
> American families had refrigerators, and nearly three-quarters had washing
> machines, telephones, vacuum cleaners, and gas or electric stoves. . . . No
> wonder people were happy. Suddenly they were able to have the things they
> never dreamed of having, and they couldn't believe their luck.

The Thunderbolt Kid and his fellow boomers were, indeed, lucky. Mired
in depression and war for the better part of two decades, Americans were

---

1. New York: Broadway Books, 2004.

now, finally, comfortable. The economy was certainly booming. Average family income rose from $3,000 in 1947 to $5,200 in 1957, and the gross national product (GNP) rose from $200 billion in 1945 to $500 billion in 1960. The most rapid economic growth came in the first part of the decade, thanks to expenditures from the Korean War; the economic decline toward the end of the decade was slight, but it would prove to be ammunition for the 1960 Kennedy campaign.

As a result of the bulging economy, more and more Americans could partake of the proverbial "American Dream"—the desire, long deferred by depression and war, to advance one's social and economic status. For many, this meant a final abandonment of cities that had become overcrowded, filthy, and chaotic, and a move to the outlying suburbs. The 1950s saw a suburban revolution—by 1968, one-third of the nation's total population lived in the suburbs. Suburban growth rested on the ability of most postwar families to buy a car, a newfound ability to afford a home (Federal Home Loan policies and the GI Bill made them ultra-affordable), and the creation of superhighways that linked workplaces in the city with a home far away from that workplace.

For other Americans, the new prosperity meant the ability to fill that suburban home with stuff—stuff that most families of the 1950s could not remember being able to afford. The number-one consumer item of the 1950s was the television set—in 1947, fourteen thousand families had one; by 1957, ten million families had one. The social consequences of staring for hours at what Federal Communications Commission (FCC) chairman Newton Minow would call a "vast wasteland" of programming would not become an issue until the next decade. In the 1950s, television provided a way to spend more leisure time than middle-class families were used to having in the much more Spartan existence of the 1930s and 1940s. They also had time to acquire and enjoy a plethora of other consumer goods: electric refrigerators; washing machines; dishwashers; prepared foods (including the infamous "TV dinner"—instantly heatable and presented in a flimsy aluminum tray, which seemed to negate the need for the dishwasher, but little matter); FM radio; automatic transmissions. . . . America in the 1950s had indeed, in the words of the economist John Kenneth Galbraith, become an "affluent society."

But not for all Americans. Galbraith was no cheerleader for what America became in the 1950s—his 1958 book instead criticized that society, pointing out that as white, middle-class America raced to affluence, it continued an American tradition of ignoring those who by virtue of their race, gender, or economic status could not compete. Between 1945 and 1965, only 1 percent of the government-insured homes built went to blacks. That actually mattered little—local zoning laws kept blacks from even *thinking* about moving to the suburbs. And the poor did, indeed, get poorer. During the decade, more than one-fifth of the nation lived below the poverty line, and the cities, which had lost most of their wealthy residents to the suburbs, no longer had the funds to combat the problem adequately.

Many intellectuals writing in the 1950s argued, then, that the affluence found in American society had become less defensible. Sociologist David Riesman described the members of the culture of affluence as a "lonely crowd," one that had become shallower, more worried about approval, and more desirous of conforming than *thinking* about their existence. The fiction of many writers pointed out this same tendency to conform. The classic expression of this feeling in the literature of the period was J. D. Salinger's *Catcher in the Rye* (1951), whose protagonist, Holden Caulfield, came to the conclusion that the whole adult world was so phony that there was no escape—except through mental illness. The artists of those who pronounced American society "beat"—writers such as Jack Kerouac, who escaped the affluent society by going *On the Road* (1957), and poet Allen Ginsberg—began a rebellion against what would soon be termed "straight society" that would startle America in the following decade. Indeed, Ginsberg's influential 1956 poem "America" would prove to be remarkably prophetic:

America I've given you all and now I'm nothing. . . .
America when will we end the human war? . . .
Your machinery is too much for me. . . .
There must be some other way to settle this argument. . . .
I smoke marijuana every chance I get. . . .
America you don't really want to go to war. . . .
The Russia wants to eat us alive. . . .
America this is quite serious.
America this is the impression I get from looking in the television set.
America is this correct? . . .
It's true I don't want to join the Army . . .

Moreover, the new affluence was stifling women. The majority of men and women in the 1950s had never known such family affluence; as children of the Great Depression, many of them had not known basic family stability. It is not surprising that they wanted for themselves a steady, traditional family environment. Women who had taken jobs in heavy industry during the war as "Rosie the Riveters" would be pressured to give up their jobs and return to the home. Not that much pressure was necessary—many women voluntarily left the workforce, seeking the same family permanence as were the men returning from war. Once a semblance of stability and affluence had been achieved, however, and once their children were of school age, middle-class women became restless. Some returned to the workforce—most in the traditionally female domains of clerical help, health care, and teaching, and all for decidedly lower wages than their nearest male counterparts.

But whether they stayed at home or worked outside the home, societal pressures—particularly mass-market advertising—were brought to bear on women to remain traditional housewives. In virtually every ad for every product, women were treated as mistresses of the kitchen and the princesses of the home. In one of the most telling photos of the 1950s, published in *Life* magazine, the viewer sees rows of automobiles waiting at a suburban train stop to pick up commuters returning home from work. The women who had driven those cars to the station have all moved over to the passenger seats—so that their men can drive them home. On television, there were few images of working women—the ever present "Mom" of *Leave It to Beaver* and *Ozzie and Harriet* reigned supreme. One exception was comedian Lucille Ball, who attempted in each week's episode of *I Love Lucy* to wheedle her way into her husband's band. It is notable that her attempts were cast as farce, and that she never succeeded. There was an equal paradox about sex. On the one hand, societal pressures to marry and have several children were overwhelming, to the point where many small all-female colleges openly billed that they taught their students the social graces needed to "catch a man." On the other hand, the statistics-laden works of psychologist Alfred Kinsey (*Sexual Behavior in the Human Male,* 1948; *Sexual Behavior in the American Female,* 1953) clearly showed that young Americans practiced various forms of sex—premarital, homosexual, and what Kinsey labeled as "perverted."

Thus, women were faced with conflicting demands. On the one hand, a male-centered society wanted women as housewives. On the other hand, they had grown out of the role during World War II and were having difficulty returning to that role in the postwar period. The majority of women resolved this tension by remaining housewives. Yet this choice left many housewives feeling unfulfilled, lonely, and guilt-ridden. These feelings of entrapment often led to real physical maladies—headaches, menstrual problems, and clinical depression. For many, alcohol and drug abuse was a socially acceptable cover for their ailments. For many others, there was a feeling that even beyond the job market there must be more. It was a yearning that they could not identify when interviewed about their lives; they were being pursued by a personal crisis that one of the most influential intellectuals of the twentieth century would soon term "the problem that has no name."

In the 1950s most Americans ignored these critics. Indeed, most of America did not question affluence and instead celebrated its escape from depression and war. However, one area of American life—the turbulent relationship between the races—refused to accept the status quo; its explosion in the South challenged some of the nation's fundamental beliefs about itself and threatened to throw the nation into a second war within.

If the hula hoop represented for many critics the nature of American society in the 1950s—moving fast, in a circle, and going nowhere—another symbol of the 1950s—the missile—might well represent the civil rights movement in the South. Explosive, surprisingly fast, soaring to unexpected heights, those who confronted the racist terrorism of the South did so in a manner that, for the first time since the Civil War, brought the issue of racial equality to a national audience. With a television now in virtually every home, those who confronted this evil tried to do so in front of a camera. As a result, white America could no longer ignore racism as an isolated, local issue—it had, by 1960, become an issue of the national conscience. This was what "movement" meant—confronting evil on a mass scale and demanding for black Americans the immediate and full protection of the law, protection that had been promised under the Fourteenth Amendment and ratified in 1868.

By the 1950s, black Americans were ready for movement. During World War II, almost one million blacks served in uniform, in both the European and Pacific Theaters of Operation. They would return home—as did all combat veterans—changed people, ready to stand up to racist demagogues as they had stood up to Hitler, Mussolini, and Tojo. The gains made by blacks on the home front ennobled their cause. Between 1940 and 1944, the number of blacks employed in manufacturing and processing had increased from 50,000 to about 1.2 million, bringing with it the rise of a black middle class that was better suited for organization and protest than any preceding generation. Established interest groups like the Congress of Racial Equality (CORE) and the National Association for the Advancement of Colored People (NAACP) began to push harder.

There were victories. The summer of 1947 saw the integration of major league baseball, albeit for largely commercial reasons, with the addition of Jackie Robinson to the Brooklyn Dodgers. There were victories in the legal battle to win integrated educational opportunities—in 1949, Ada Sipuel was granted admission to the law school at the University of Oklahoma, and the following year the Supreme Court demanded that the University of Texas open its doors to black students. In May 1954, the Supreme Court dealt what its supporters assumed to be a death blow to segregated schools when, in *Brown v. Board of Education of Topeka, Kansas,* a unanimous court concluded that "in the field of public education . . . separate educational facilities are inherently unequal."

But no court could stop the random acts of racial terrorism that had long been an accepted part of southern society. On August 28, 1955, fourteen-year-old Chicagoan Emmett Till, while visiting relatives in Money, Mississippi, committed an unpardonable breach of southern racial etiquette. When leaving a dime store after buying some candy, he turned to a white girl and quipped, "Bye, Baby." That night, vigilantes kidnapped Till from his uncle's home, took the boy to a back road, shot him in the head, and brutalized him so badly that the body was disfigured beyond recognition. This was a lynching in the finest southern tradition. But the reaction to Till's murder did not follow true to form. This time, vigilantism encountered a very public resistance. Till's mother, Mamie, insisted on an open casket funeral, so that the world could see what had been done to her son, and she held many press conferences, which were replayed on the nightly television news. Till's uncle, Mose Wright, literally took his life into his hands when he took the stand, pointed to the two men charged with Till's murder, and identified them as the men who had abducted his nephew. The result was never in doubt—the defendants were acquitted. But massive resistance had been met by movement—what was to follow would be the organization of that movement.

The murder of Emmett Till—not the announcement of *Brown*—marked the beginning of the Civil Rights Movement. Martin Luther King, Jr., would be the first black leader to define the rules of engagement for that movement. Shielded from racism in his Atlanta upbringing, a moderate by both training and character, King was thought by many to be an unfortunate choice to lead in a situation that seemed to cry for immediate activism. That situation was sparked by an event later described by future Black Panther leader Eldridge Cleaver as a moment when, somewhere in the universe, a gear in the machinery shifted—the December 8, 1955, refusal of Rosa Parks to move to the back of a segregated bus in Montgomery, Alabama, and the subsequent eleven-month boycott of that city's buses by its black population. Montgomery's ministers chose King to lead the boycott because he had been in town for too short a period of time to be corrupted by city officials. He succeeded in large part because his training as both a theologian and a philosopher led him to accept the nonviolent beliefs of Mahatma Gandhi, and to adopt those views as a strategy to face down southern racism. Faced with a reaction to the boycott that included physical threats and the firebombing of both churches and his own home, King demanded that his followers turn the other cheek and quietly continue their boycott. Much like Mamie Till, who had forced the nation to look at her son's destroyed body, King forced the nation to look at its own disfigured system of racism. In the 1960s, King's strategy of nonviolence would face many challenges, as it struggled to meet the needs of a growing, more diverse movement. But in Montgomery in 1955–56, the strategy worked. After eleven months, the Supreme Court declared that Montgomery's segregated bus system was unconstitutional.

But buses were not public schools. Quite simply put, *Brown* never worked as advertised. The Court itself refused to put a deadline on integration, demanding that schools integrate not immediately, but with "all deliberate speed." This allowed southern school districts to organize what southerners called "massive resistance" and to find ways to obstruct the ruling of the Court. By 1957, less than 20 percent of the school districts in the South had complied with *Brown*. That year saw the first full-scale counterattack on desegregation when an Arkansas court issued an injunction stopping the integration plans of Central High School in Little Rock. A federal court countermanded the injunction, but the night before school was to open, Governor Orval Faubus stationed Arkansas National Guard troops around the school to stop nine black students from registering for classes. The mob that had formed outside the school chased the teens from campus, screaming racial epithets and spitting on the youngsters as they boarded

escape buses. Defended by Thurgood Marshall (who had been the victorious lawyer in *Brown*), the students won affirmation of their right to attend
Central High. President Dwight D. Eisenhower begrudgingly protected that
right, sending federal troops to escort the students to class. They enrolled,
and endured a year of unparalleled harassment. The following year, Faubus
closed all the state's high schools for the entire year rather than endure the
protests again. The mob violence in Little Rock, despite the Pyrrhic victory
that surrounded the graduation of one black senior in June 1958, made it
clear that while *Brown* might be the stated law of the nation, it was far from
being the acknowledged law of the South.

Many wondered why the president of the United States refused to lend the
moral power of his office to the movement. In the two decades prior to the
1950s, Americans had gotten used to having activists in the White House.
Both Franklin Roosevelt and Harry Truman had been engaging public figures who relished using the various powers of the presidency to attack problems. Both men believed that if there *was* a balance of power in American
government, the scales *should* tilt toward 1600 Pennsylvania Avenue.

This was *not*, however, Dwight D. Eisenhower. Hardly a political activist, Eisenhower envisioned a different, more collegial, more "businesslike"
presidency. As a result, for almost a decade after the end of his presidency,
no one—not contemporaries, not the press, not historians—gave Dwight D.
Eisenhower credit for being anything but a kindly caretaker of the executive
office. His domestic policy seemed to be a direct response to the demands
of big business, while his foreign policy appeared to be the exclusive creation
of his secretary of state. Treating Eisenhower as a man who relied on others
but rarely initiated anything, critics dismissed the Eisenhower presidency as
a passive interlude between the tenure of two boisterous activists. The contemporary press concentrated on his health, and historians concentrated on
his pleasant personality. Simply put, Dwight Eisenhower received the kind of
deference that one would reserve for an aged relative in a nursing home.

However, historians rejuvenated Eisenhower and his presidency with a
haste that was startling even for often impetuous revisionist historians. The
Eisenhower of recent history is a much younger man than the one who was
written about in the 1950s and 1960s. He is no longer the doddering "Ike."
He has instead become "President Eisenhower," a calculating, often shrewd
politician who ruled his administration with the cunning of a career officer.

To the revisionists, no one controlled Eisenhower. While these historians judge his refusal to push for the enforcement of *Brown* to be less than meritorious, they argue that Eisenhower's minimalist attitude toward civil rights kept even greater violence from breaking out in the South on his watch. Even the deception of the U-2 Affair became the badge of a tough Eisenhower. The most telling facet of the new Eisenhower is that it took *real* guts to say no in Vietnam; one could not say the same about his activist successors.

Taken on his own terms Dwight Eisenhower was indeed a success as president. It can be argued, in fact, that he has been the only true success in the White House since 1945. But this was not because he was a closet Machiavellian. Eisenhower was a success because he did not choose to push the status quo too hard. He was neither a reactionary, wishing to turn the clock back to 1928, nor a New Deal liberal, hoping to push America forward into the acceptance of a more positivist state. He went neither forward nor backward, and to his credit, he promised neither to the American public. Neither as passive as the early historians of his administration made him out to be nor as activist as the revisionists have tried to make him out to be—indeed, Eisenhower would have shunned either label—Dwight Eisenhower's gift was an innate refusal to rock the boat.

First and foremost, Eisenhower was a businessman's president, and quite in line with the economic emphasis of the decade. But he was no Warren Harding redux. Eisenhower did not undertake to rein in the spending of the New Deal and the Fair Deal. Truman left office proposing a budget of $76.6 billion—about $10 billion more than revenues. Such an imbalance bothered Eisenhower, who during the 1952 campaign had promised to balance the budget. That, however, never happened. A recession in the fall of 1953 was halted only by reducing taxes by $3 billion, thus incurring an even greater deficit. Also, Eisenhower never slashed spending as a method of budget balancing. He took some token measures—between 1954 and 1956 he cut the number of federal employees from 2.4 million to 2.2 million. But in 1955–56, the administration spent freely. Defense was the first priority, but the administration also tried to stimulate the domestic economy with spending. The minimum wage rose in 1956 from 75 cents to $1.00 an hour, and Social Security benefits were increased. The St. Lawrence Seaway, first proposed under Harding, finally began construction in 1954. The Housing Act of 1955, while not as strong as its supporters had wished, stimulated the public housing boom of the 1960s. Perhaps the most successful venture along these lines was the Interstate Highway System. Although Eisenhower sold the program in a military fashion (arguing that a sophisticated road system would make for a more orderly retreat from cities that had suffered a nuclear attack), the plan provided for an incredible construction program and a large number of jobs.

When faced with crisis, Eisenhower responded with patience, stealth, and willingness to let his advisors play the primary public role—what political scientist Fred Greenstein called the "hidden-hand presidency." The major domestic crisis of the first term centered on the wildly flaying investigations of Joseph McCarthy. McCarthy had easily won reelection to the Senate from Wisconsin in 1952, running only a bit behind Eisenhower in the state. Yet McCarthy's national popularity, if anything, had grown during the campaign. In 1953, most Americans (53 percent) approved of the senator's crusade. That was a good thing for McCarthy because he did not plan to allow the election of a Republican president to stop his search for communists in the State Department. Indeed, the senator declared that there were still communists in the foreign service, but that he had faith that the new secretary of state, John Foster Dulles, could ferret them out.

McCarthy's role as chairman of the Committee on Government Operations, as well as the chair of the committee's most powerful subcommittee, the Permanent Subcommittee on Investigations, gave him a public platform. While remaining carefully aloof from the administration during its first days, McCarthy took his traveling fear show to Europe, where two assistants, Roy Cohn and G. David Schine, investigated the State Department and the U.S. Information Agency. Their efforts resulted in several resignations, as well as a campaign designed to purge the shelves of all overseas U.S. libraries of any books that were deemed to contain seditious material. Eisenhower largely ignored these revelations. But then McCarthy lashed out against the U.S. Army. In January 1954, McCarthy revealed that Major Irving Peress had refused to sign his loyalty certificate but had nevertheless been granted an honorable discharge from the army. Secretary of the Army Robert Stevens admitted that the Peress case had been poorly handled, but that did not satisfy McCarthy. He called several officials to testify, including Brigadier General Ralph Zwicker, who was ostensibly responsible for the decision to discharge Peress. McCarthy bellowed to Zwicker: "You are a disgrace to the uniform. . . . You're not fit to be an officer. You're ignorant." Although McCarthy and Stevens worked out a compromise package, McCarthy had sown the seeds of his own destruction. Eisenhower, who just happened to be an alumnus of the Army, struck back.

Two weeks after the meeting that produced their "compromise," Stevens charged that McCarthy had used his political power to prevent Schine's induction into the army. Caught off guard by the charge, a livid McCarthy wanted revenge. It was Vice President Richard Nixon, dispatched by Eisenhower to be the broker between McCarthy and the White House, who convinced the senator to do it on television. For McCarthy, this made sense. Television had already begun to aid the careers of politicians—there was no reason for McCarthy to think that he could not control the media. He was wrong. For the first time, American *saw* both his method and his demeanor—and there was an instantaneous rejection. Glued to a TV set for thirty-six days, Americans witnessed McCarthy's thinly veiled accusations against Eisenhower ("treason that has been growing over the past twenty—twenty-*one*—years."). But it was the chief counsel for the army, Bostonian Joseph Welch, who drove the stake into McCarthy's heart. McCarthy had linked a young associate of Welch's with a communist "club." Once proclaimed on television, this disclosure meant the end of the young man's career, and that was too much for the placid Welch. Looking directly at McCarthy, Welch moaned: "Little did I dream you could be so reckless and so cruel as to do an injury to that lad. . . . If it were in my power to forgive you for your reckless cruelty, I would do so. I like to think I am a gentle man, but your forgiveness will have to come from someone other than me." As McCarthy tried to go on, Welch interrupted once more: "Have you no sense of decency, sir, at long last?" As McCarthy fumbled for the next question, the Senate Caucus Room burst into applause. With that spontaneous outburst, McCarthy's career was finished.

Eisenhower had avoided a direct conflict with McCarthy, and as a result he kept the loyalty of the conservative wing of his party through 1956. Using Nixon as an intermediary was a master stroke. The vice president already had the trust of the party's right, and he sympathized with McCarthy's ends if not necessarily his means. Several historians have claimed that Nixon suggested that McCarthy televise his hearings *knowing* that the media would be his undoing. Regardless, the president had another do his bidding, stayed above the fray, and achieved the desired result—"hidden-hand" leadership.

In the area of civil rights, Eisenhower did not extend his hand, hidden or otherwise. He felt that a presidential presence in that debate was politically unwise, a violation of state's rights, and against his own personal support of southern segregation. Therefore, he did as little as possible. Although he privately referred to the 1953 appointment of Earl Warren as chief justice as the biggest mistake he had made as president, Eisenhower publicly claimed that the *Brown* decision must be enforced and did so only when faced with certain bloodshed in Little Rock. The Civil Rights Act of 1957 was a gutted affair that was largely the work of the Senate majority leader, Lyndon B. Johnson. This was hardly the stuff that moral leadership was made of. But when push came to shove, Eisenhower did not ignore his constitutional duty. What can be said of Eisenhower and civil rights can also be said of his successor—the movement dragged him along kicking and screaming.

The image of Eisenhower as a do-nothing president has been at its strongest when considering his administration's foreign policy. All too many observers have argued that Eisenhower left diplomacy up to the State Department, and Secretary of State Dulles engineered a foreign policy of boisterous, dangerous confrontation with the Soviet Union. This conclusion seems to stem from the assumption on the part of many scholars that a president and his secretary of state must be of one mind on foreign policy. However, the evidence suggests that there were *two* theories of diplomacy present in the Eisenhower White House—that of the president and that of Dulles. The fact that it was clearly Eisenhower's view that prevailed throughout the administration not only leads to a reinterpretation of his foreign policy, but can also be used to explain what many observers have seen to be the chief success of his administration—he kept the nation out of war.

John Foster Dulles mixed the small-town Presbyterian moralism he had learned as a boy in northern New York with the conservative value system he had learned while a student at Princeton. A career diplomat, Dulles came quite naturally to view the Soviet Union not only as a threat, but as morally wrong. Such a view made him an ideologically perfect choice to be Truman's token Republican in the State Department. Firsthand observation of Truman's policy of containment only hardened Dulles's anti-Soviet stance and convinced him that was not enough. He embraced the theory of liberation— that the United States should actively pursue a foreign policy that would *free* the captive nations from the yoke of communist aggression.

Eisenhower disagreed with Dulles's assessment. To him, containment— the threat of a military or a nuclear response to further Soviet aggression—had worked. It was when containment had been *abandoned* in Korea—when Truman pushed into North Korea, past the thirty-eighth parallel in an attempt to liberate that nation from the communists—that a bloody stalemate had occurred. Eisenhower believed that a reinstitution of the policy of containment would freeze the Soviets in their tracks and make another Korea unnecessary. That would particularly be so if Eisenhower threatened to use not traditional military troops against the Soviets but a nuclear strike. It was this policy, soon to be christened "massive retaliation," or "brinksmanship," that became the modus operandi of the Eisenhower foreign policy. Dulles defined the policy for *Life* magazine, arguing that "the ability to get to the verge of war is the necessary art. If you cannot master it, you eventually get into wars." Such a policy called for Eisenhower to be a bluffer with the guts of a burglar, threatening the use of military might of the United States, particularly its nuclear capability, and hoping that the threat would render unnecessary the use of such force.

The Eisenhower administration brought several key crises to peaceful conclusions using the threat of massive retaliation. Three weeks after he was elected, Eisenhower made good on his campaign promise and went to the front in Korea, an act that Truman criticized as "demagoguery." Yet there was a surprise for those who expected that the military man would be a militant president—when conferring with General Mark Clark, Eisenhower was less interested in how the war could be *won* than he was with his commander's ideas on how to get the peace talks moving. Dulles pushed for a new military initiative to break the stalemate, but Eisenhower was adamant—the war would be ended at the peace table, before it had a chance to destroy his administration, as it had Truman's. The new administration met with resistance from both the North and the South Koreans. The North refused to negotiate a wholesale release of its prisoners of war, and in the South, President Syngman Rhee was holding out for a completely unified Korea under the South's control. As the stalemate moved into mid-1953, Eisenhower took bold action. He threatened that if the talks did not move perceptibly forward, he would feel free to move decisively "without inhibition in our use of weapons"—a thinly veiled threat to use nuclear force. Whether or not Eisenhower was bluffing is impossible to gauge, but it was definitely a threat, and the threat worked. On July 27, 1953, an armistice was signed, ending the Korean War some three years after it had begun.

Eisenhower's handling of the French collapse in Indochina was equally shrewd. In April 1954, the hapless French forces, which had been fighting the Viet Minh revolutionaries since the end of World War II, had allowed themselves to be surrounded at the indefensible fortress at Dien Bien Phu. Dulles and Nixon pushed for an American intervention, on the grounds that its North Atlantic Treaty Organization (NATO) commitment to the French had to be honored. Eisenhower agreed; but with the war in Korea only recently over, he was not about to commit American forces to another Far East expedition. On April 7, Eisenhower used a press conference to proclaim that if Indochina fell to communism, the rest of the Far East was next: "You have a row of dominoes set up, you knock over the first one, and what will happen to the last one is the certainty that it will go over very quickly." However, Eisenhower and Dulles devised a way for the United States to avoid committing its troops to help the French. The strategy was put forth in a speech to the Overseas Press Club on March 29. While proclaiming that the situation in Indochina was "a grave threat to the whole free community," Eisenhower made it clear that the United States would not help the French unless *other* members of the free community, supposedly so threatened by the situation, *also* helped the French—what Eisenhower called "united action." Not surprisingly, since the rest of the free community also still had open wounds left from the Korean War, there were no takers—a fact that could have surprised neither Eisenhower nor Dulles.

Although Eisenhower's refusal to help the French was, in large part, the reason for the fall of Dien Bien Phu on May 8, that was far from the end of America's involvement in the region. On July 21, 1954, the Geneva Conference, borrowing one of the most tragic pages from the history of the Korean peninsula, temporarily divided Indochina in half along the seventeenth parallel until elections could be held. The northern portion, led by Ho Chi Minh, and more formally known as the Democratic Republic of Vietnam, received immediate promises of aid from the communist bloc; Eisenhower quickly moved to fill the power vacuum that the French had left behind in the south. Immediately following the Geneva Accord, the United States threw its support to Ngo Dinh Diem as a potential ruler in the south. Rabidly anti-French and a devout Catholic, Diem had wandered the world while the French controlled his homeland—even spending time in a Catholic seminary in New Jersey. A rigid true believer and a corrupt bureaucrat, Diem nevertheless promised the type of stability of leadership for the South that the hapless Emperor Bao Dai could never provide. In 1956, with the backing of the Americans, Diem was elected premier of the newly proclaimed Republic of Vietnam, more commonly known as South Vietnam, thus ending any hopes of an eventual political unification of the two Vietnams.

Diem, however, quickly proved to be a millstone around Eisenhower's neck. His corruption, quiet intransigence, and, most important, his complete distance from his people—as a Catholic, he showed nothing but disdain for the Buddhist majority in his nation—strained relations between Washington and Saigon almost to the breaking point. But, playing to a key theme in modern American history, the United States chose to stay with the corrupt devil they knew rather than chance a takeover by another devil they knew—Ho Chi Minh. Between 1955 and 1960, the United States gave South Vietnam almost $127 million in direct economic aid, and over $16 million in technical aid, in order to prop up the Diem government from outside pressure. Eisenhower also recognized a need to help Diem build an army, literally from scratch. During those years, the United States committed between 750 and 1,500 military advisors to assist the Diem government in establishing an effective army; the advisors were organized as the Military Assistance and Advisory Group (MAAG), Vietnam. MAAG would eventually be criticized for preparing the South Vietnamese for the wrong type of war—for not training them in the finer arts of jungle, guerilla warfare.

The need for such training would soon become apparent. Diem's heavy-handed tactics led to outcries of dissatisfaction from his own people. He proved to be incapable of controlling the protests without American help, thus playing into an anti-American sentiment in the South that was a natural outgrowth of the anti-French sentiment that the nation had experienced for decades. This gave Ho Chi Minh the opening he needed to organize an insurgency in the South. In 1960, Ho announced the existence of the National Liberation Front (NLF), an umbrella group that promised to organize all the anti-Diem revolutionaries in the South and train them in a manner that would allow them to overthrow Diem's regime. Diem proved to be a cagy adversary, however. With American assistance, particularly the covert, clandestine aid provided by Central Intelligence Agency (CIA) operative Colonel Edward Landsdale, he held the NLF at bay, derisively and inaccurately labeling the group "Vietnamese Communists"—Vietcong. At no point did Eisenhower consider putting any American ground troops in Vietnam. Financial, advisory, and covert support—support not seen by the American people until the release of the *Pentagon Papers* (see chapter 7)—was all that Eisenhower had to offer, along with American participation in the Southeast Asian Treaty Organization (SEATO), giving it a symbolic presence in the region. To those few Americans who even bothered following the American role in Vietnam in 1955–60, Eisenhower had honored America's alliances and kept troops out of war.

The 1954 crisis over Quemoy and Matsu further illustrates Eisenhower's diplomatic skills. To Eisenhower, the loss of China to the communists in 1949, a loss that both he and most conservative Republicans ascribed to Truman's refusal to intercede in the Chinese Civil War, was "the greatest diplomatic defeat in this nation's history." After China had fallen to the communist army of Mao Zedong, thus creating the People's Republic of China, Chiang Kai-shek's nationalists had escaped to the tiny offshore island of Taiwan (Formosa), soon to be dubbed the Republic of China. Chiang mixed peculiarity with patriotism; continuing to insist that he was the rightful ruler of all mainland China, his troops began every morning by firing a volley of artillery fire at the mainland, volleys that usually sputtered into the sea far short of their mark. Despite his idiosyncrasies and reports of widespread corruption in his regime, Chiang had the treaty support of the United States. For his part, Mao had threatened to invade Formosa ever since they had banished Chiang there. Both nations claimed the tiny twin islands of Quemoy and Matsu, off the Formosan shore, as their own. When Mao's troops began an artillery attack on the two islands on September 3, 1954, it was the culmination of several months of threats from both sides. Eisenhower faced the same quandary he had faced only five months before in Indochina—should he send U.S. troops to aid an ally?

The answer was once again no, despite Dulles's protests to the contrary. Despite the fact that there was a sizeable China lobby in the ranks of the Republican Party who, despite Chiang's oddities, had been consistent supporters of the Formosan government, Mao's army was a much more formidable enemy than even the Viet Minh. Consequently, Eisenhower waited the crisis out. Indeed, as historian Robert Divine has pointed out, Eisenhower was deliberately ambiguous, leaving Mao guessing as to whether or not the Americans would intervene. It was this patience, with the threat of massive retaliation lurking in the wings, that eventually cooled the crisis. By the end of April, both Chiang's and Mao's rhetoric had cooled, and the crisis passed. Despite the opinion of his detractors, Eisenhower had not taken the United

States to the brink of World War III over Quemoy and Matsu; Chiang and Mao had done that for themselves. Indeed, Eisenhower had once again shown a penchant for patience in a crisis.

A key diplomatic development of the Eisenhower period was the new attention paid by both the Soviets and the Americans to the Third World, thus signaling a basic change in the temperament of the cold war. For both nations, a characteristic of this change was their renewed interest in Middle East oil. For both nations, the Suez Canal was of primary importance. Without access to the canal, the shipping of oil from the Middle East would effectively grind to a halt. No one knew this better than the flamboyant Gamel Abdul-Nasser, president of Egypt. While Nasser had reacted to American support of Israel by signing a pact with the Soviet Union, he was willing to deal with either nation to further his domestic projects. His pet project was the building of a dam on the Nile River to provide cheap power for his people. The Aswan Dam had become a symbol for Egyptian modernization, and Nasser had leveraged much of his popularity to buy support for its construction. To finance it, he borrowed money from the United States, Britain, and the World Bank.

Yet Nasser's ideology soon got in the way of his construction. After Nasser had formally recognized Communist China in May 1956, Dulles recommended to Eisenhower that the Americans withdraw their loan offer. Eisenhower ordered it to be done, and as soon as Nasser found out, he nationalized the Suez Canal, using the tolls he now collected from all shipping to pay for his dam. Despite Dulles's entreaties, Eisenhower consistently ruled out the use of the American military to force Nasser to reopen the canal. Other nations saw the situation differently. Britain and France, trying to reclaim the glory of their pre–World War II empires, and Israel, trying to solidify its claims to legitimacy in the Middle East, saw in the Suez Crisis an opportunity. On October 31, less than two weeks before the American presidential election, the three nations invaded Egypt, assuming that they would be supported by Eisenhower.

They were not. Eisenhower immediately called the British prime minister, Anthony Eden, and made his displeasure abundantly clear. The United States rammed a cease-fire resolution through the United Nations, which the Israelis immediately obeyed. As Britain and France tried to decide what to do, Eisenhower heard rumblings from the Kremlin that suggested that the Soviets were planning to enter the crisis actively. Calling the Soviet's bluff, Eisenhower put American armed forces on alert. For his part, Eden also heard the Russians coming. He continued this quest for empire for one more week, until, faced with the possibility of Soviet intervention, he too withdrew his troops. Soon after, France also withdrew.

There was a cost, however, to Eisenhower's use of brinksmanship. Eisenhower's greatest failure as president was his inability to gain a closer relationship with the Soviet Union. While the death of Joseph Stalin on March 5, 1953, seemed to offer hope for a thaw, the fact that in August of the same year the Soviets detonated their first hydrogen bomb seemed to highlight the need for a formal discussion between the two nations. Eisenhower was sincerely committed to a thaw in the cold war. But each time that he came close to his goal, he shot himself in the foot.

There had been no superpower summit since 1945, in Potsdam. It was Eisenhower who pushed for a new summit. The Soviets met his request with a surprising willingness to cooperate. Eisenhower and Soviet leaders Nikolay Bulganin and Nikita Khrushchev met in Geneva in July 1955. While they got along well enough for the press to declare a "Geneva Spirit" of good will, a serious breakthrough was scuttled by Eisenhower's absurd proposal that the Soviets open their skies for U.S. spy planes, and that the United States would do the same. The Soviets rejected the plan at face value. Indeed, Khrushchev charged Eisenhower to his face with trying to get the Soviets to accept a "very transparent espionage device." Although Khrushchev visited the United States in the fall of 1959, and the two leaders made plans for a new summit in 1960, tension continued to mount.

Evidence of this tension was Eisenhower's commitment to the U-2 program. Developed by the CIA, the U-2 was a high-altitude spy plane. Its wide wingspan and slender fuselage gave it the appearance of a pterodactyl in flight. Its powerful camera could take a picture from several miles altitude that would enable the viewer to count the number of people on the street below. Eisenhower personally approved each mission, each of which emanated from U.S. bases in Turkey. The Soviets also knew about the missions, but the U-2 planes stayed just out of the reach of Soviet interceptor missiles. That is, until May 1, 1960. In a scenario that seemed scripted for Khrushchev, the Soviets shot down a U-2 and captured its pilot, Francis Gary Powers, on May Day—the Soviet Fourth of July. Khrushchev at that point took an incredible gamble. He held back releasing the information on the fate of the plane and waited to gauge the American reaction when they found out that one of their spy planes was missing. Once the disappearance had been reported in the press, Eisenhower went with the prearranged denial—that the U-2 had been gathering information about world weather patterns. When Khrushchev released photos of both the plane and pilot, Eisenhower was seen to be a liar. In spite of Eisenhower's successes in foreign policy, the U-2 debacle would give ammunition to a young Democratic senator angling for the presidency, who would charge that in world affairs, America in the 1950s had gone soft.

On January 20, 1961, in the aftermath of a snowstorm that had brought the city of Washington to a standstill, Eisenhower passed the mantle of national leadership to a young, completely untested legislator with a record of little else than name recognition. The difference between the seventy-year-old Eisenhower and his forty-four-year-old successor could not have been clearer; what remained to be seen was whether the inauguration of John F. Kennedy would also inaugurate a new era in American history.

Recommended Reading

Begin your reading on the 1950s with a laugh, and know that Bill Bryson's *Life and Times of the Thunderbolt Kid* (New York: Broadway, 2006) serves as one of the best case studies of American society during the decade. Andrew J. Dunar, *America in the Fifties* (Syracuse: Syracuse Univ. Press, 2006), is an excellent introduction to the decade. John Kenneth Galbraith, *The Affluent Society* (Boston: Houghton Mifflin, 1958) offers the most important contemporary view of the period. A recent view of the society of the 1950s is Elaine Tyler May, *Homeward Bound: American Families in the Cold War Era* (New York: Basic Books, 1999). Of the many books on the Eisenhower presidency, the one that set the stage for a revision of his place in history was Fred I. Greenstein, *The Hidden Hand Presidency: Eisenhower as a Leader* (New York: Basic Books, 1982). The most thoughtful view of Eisenhower's foreign policy continues to be Robert A. Divine, *Eisenhower and the Cold War* (New York: Oxford Univ. Press, 1981). The best concise history of the war in Vietnam is still George C. Herring, *America's Longest War: The United States and Vietnam, 1950–1975*, 3d ed. (New York: McGraw Hill, 1996).

2

"The Torch Has Been Passed to a New Generation"
The Myths of John F. Kennedy

THE PROBLEM WITH THE PRESIDENCY of John F. Kennedy is a problem of evidence. There seems to be nowhere that the historian can turn for an objective opinion of Kennedy's short tenure. No president was analyzed so quickly, and so shoddily, by both contemporary observers and historians, until fact, myth, and just plain nonsense were irretrievably mixed. Yet what was perhaps more important, the all too few balanced studies of Kennedy and his administration that have appeared in the past five years have met with an interesting and telling fate; the general American public has shown that it wants to *ignore* any historical attempt that purports a balanced treatment of Kennedy and his administration. People do not want to *think* about Jack Kennedy. More than any other modern president, he was a president to whom the country *reacted*. Revisionism comes and goes; with Kennedy, it has come, and few Americans care.

What remains is the Kennedy Myth, a myth that began the second that Kennedy died in Dallas. The assassination of John Kennedy not only stopped his life, it effectively stopped the flow of evidence on his administration. All attempts to probe were squelched, either by the grieving family, or by the protective staff. What replaced the evidence was mythology—Kennedy had restored grace, style, and wit to a presidency that had aged with Eisenhower; Kennedy had faced down the Russians; Kennedy had been the first great friend of the black man in Washington. He had, in the words of a Democratic partisan, "made America look good." His presidency became a classical tragedy, in which the hero did the best he could, won a few, lost a few, and was killed while trying. However, when the historian questions the Kennedy Myth, as all myths must be questioned, and delves into the vast amount of evidence on the Kennedy presidency, a diametrically opposite hypothesis both appears and can be supported by the evidence—that Kennedy was an amoral warmonger, a man who took the country to the brink not for defense, as did Eisenhower, but just for the hell of it. Not a hero, but a Machiavellian Black Prince.

Can one escape the Kennedy Myth—so eloquently labeled by the grieving widow when she told a reporter that her husband's favorite phonograph record was the soundtrack to the Broadway musical *Camelot*—and embrace a study of John F. Kennedy that reaches a conclusion that is somewhat less harsh than that of historian/journalist Garry Wills: "His real legacy was to teach the wrong lesson, over and over"?

Probably not.

America's fascination with the lifestyles of the rich and famous is a cornerstone of its popular culture. It is certainly a cornerstone of the Kennedy Myth. The Kennedy family has been the subject of almost as many books as the Kennedy presidency. It is the classic family that you love to hate. The patriarch, Joseph Kennedy, Sr., was a bootlegger, stock speculator, money maker, and womanizer—all done to gigantic proportions. His wife, Rose, was the gentle matriarch, loyal despite her husband's infidelities, taking refuge in the strict practice of her faith. The family's Catholicism clashed with the puritanical Protestantism of the ruling Boston Brahmins. Kennedy found that despite his wealth and influence—indeed, despite the fact that he had married the daughter of one of the most popular politicians in the Bay State—he was shut out of Boston politics (it was said that the one position Kennedy wanted more than any other, one that because of his religion he never received, was appointment to the Board of Overseers of Harvard University). Vacation retreats to the family's summer home at Hyannis, on the more cosmopolitan southern coast of Cape Cod, became permanent.

The combination of their faith and their wealth placed the Kennedy family into a microscopic minority. Lest they fall prey to sloth, Kennedy maintained a rigorous family discipline. Stories abound of the family dinners where the boys (Joe Jr., Jack, Bobby, and Teddy) and the girls (Rosemary, Kathleen, Eunice, Patricia, and Jean) played the roles of the founding fathers, as they recited memorized passages from *The Federalist Papers*. The touch football games have also become legend; they were bruising, often bloody affairs. Should Kennedy guests misjudge the competitiveness of their hosts and treat the game as no more than a pleasant diversion, they were more often than not severely injured or humiliated. Joe Kennedy taught his children to take life in a Protestant world quite seriously; he bred a family that relished contests.

As biographer Herbert Parmet has observed, young Jack, born in 1917, was, in many ways, "not a typical Kennedy." A voracious reader, Jack was prone to severe bouts of asthma and other maladies. His sickly nature, however, did not prevent him from being fiercely competitive with Joe Jr., who was clearly most like his father, and just as clearly his father's favorite. It was Joe, not Jack, who was expected to enter politics and win the respect that the father felt he and his family deserved. For his part, Jack grew up as Joe's tagalong. He went to Choate Prep School, where Joe went. Unlike Joe, however, Jack did not distinguish himself in school; like many bookish young boys, he read more than he studied, and the results were grades that were quite average. Yet he surpassed his brother in the area of charm. Jack was instantly likeable, and his smile was both quick and sincere. There were few people—then, or in 1960—who didn't like him when they first met him. Jack followed Joe Jr. to Harvard as well. It was no great surprise to anyone that Jack was more interested in football than in his studies. Although the reed-thin young man never made the first team, it did not stop him from playing whenever he got the chance, as if his opponents were once again his brothers and sisters. Jack's football career was highlighted by a painful (and poorly treated) back injury, an injury that would color the rest of his life.

Joe Jr. was not Jack's only rival within the family. He also took on his father. In 1938, Franklin Roosevelt showed Joseph Kennedy, Sr., his appreciation for his financial help by appointing him ambassador to England. Kennedy was immediately embroiled in the preparedness controversy, and he took the unpopular stance that America was not ready for war with Adolf Hitler, would lose it if it came, and should avoid it before it did. Jack did not share his father's sentiments. His 1940 senior essay at Harvard was a hawkish little piece—not particularly well written—that argued that British prime minister Neville Chamberlain's policy of appeasement, a policy with which his father largely agreed, was an open invitation for war with Germany. Yet the essay did not inflame the ambassador as its author thought it might. Joe Kennedy elicited the help of *New York Times* columnist Arthur Krock, who rewrote the manuscript, and the essay appeared in book form before the year was out, under the title *Why England Slept*. The book was a mild success, and it was assumed that while Joe Jr. entered politics, Jack would enter the more sedate life of academe, or perhaps follow his father into the business world.

As it did for every man, World War II changed Jack's direction. It did so not only through his experience in combat, but by changing his perception in his father's eyes. Despite his health, and probably with the influence of his father, Jack received a commission in the navy. As commander of a Patrol Torpedo (PT) Boat—a small, fast, lightweight vessel perfectly suited for channel warfare—Jack's skill and courage were incontestable. While on night patrol on August 2, 1943, PT 109 was gored by the Japanese destroyer *Amigari*. The crew swam to neighboring Plum Pudding Island, one that was held by the Japanese, for safety. Despite pain from his back, Jack dragged one badly burned member of the crew behind him by tying a shirt around the two of them and then grasping it in his teeth. Once on the island, Jack made contact with natives, who transmitted his message for help—carved in a coconut—to Australians in the area, who eventually rescued the crew. It was while convalescing from this experience that Lt. Kennedy learned that his brother Joe had been killed in a bombing raid. The mantle had been passed.

Young, wealthy, successful, handsome, charming, and a hero. It was more than enough to get Kennedy elected Democratic congressman from Massachusetts's Eleventh District in 1946. And that was in spite of a rather severe political handicap—Jack was a poor public speaker. Yet he more than made up for that fact by meeting as many voters one-on-one as he could. A handshake and smile from the young candidate was magical. However, Kennedy disliked the Congress. His attendance was poor, and his interest level low. He palled around with another freshman, Senator Joseph McCarthy of Wisconsin. The boorish, earthy McCarthy was a perfect traveling companion and foil for the sophisticated Kennedy, and the two men quickly developed a reputation for their after-hours lifestyle and their sexual conquests. Following his February 9, 1950, speech in Wheeling, West Virginia, where he charged that there were 205 communists working in the State Department, McCarthy's influence soared. In 1952, he helped Kennedy defeat incumbent senator Henry Cabot Lodge by choosing not to come to Massachusetts to campaign for his fellow Republican. Kennedy's victory, being one of the few shining spots for the Democrats in the first year of Ike, was immediately noticed and widely reported.

Kennedy was as bored in the Senate as he had been in the House. Again his attendance record was low, as was his participation level. This was not to say, however, that Kennedy refused to carve out his area of expertise. Hoping to broaden his national appeal, Kennedy moved to make himself the senator of record on the problems of the Northeast. He also latched onto an investigation of racketeering in organized labor; yet his participation on the Select Committee on Improper Activities in the Labor or Management Field—better known as the McClellan Committee—was far less impressive than the performance of the committee's young junior counsel—Kennedy's brother Bobby. Jack's time in the Senate was clearly a time of waiting and planning for higher office.

In many ways, the presidential election of 1960 was the most important of the postwar period. It was not a mandate for Kennedy, nor did it end the career of his defeated opponent, Vice President Richard Nixon. The election was not what political scientist Walter Dean Burnham has called "realigning"; Kennedy was not able to increase significantly the percentage of Democratic control of the Congress. It was, as Eisenhower's had been in both 1952 and 1956, a personal victory, a victory of the candidate rather than his party. Yet 1960 was of critical importance for other reasons. The unprecedented early start for the 1960 Democratic presidential nomination would revolutionize political campaigning. Kennedy also shattered two barriers—those of youth and religion—with his fall victory. Yet most important, the 1960 election impressed the charisma of John F. Kennedy in the minds of the American people and established the perception of him as a youthful, vigorous leader who would rescue the country from the abyss of aged leadership; in short, it began the Kennedy Myth.

In 1960, the only candidates who truly placed their fate in the hands of the primary electorate were Kennedy and Minnesota senator Hubert Humphrey. Although he had become more of a party man since his rousing civil rights speech to the 1948 convention that resulted in the walkout of southern conservatives—the "Dixiecrats"—Humphrey could be assured of the lion's share of the New Deal–liberal support, that is, if two-time loser Adlai Stevenson stayed out of the race. Both Humphrey and Kennedy had to prove that they could command a national constituency; thus, both had to enter all the primaries and hope for an early knockout of the other. Despite his superior organization and financing, Kennedy could not score a knockout blow in any of the early primaries—he was uncontested in New Hampshire, and his margin of victory in Wisconsin (56 percent) was unconvincing. The decisive battleground was West Virginia—predominately Protestant, rural, and unemployed, the state looked upon both Democratic candidates with suspicion, and they were particularly wary of a Catholic candidate. Clearly, whoever lost in West Virginia was out of the race. It was here that Kennedy decided to take the religious issue head-on, asserting that "I refuse to believe that I was denied the right to be president on the day I was baptized." That swayed votes; however, it was the Kennedy money that swung the primary their way. Humphrey was hopelessly outspent, and he never mounted a serious campaign in the state. (Local wags remember the senator speaking from the roof of a station wagon, when, in midspeech, an airplane flew noisily overhead. Humphrey, with a tired yet defiant tone in his voice, looked up and shouted, "Goddammit, Jack. Come down here and fight fair!") Kennedy won better than 60 percent of the vote, and Humphrey was out.

However, the nomination was not yet Kennedy's. Former president Harry Truman was never comfortable with the young man from Massachusetts, who he felt had not paid his dues, and was supporting the late-blooming candidacy of Senator Stuart Symington of Missouri. Senate majority leader Lyndon Johnson also threw his ten-gallon hat into the ring, assuming that his congressional chits would translate into delegates. And then there was Stevenson, who refused to commit to the race. However, by the time of the Los Angeles convention, Kennedy's delegate lead was insurmountable, and none of the power brokers was able to budge him. Kennedy's first ballot victory was the result of his early work in the primaries; every nomination after 1960 was decided long before the convention ever met.

Dismissing Richard Nixon as an unattractive, almost plodding campaigner who was run over by the handsome, eloquent Kennedy is doing the vice president—and history—a grave disservice. Nixon had proven his loyalty to the Eisenhower administration in times of supreme stress—a loyalty that was neither appreciated by the president nor reciprocated. Nixon's foreign trips, cabinet experience, and closeness to the temples of power had established him as the Republican Party's heir apparent. Yet his fall campaign was snakebit from the opening gun. A half-hearted challenge by the darling of the Republican Left, New York governor Nelson Rockefeller, forced

Nixon to make a humiliating pre-convention compact with the governor. This liberalization of the party's platform, without the advice or consent of the Platform Committee, not only angered the party leadership—including Eisenhower—but it also cast doubts onto Nixon's ability to run an independent campaign. His choice for his running mate was a poor one—Henry Cabot Lodge would run as if he wasn't tied to Nixon in any way, and he would make several embarrassing gaffes. Nixon's health affected his performance—a car door slammed against Nixon's leg, sending him to the hospital with a wound that would bother him for the rest of the campaign. Yet the clincher was Nixon's decision to campaign in all fifty states. It was strategically foolish—the candidate had to visit Alaska during the last week of the campaign in order to honor his commitment. It was also exhausting; Nixon drained both himself and his press entourage, and the press would not give him a break when it really counted—after the first debate.

The Kennedy-Nixon debates have taken on a mythic quality all their own: Kennedy won by his looks; Nixon sweated away votes under the hot lights and forgot to shave; Nixon's Spartan preparation only got him the debating points of his radio audience; Kennedy's self-assurance won him the infinitely larger television audience. Much of this is true. The Kennedy staff was as concerned about whether the stage background clashed with their candidate's suit and about their candidate's being properly tanned and fit for the occasion (he prepared by taking a brief vacation in Bermuda) as they were with his knowledge of the issues. Nixon prepped himself by hiding in a hotel room for several days with his briefing books. As Americans viewed the debates, the contrast was stark. Kennedy did not look directly into the camera, except in passing. He lunged forward just a bit and had an air of authority in his voice. Nixon, on the other hand, looked directly down the throat of the camera and spoke with a pleading quality in his voice. He looked as tired and as ill as he truly was. His appearance was not helped by a suit jacket that was too big for him, and its dull earth color blended right into the background of the studio set.

To put the campaign into its simplest terms, Kennedy offered youth, vigor, and promise for a new decade; Nixon offered four more years of Eisenhower-like stability. Yet the conclusion that many have drawn from Kennedy's victory flows only from this observation—that the nation chose to move forward with Kennedy's youth, rather than stay put with Nixon's experience. Indeed, the nation as a whole was not quite sure which way it wanted to go.

Kennedy won 303 electoral votes, to Nixon's 219. But in the popular vote the results were razor close—both Kennedy and Nixon had less than 50 percent of the total, and the margin of Kennedy's victory was one-tenth of 1 percent. Although the election was a personal victory for Kennedy, it was no mandate, to be sure. It was also not a victory for Kennedy's party. While the Congress had not fallen to the Republicans, they had nonetheless made a net gain of two Senate seats and twenty-one House seats.

The closeness of the election indicated something significant for the Kennedy administration, and for the next twenty years of American politics. Both Kennedy and Nixon had struck a chord with the American people. The presidential election of 1960 boasted the greatest voter turnout in American history—some 69 million voters came to the polls, 63.1 percent of the voting-age population, a full 11 percent greater than in 1956. And these voters as a whole were not ready to join Kennedy in his vision of the future. The Republican party—and Richard Nixon—were alive and well, as was, by association, Eisenhower's view of America and of the presidency. America in 1960 was nowhere near fully committed to radical change, liberal reform, or knee-jerk moves into an uncharted future. Neither was Kennedy.

Yet Kennedy *looked* ready. The new president and his cohort exuded a youthful attitude. While Kennedy's inaugural address is best known for the line, "Ask not what your country can do for you, ask what you can do for your country" (a thinly veiled stab at the outgoing administration; of course, Eisenhower had asked nothing of the American people . . .), there is a far more telling line. With Eisenhower by his side on the dais, Kennedy proclaimed that "the torch has been passed to a new generation of Americans, *born in this century*"—noting the significant difference between the administrations of Kennedy and Eisenhower. Kennedy's entire administration would not only be chronologically young, but would be expected to *act* young, as well. The outward trappings of Camelot—the balls, the concerts, the parading of the two young children before the cameras, the beautiful wife—would be signs of youth; so, ironically would the velocity of Kennedy's extramarital sex life.

One other difference that would soon make itself evident was Kennedy's almost uncontrollable urge to test his own toughness and that of his administration. This was not a quixotic strain in his character—Kennedy could not have cared less about fighting for a lost cause. But once the cause had been evaluated and had been seen to be worth the effort, tremendous chances were taken to ensure its success. Historian Garry Wills crudely but pointedly called this tendency "ballsiness." It was the outward expression of this toughness that separated him from Eisenhower, who, while perhaps even tougher than the kid from Cape Cod, kept that part of his character very private. Kennedy enjoyed flaunting how tough he was; in the South, in Vietnam, in Cuba. It, too, was part of the Kennedy Myth.

Yet the third difference was the most often noted: charisma. It is an incredibly elusive term, of course. Kennedy was hardly the first president to captivate the American people. In no small sense, his three immediate predecessors had charisma—Roosevelt's charm, Truman's candor, and Eisenhower's smile were all quite disarming, quite natural and real, and all used to further their political career. But Kennedy seemed to have the market cornered on charisma. Americans may have been wild about Harry, and they certainly liked Ike. But they loved Jack; loved him in a visceral sense that the American public has not loved a president since. It is the backbone of the Kennedy Myth, to be sure. Nevertheless, it must be considered when evaluating his presidency; to ignore it would be to ignore his strongest asset.

In his acceptance speech before the Democratic Convention, Kennedy had announced that it was his belief that America was about to enter a "new frontier—the frontier of the 1960s—a frontier of unknown opportunities and perils." The idea that there were American frontiers that had yet to be explored fit in perfectly with Kennedy's attitude of toughness. Given the penchant of historians to label presidential administrations, Kennedy's was quickly christened the New Frontier. However, there was little new about the way that Kennedy ran his administration, particularly in domestic policy. His domestic policy was based upon the age-old restrictions and assumptions of pure power politics played out in a Democratic Party divided into a northern liberal and a southern conservative wing that often voted with conservative Republicans against any measure that smacked of liberalism. Running for reelection from the moment he occupied the Oval Office, Kennedy's policies looked more moderate than liberal—more safe than New Frontier—and even had he taken a chance with legislation, he had little chance of getting it passed.

Kennedy had not been a particularly good congressman or senator; there was no reason to assume that as president, he would automatically understand the complexities of Congress. Nor could it be assumed that he would be welcomed with open arms by his former colleagues in the Senate, many of whom saw him to be little more than an opportunistic rich kid. Knowing this, Kennedy could not bring himself to call them personally, except on very rare occasions. Kennedy simply never found the right formula for presenting his legislation to Capitol Hill and guiding it through to its passage. The fact that his electoral victory had been transparently thin did not enhance his bargaining power. As a result, the Eighty-seventh Congress manhandled most of the New Frontier's domestic proposals.

During his first year, Kennedy was the beneficiary of the traditional "honeymoon" between president and congress. The federal minimum wage increased from $1.00 to $1.15 per hour, and those job areas that were required to pay their workers a minimum wage broadened. Congress passed a sweeping $5.6 billion Housing Act, as well as the Area Redevelopment Act of 1961, which provided loans for new businesses and grants for retraining the unemployed. Kennedy was also successful in getting a Trade Expansion Act in 1962, which allowed the president to negotiate trade agreements with much more latitude that he had previously held. These measures were arguably liberal, but they were no real test for the new administration; on all of them, Kennedy had help from many Republican congressmen.

However, when Kennedy moved to introduce legislation that he hoped would cement an image of Kennedy the Reformer, he met with failure. His most notable legislative disappointment was his inability to pass the King-Anderson Bill, under which Social Security recipients would receive hospital care and other benefits for ninety days—under his successor, this would become Medicare. Kennedy could not solve the challenge presented to his bill by the powerful American Medical Association (AMA). Foreseeing a distinct drop in their personal paychecks if the bill passed, doctors in the AMA began to shout that Kennedy's bill was a step toward British socialized medicine. The AMA gained the support of the nation's insurance carriers, who foresaw a drop in premium payments. The "Southern Coalition" of conservative Democrats and Republicans was more than happy to climb on the public-opinion bandwagon, and, despite Kennedy's personal appeals to the nation for the bill, it went down to defeat.

The same fate met Kennedy's proposed bill to aid education. During the debate, the religion issue once again haunted Kennedy. This time, it was the nation's Catholics who refused the president their support, arguing that the government should be sending tax dollars to *both* private and paro-chial schools. Hoping to defuse the lingering criticism that he was a tool of the Vatican, Kennedy designed his education package so that only public elementary and secondary schools would receive aid. This gave an open-ing for Kennedy's conservative opponents. In the 1960 election, Republi-cans and southern Democrats alike had tarred Kennedy as the pope's lackey; now they sided with the Catholic Church and criticized Kennedy for giving money only to public schools. Despite the contradiction in their position, the Southern Coalition seized upon the opportunity to hand Kennedy another major legislative defeat. Kennedy also met with defeat when he attempted to improve the sagging economy by cutting taxes. Kennedy called for a $13.5 billion tax cut, but it, too, was blocked in Congress.

The area of civil rights will be explored in detail in the next chapter. Suffice it to say here that Kennedy knew that any moves toward a civil rights bill would be met with congressional opposition. Thus, he did nothing to push for such a bill until events in the South forced his hand. In a June 1963 speech to the nation, Kennedy had indeed proposed a civil rights bill, but southern conservatives immediately bottled it up in committee. The Southern Coalition was also instrumental in defeating Kennedy's pro-posal for a Department of Urban Affairs; it was defeated when Kennedy announced his appointee to lead the new department: Robert Weaver, who was African American.

Kennedy's record in domestic legislation, then, shows a record of almost total defeat. With few exceptions, Kennedy's foreign and national security policies show the same record. Indeed, quite apart from the picture of a cou-rageous president who faced down the Soviet Union and avoided World War III, an equally compelling hypothesis can easily be defended that charges Kennedy with being at best a youthful blusterer, and at worst a warmonger.

Kennedy's primary concern was never domestic policies; it was America's place in the world. A major Kennedy campaign theme in 1960 was that of the "missile gap" between the United States and the Soviet Union. Although his charge was that under Eisenhower, the United States had fallen behind in the arms race, Kennedy knew better; indeed, the United States held the basic first strike and had a retaliatory second-strike capability. Nevertheless, the issue was an emotional one, and Kennedy's hard-line stance allowed him to separate himself from Nixon, who could not defend the Eisenhower administration from Kennedy's charges without publicly discussing classified defense information—something Nixon would not do. Once in the White House, Kennedy found out that, gap or not, the arms race was pushing forward. In September 1961, Nikita Khrushchev restarted his nation's nuclear test program—one of the detonations was an unprecedented fifty-seven megatons. Not to be outdone, Kennedy resumed American testing the following spring, with blasts twenty-five hundred times bigger than those inflicted on Hiroshima and Nagasaki.

Yet despite his saber-rattling in 1960, and despite his keeping pace with the Soviets test-for-nuclear-test, Kennedy dramatically changed America's defense strategy by pulling back and away from Eisenhower's reliance on overwhelming nuclear force. This plan began as a cost-cutting measure. Kennedy had chosen for his defense secretary a cost-cutting CEO from the private sector, who had been successful in cost effectiveness in one of the world's most volatile businesses. Ford Motor Company's Robert McNamara, and his equally talented young analysts, began to trim back the fat that had been put into the defense budget. Pet projects were inevitably scrapped, and the military—already concerned about serving so young and untested a commander-in-chief—was appalled.

But this policy was hardly an abandonment of the nation's security interest, as it had evolved and been defined during the cold war period. Both McNamara and, ultimately, Kennedy became enamored of protecting American interests with an elite surgical military force, rather than with threats of nuclear Armageddon. Very much in tune with Kennedy's personality—action, bravado, and recklessness—the U.S. Army Special Forces reflected Kennedy's belief that this flexible fighting force could meet the Soviets on the ground and come up winners. It also allowed him an explanation for trimming back the U.S. nuclear arsenal to fallback capability—phasing back on first-strike systems and developing second-strike (counterattack) missiles like the Triad. What would become known as the "McNamara Doctrine"—Special Ops and Second Strike—would drive the Kennedy foreign policy decision-making. Special Ops became the basis of Kennedy troop involvement in Vietnam (see chapter 7); it would also be key to events in both Europe and Cuba.

To be sure, Kennedy had inherited the cold war with the Soviet Union. It was, however, not a conflict from which he intended to shrink. Where his predecessor had been more guarded, the new president was, initially at least, publicly bellicose. When in his inaugural address Kennedy promised that the United States would "pay any price and bear any burden" as it struggled for mastery of the modern world, it was hard not to hear the saber rattling. Always looking for ways to prove himself, it is not surprising that within weeks of his taking office Kennedy jumped at the opportunity to bloody the nose of communism in the Western Hemisphere. Initial American support for Fidel Castro, the victor in the 1959 overthrow of the dictatorial government in Cuba, had evaporated, as Castro quickly cast his lot with the Soviet Union. Eisenhower had placed an economic quarantine on the island and had approved a top-secret mission to overthrow the Castro government using a force of some fourteen hundred Cuban exiles who had been armed and trained by the Central Intelligence Agency. Despite being presented with evidence that hinted at disaster (Kennedy was shown a map of Cuba overlaid on a map of the United States—the eight-hundred-mile island stretched from New York to Chicago), the CIA held firm to their plan and quickly sold Kennedy on their assessment—that Castro's government was weak and that the landing of a group of guerillas would spark a national uprising against Castro. Kennedy approved the mission for many of the same reasons that Eisenhower had withheld his approval—it was clandestine, surgical, and run essentially without military control. The code name for the operation would turn out to be quite apt: Operation Bumpy Road.

On April 17, 1961, the guerillas landed at the Playa Giron—the Bay of Pigs. From the start, it was a catastrophe. Already tipped off to the invasion, Castro lay in wait; the vast majority of the invading force was either killed or captured on the beach. Quickly realizing his blunder, Kennedy refused to compound the error by committing American air forces to the battle. His refusal to give air cover to the hapless invaders sealed their doom but ironically helped Kennedy. That decision, along with a televised presidential address in which Kennedy took public responsibility for the debacle, resulted in a stratospheric leap in his polls, hitting an 83 percent approval rating in late April 1961. For Kennedy, the lesson of the Bay of Pigs was not that he had erred in judgment; rather, it was that he has lost control of his administration early in the game. He fired CIA director Allen Dulles and his deputy, Richard Bissell; Attorney General Robert Kennedy was given the task of policing the CIA. President Kennedy never fully trusted the Joint Chiefs of Staff again, preferring to turn instead to his ad hoc groups when dealing with national security issues.

It was a newly sobered John F. Kennedy who went to Vienna June 3–4, 1961, to meet with his Soviet counterpart. Nikita Khrushchev had snidely observed to his advisors that his own sons were older than the American president; in Vienna, Khrushchev treated Kennedy with undisguised contempt. Gauging him as both a weakling and politically wounded after the Bay of Pigs, there was no need for Khrushchev to give ground on Berlin or on nuclear testing, and he didn't. A visibly shaken Kennedy understated the case when he characterized the summit as "a very sober two days."

Sensing the onset of a new crisis, thousands began to stream across the border from East to West Berlin. Khrushchev's saber-rattling had created this problem, and he solved it with a mailed fist. On August 13, Khrushchev closed the borders that divided Berlin and erected a twenty-five-mile-long barrier of barbed wire and fencing that was heavily patrolled by Soviet troops. Within four years the Soviets replaced much of the wire barrier with a concrete wall that averaged 11.8 feet in height. Ignoring the military hawks in his circle who called for American tanks to break the Berlin Wall, and those political advisors who told him that his administration needed a victory, Kennedy once again would not commit American troops to conventional battle. He sent in fifteen hundred troops—a token force—but made no attempt to tear the barrier down. The crisis passed slowly, and again, as in the Bay of Pigs, Kennedy came out of the Berlin Wall crisis smelling like a rose. A press that was already smitten with the Kennedy style gave the president additional points for restraint, choosing to ignore the fact that it was Kennedy's precipitous behavior at Bay of Pigs that led Khrushchev to believe that Kennedy could be trumped without a fight—the Berlin crisis only served to solidify this assessment in Khrushchev's mind.

Unlike Eisenhower, Kennedy was not by nature a patient or prudent leader. Throughout 1961, he clearly understood that he was perceived either as feeble or at best a beginner, on the world scene. Living through a phase that was labeled for a future president the "wimp factor," Kennedy wanted to change that perception—if possible, before the upcoming 1962 congressional elections. One area where the president could declare open warfare on the Soviets was in space. By 1962, Kennedy had decided to ratchet up the space program. The Soviets had been the first to put a man into space—on April 12, 1961, cosmonaut Yuri Gagarin had orbited the earth for 108 minutes and returned safely home. The Americans put their first man into space twenty-three days later, as Mercury astronaut Alan Shepard rode a Redstone

BAKER COLLEGE OF CLINTON TWP

Rocket for a thrilling, but suborbital ride. While Shepard was feted as a hero, the entire national security community knew that if the United States was to keep pace with the Soviets, a commitment must be made to a manned orbital flight—and soon. This Kennedy did, and more. In what was to be one of his most famous speeches, on May 25, 1961, Kennedy threw down an intergalactic gauntlet to the Soviets before a joint session of Congress, convened to discuss "urgent needs" of national security that had come up and would not keep until a formal state of the union opportunity. In his speech, Kennedy demanded that significant new monies be appropriated for the space program, with the goal in mind of meeting what seemed to be an impossible deadline: "I believe that this nation should commit itself to achieving the goal, before this decade is out, of landing a man on the moon and returning him safely to earth." With the help of Vice President Johnson, to whom Kennedy had given the space portfolio, the National Aeronautic and Space Administration (NASA) got its money. By the time of Kennedy's death, the Mercury Space Program had, in the person of John Glenn, sent an astronaut to orbit the earth. Plans were also underway for a two-astronaut training program (Project Gemini), and the three-man mission (Project Apollo) that would eventually land an American on the moon in July 1969. Thanks to Kennedy's public commitment, the United States had surpassed the Soviets in space and would never look back.

Another way that Kennedy could challenge the Soviets was with an extraordinary volunteer army. In March 1961 Kennedy announced, through an executive order, the creation of the Peace Corps. He named his brother-in-law, R. Sargent Shriver, as the organization's director, and together they won congressional approval of the organization that fall. The Peace Corps took young American volunteers, trained them (albeit, said critics, too briefly) and sent them to some of the most destitute areas of the planet—particularly on the continent of Africa—to teach, build, support, and become agents for change. The alumni of the Peace Corps—by 1963, there were over seven thousand such volunteers serving around the world—would, not surprisingly, remember their experience as life-altering. When coupled with the Alliance for Progress, an expensive Kennedy initiative to send aid to the poorest countries of Latin America, it gave the appearance of a Kennedy commitment to the third world.

Kennedy's commitment to the space race, the Peace Corps, and the Alliance for Progress was not halfhearted, and his victories in funding those projects represented some of the best examples of congressional lobbying that his administration was to produce. However, in the realm of national security, Kennedy wanted nothing more than he wanted a victory against Fidel Castro, who continued to hold the prisoners from the Bay of Pigs in Cuban jails and who had become a living symbol of defeat to the Kennedy brothers. The Kennedys' behavior toward Castro was obsessive. They ordered the CIA to assassinate the Cuban leader (Operation MONGOOSE), although plans such as sprinkling drugs on the steering wheel of Castro's car so that he would get into an accident smack of absolute stupidity. Kennedy had also ordered regular aerial photographic flights over Cuba by American U-2 spy planes. In early October 1962, these flights yielded fruit. Photos showed that the Soviets were installing about forty intermediate-range missile sites in Cuba—all of which were capable of hitting as far north as northern Georgia.

Remembering his experience during the Bay of Pigs invasion, Kennedy kept the disclosure of the missiles a secret from much of his own administration, deliberating in secret with a small group of carefully chosen advisors, christened the Executive Committee, or EX-COMM. The group debated the options, both with and without Kennedy's presence, arguing whether the missiles were a real threat to the United States, as America had the clear retaliatory superiority. Kennedy was also reminded, to his disgust, that American Jupiter missiles in Turkey were even *closer* to Soviet soil than were the missiles in Cuba. The leader of this faction, U.N. ambassador Adlai Stevenson, called for negotiating with the Soviets by bargaining away the Turkish missiles. On the other hand, Kennedy's military advisors recommended surgical air strikes that would neuter the missile sites before they had become operational.

Many historians have given Kennedy credit for steering a middle path between these two extremes and calling instead for a naval blockade of Cuba that would squeeze out the missiles. After two tension-filled weeks, the tactic worked. Like Kennedy at the Berlin Wall, Khrushchev refused to pierce the barrier; on October 28 he turned his supply ships around and eventually dismantled the missiles. Publicly Kennedy agreed never again to invade Cuba; only decades later would it be learned that Kennedy had also agreed to dismantle the Turkish missile sites.

More so than any other event in his administration, the Cuban Missile Crisis has been interpreted as evidence that Kennedy was growing in the job, and that he did not make the same mistake as had been made at the Bay of

Pigs of acting precipitously on the confrontational advice of his military advisors. This assessment has merit, but it must be tempered by the understanding that Kennedy also refused to accept the option of walking away from the revelation of the missile sites, with an understanding that those sites were no more or less harmful to the United States than the Turkish sites were to the Soviet Union. There is also merit to the point made quite vociferously at the time that a blockade is, in itself, an act of war. Put simply, Kennedy needed a victory against the Soviets for both psychological and political reasons. Psychologically, Kennedy needed to stand up to Khrushchev—he privately told James Weschler that "if Khrushchev wants to rub my nose in the dirt, it's all over." Politically, Kennedy was being bashed by Republicans in that fall's off-year elections as being weak; his hopes for personal reelection in 1964 might well hinge on that perception being taken out of the debate. The Cuban Missile Crisis was not, as some have claimed, a manufactured crisis—there were real missiles, on both sides, poised to strike. But by not ignoring the revelations, or using diplomatic backchannels to resolve it, Kennedy took the world to the brink of war.

Despite this debate, there is no question but that Kennedy immediately profited from the outcome of the crisis. His popularity soared to new heights, a development that immediately translated into votes. In November 1962, the Democrats avoided the usual off-year slap from voters, losing only six seats in the House and actually gaining four in the Senate. Capitalizing on this victory, which gave new strength to his upcoming reelection bid, Kennedy brokered a significant thaw in the cold war. He began with his commencement address to the graduates of American University, delivered on June 10, 1963. In it, Kennedy cooled his own anti-Soviet rhetoric and instead reflected upon the human experience that both Soviets and Americans shared:

> So let us not be blind to our differences, but let us also direct attention to our common interests and the means by which those differences can be resolved. And if we cannot end now our differences, at least we can help make the world safe for diversity. For in the final analysis, our most basic common link is that we all inhabit this small planet. We all breathe the same air. We all cherish our children's futures. And we are all mortal.

The American University address was the opening salvo in what would quickly become heated negotiations over a significant treaty between the

Soviets and the United States on the issue of the testing of nuclear weapons. Such a treaty presented significant political risks for both Kennedy and Khrushchev, neither of whom could afford to appear soft on the issue of nuclear development, lest they risk the ire of the conservative wings of their parties. But the Cuban Missile Crisis had sobered both leaders toward the prospect of a World War III (ten days after the American University address, the two leaders had installed a private teletype so that they could have instant communications in times of crisis, and before the end of the summer, the famous telephone "hotline" had been installed on desks in the Oval Office and in the Kremlin). In October 1963, the United States Senate approved a treaty with the Soviet Union, banning the atmospheric testing of nuclear weapons. The process of advise and consent by the Senate showed promise for the legislative initiatives of a second Kennedy term—the president had managed to cajole several Republican leaders, including future minority leader Everett Dirksen of Illinois, into supporting the treaty. It was a newly emboldened and politically strengthened Kennedy who, in November 1963, left for Dallas, Texas, to broker a compromise between warring factions of the Texas Democratic Party and to jumpstart his own campaign for reelection the following fall.

All that can be said with absolute historical certainty about the events of November 22, 1963, is that John F. Kennedy was assassinated while riding in a motorcade through downtown Dallas. Beyond that statement of fact, the historian faces speculation, gossip, hearsay, nonsense, and contrived Hollywood versions of the event—as well as a massive amount of audio, video, oral history, and journalistic evidence. To suggest that this book could offer a fair analysis of this evidence, and postulate "Who Killed Kennedy"—is ridiculous. Thus, the fairest way to treat the assassination in these pages is to fall back on the observation of Theodore Sorensen, one of Kennedy's closest aides, who wrote in his memoirs: "I must ask to be excused from repeating the details of that tragedy. How and why it happened are of little consequence compared to what it stopped."

What *did* it stop? It most certainly did not stop a universally successful administration. But did it stop a liberal one? Most certainly no twentieth century president, save Franklin Delano Roosevelt, has been so often *labeled* a liberal, by scholars and generalists alike. Kennedy himself eschewed philosophical labels, so any labels that we might attach will receive no help from him. It seems that in foreign policy particularly, Kennedy fits the mold of the classic post-1945 cold war liberal—he shared their passionate anticommunist zeal, and he believed in governmental support for social welfare. When dealing with the economy, Kennedy showed a penchant for deficit spending that could place him as an inheritor of the New Deal. However, this persistent labeling of Kennedy as liberal is, in itself, a myth. The results of the Kennedy administration fall far short of anything *close* to that which might be considered a "liberal presidency." No quixotic warrior, Kennedy fought few battles in the name of any philosophy. He was a pragmatist, a politician, if you will—indeed, one fact that is often omitted from Kennedy hagiography is that he was serving only his first term in office, and as a politician, all his actions centered on his getting reelected in 1964. He could no more abandon the conservative southern Democrats in his party than he could abandon the northern Democratic liberals and expect to get reelected. His entire administration—his incredibly brief, single-term administration—was a tightrope walk toward reelection.

This brings up the parlor game of whether or not Kennedy would have changed had he been reelected to a second term, and, perhaps, *become* the liberal that his supporters believe that he was. There is evidence to suggest both possibilities. In foreign affairs, he had become more progressive in his thinking about the Soviet Union's place in the bipolar world, as evidenced by his support of the Test Ban Treaty. But to term him anything other than a cold warrior is to ignore the fact that at the time of his death, as we will see in chapter 7, Kennedy was increasing the American commitment to South Vietnam. In domestic affairs, there is a case to be made that Kennedy had turned the corner on civil rights after Birmingham, and with the introduction of his civil rights bill he had taken an overtly moral stand against the evil of American apartheid (to be discussed in the following chapter). However, one is left to wonder, given Kennedy's track record on Capitol Hill, whether he would have stayed that course and fought for a bill—even in his second, final term—that most certainly would have been met with strong resistance in Congress, or whether he would have accepted a gutted bill, more like the 1957 bill, that would have done little for his progressive legacy.

Dallas leaves us with no answers, only an unfinished presidency. And as it was unfinished, and at best evolving, the most accurate thing that a historian can conclude about the Kennedy years is that they were transitional. Neither the active conservativism of the Eisenhower years nor the liberal activism of the Johnson years, the Kennedy years did not begin the "sixties" in American history. Rather, the Kennedy years showed Americans the struggles that they were about to face in the last seven years of the decade, struggles they would face not through the pragmatism of John F. Kennedy, but through the prism of the unabashed liberal activism of his successor.

Recommended Reading

More books have been penned on Kennedy's brief presidency than on that of any other, save Abraham Lincoln. Much of it is thinly researched hero-worship, but selected pieces of the Kennedy literature stand as some of the best works on the modern American presidency. James Giglio, *The Presidency of John F. Kennedy*, 2d ed. (Lawrence: Univ. Press of Kansas, 2006) is a graceful, impeccably researched synthesis. Kennedy has been well served by two of his many biographers: Herbert Parmet's two volumes, *Jack: The Struggles of John F. Kennedy* (New York: Dial Press, 1980) and *JFK: The Presidency of John F. Kennedy* (New York: Dial Press, 1983) are the best biography; David Burner's brief *John F. Kennedy and a New Generation*, 3d ed. (New York: Pearson Longman, 2009) is both a worthy introduction to Kennedy's life for the student and a critical, evaluative essay for the specialist. Theodore White's *The Making of the President, 1960* (New York, Atheneum, 1961) stands as one of the best books written on American politics; his other books pale in comparison. Of specialty studies on the Kennedy domestic policies, there are few to record. Foreign policy, however, has a much stronger Kennedy literature. On the great events discussed in this chapter, consult: Trumbull Higgins, *The Perfect Failure: Kennedy, Eisenhower, and the CIA at the Bay of Pigs* (New York, W. W. Norton, 1987); Robert Slusser, *The Berlin Crisis of 1961* (Baltimore, Johns Hopkins Univ. Press, 1973); and Elie Abel, *The Missiles of October: The Story of the Cuban Missile Crisis* (New York: Dell, 1968).

3

"We Shall Overcome"
Civil Rights in the South, 1960–1965

THE CIVIL RIGHTS MOVEMENT of the 1950s changed—as did virtually everything in the 1960s—at the hands of college students. Inspired by Dr. Martin Luther King's rhetoric of nonviolence, and fueled by his victory in Montgomery, a group of students from traditionally black colleges in the South took action. On February 1, 1960, four freshmen from North Carolina Agriculture and Technical College in Greensboro entered that city's Woolworth's department store, sat at the whites-only lunch counter, and refused to leave until they were served. They weren't served, but they stayed until the store closed. The next day they returned, but now they were twenty-three strong; by the end of the week, hundreds of A&T students, as well as white students from a neighboring university, had joined in the protest.

The sit-in movement had begun, and it would spread like wildfire on black college campuses. In Nashville, where there were four traditionally black colleges, the students had already been engaged by Reverend James Lawson's classes in nonviolent protest. This was *far* beyond any strategy of waiting for a legal dissolution of segregation. Indeed, it was a step beyond what King had unveiled five years before as a strategy in Montgomery. Like King, Lawson was ready to confront segregation directly; but his would originally be an economic protest—he was training students to walk into the lion's mouth, sit there, invite violence, and learn what to do when it came (how to cover themselves from the beatings and be carried off by police with minimum physical damage to themselves). Two students, John Lewis and Diane Nash, led the sit-ins at Nashville's lunch counters, which began in mid-February 1960. The city ignored the protest for a few weeks, and many of the eateries closed for fear of violence, but the students continued their campaign, coming to the lunch counters when they opened, taking a seat, and staying silent until they closed.

On February 22, having had enough, the local police finally permitted pent-up white youth to retaliate. Entering the restaurants where the protesters were seated, they poured ketchup and salt over their heads, spit on them, then yanked them out of their seats onto the floor and began kicking them. As Lawson had taught them to do, the students rolled into the fetal position so as to better absorb the blows. They did, and they were immediately arrested for disturbing the peace. But once the first group was arrested, another wave took their place at the counter. Then they were arrested, replaced by their peers, and so on—until about eighty students had been arrested. They were all found guilty, but for his part, John Lewis refused to pay the fifty-dollar fine—he chose instead to serve a jail sentence.

Following the arrests, Nashville blacks now stole a few pages from King's Montgomery playbook. To protest the arrests, they organized a boycott of downtown chain stores. Both the sit-ins and the chain store boycotts spread all over the country, to more than sixty different cities. Also as had been done in Montgomery, the Nashville students directly confronted those civic leaders who could, if they wished, eliminate legal segregation. But the movement had begun to change when Diane Nash directly asked Mayor Ben West if it was morally wrong to segregate, the mayor was being publicly confronted not by an ordained minister, but by a twenty-two-year-old student. The voice of youth, now joined with the moral and economic power of movement, was compelling. Three weeks after Nash had confronted West, the mayor not only announced the desegregation of the Nashville chain stores, but publically admitted that segregation was . . . wrong.

The success of the sit-ins led students to organize. Ella Baker, a fifty-six-year-old executive secretary of the Southern Christian Leadership Conference (SCLC) put out a call for a meeting of student leaders at Shaw University in Raleigh, North Carolina. In April 1960, over three hundred students answered Baker's call, and together they formed the Student Nonviolent Coordinating Committee (SNCC; the acronym was pronounced "snick"). SNCC's statement of purpose, the first important document of the student movement of the 1960s, affirmed that theirs would be an organization founded on the ideals espoused by King: "Through nonviolence, courage displaces fear . . . each act or phase of our corporate effort must reflect a genuine spirit of love and goodwill."

In an inaugural address that spurred Americans to new service to their country, John F. Kennedy never once mentioned the civil rights movement—or African Americans, for that matter. Some scholars argue that the black vote had given Kennedy the elections, as thousands flocked to his banner after he spoke out in support of King, who had been jailed after a sit-in at an Atlanta department store. (King's father famously said, "I've got all my votes and I've got a suitcase, and I'm going to take them up there and dump them in [Kennedy's] lap.") But that was a debt that Kennedy could not yet repay. He did not intend to speak out in favor of the civil rights movement, nor did he intend immediately to honor his campaign promise to wipe out segregated public housing "with the stroke of a pen." Any hopes for the passage of a Kennedy legislative program hinged on the support of southern Democrats, whose political careers—some more, some less—had been built on race-baiting. The Kennedy approach to civil rights would go beyond the Eisenhower ennui, but not by much. It would center on the quiet appointment of blacks to political positions and the slow and equally stealthy registration of enough blacks in the South to vote, so that eventually the southern Democrats would *have* to pay attention to the demands of these new voters—all without the direct, public confrontation of Montgomery and Little Rock. Kennedy left it up to the Justice Department, led by his brother and an extraordinary band of lieutenants, to carry out this policy.

However, Kennedy's civil rights strategy was doomed from the start. The confrontations precipitated by the civil rights movement in the 1950s, as well as the sit-in movement, had been so successful that any hopes for a roll-back in activism from SCLC, the Congress of Racial Equality (CORE), or the National Association for the Advancement of Colored People (NAACP) was a pipe dream. Indeed, Kennedy himself, inspiring the nation with a call to service, inadvertently spurred the movement toward a new activism—the day after Kennedy's inaugural address, touched by the president's clarion call, a black air force veteran named James Meredith filled out an application to be admitted to the University of Mississippi. That conflict was a year away; the conflict that would force the Kennedys to deal publicly with the new activism of the civil rights movement occurred over the right to travel on a bus.

It was the perfect metaphor for the new activism—an integrated band of innocents, riding defenselessly into the teeth of southern racism. In December 1960 the Supreme Court, in *Boynton v. Virginia,* had ruled that segregation in restaurants and waiting rooms serving interstate bus passengers was unconstitutional. The Interstate Commerce Commission (ICC) had the power to enforce the decision. However, southern racists were no more willing to enforce this law than they had been to rush to desegregate their public schools after the 1957 *Brown* decision. Moreover, Kennedy would not risk the anger of southern Democrats by whipping the ICC into action. To force the issue and demand the enforcement of the law, CORE planned a mass-transit infiltration of the south. Two buses—one Greyhound, one Trailways—would journey from Washington, D.C., to Jackson, Mississippi, stopping frequently at segregated bus stations. The passengers were an integrated group of students, members of CORE and SNCC. They left the capital on May 4, 1961; they anticipated violence.

On May 8, the buses pulled into the station at Rock Hill, South Carolina. There the first bus encountered racist thugs who, unstopped by the local police, severely beat the passengers. By the time the second bus had arrived, the station was boarded up. The motorcade continued south. King had lunch with the riders in Atlanta but made no promise of support. By the time the buses hit Anniston, Alabama, on Sunday, May 14—Mother's Day—the riders had become a minor media curiosity, and a mob was at the ready. The terrorists stormed the first bus, rocking it, smashing windows, and slashing its tires. The driver tried a desperate escape, but the mob caught the disabled bus on the outskirts of town, setting it ablaze with Molotov cocktails. The passengers on the second bus also suffered beatings and, with their bloodied comrades from the first bus, continued on to Birmingham, where the riders were once again beaten in a scene of pure fury. (Birmingham police chief Eugene "Bull" Connor would later quip that since it was Mother's Day, most of his force was home, "visiting their mothers.") Rather than turn back, SNCC reinforced the riders; a bus of twenty-one students, including sit-in veteran Diane Nash, left from Nashville for Birmingham. When they reached Birmingham, Bull Connor immediately arrested them, putting them into what he called "protective custody."

The Freedom Rides were now a national cause célèbre. For the first time, Americans were seeing the civil rights movement played out on their tiny television screens. The pressure on the Kennedy administration to end the crisis was white-hot. It had been less than a month since the humiliation at the Bay of Pigs (see chapter 2), and the president needed to avoid a calamity at home. Attorney General Robert Kennedy tried to talk the arrested students into accepting a release from jail—but they would not go. For his part, Alabama governor John Patterson made it clear that he would not protect the safety of the riders. It took Bull Connor to break the stalemate temporarily. He put the students into police cars, took them to the Tennessee state line, and left them there, telling them to find their own way home. But the riders would not be deterred. They returned to Birmingham and bought tickets for Montgomery.

By this point, the Kennedys were as frustrated with the Freedom Riders as they were with their racist attackers. Representing the Justice Department in Montgomery, Assistant Attorney General John Seigenthaler finally brokered a deal with Patterson—the governor would guarantee the protection of the Riders out of Birmingham and into Montgomery. On the morning of May 20, the twenty-one reinforcements planned to leave for Montgomery (the students had asked King to accompany them, but he refused, saying that he was still on probation from a Georgia traffic arrest the previous year), and state troopers were at the ready to escort them. But no Greyhound driver would board the bus to start them on their way. Incensed, Robert Kennedy shouted into the phone: "Well surely somebody in the damn bus company can drive a bus, can't they? I think you had better get in touch with Mr. Greyhound or whoever Greyhound is, and somebody better give us an answer to this question." A driver was found, and the bus departed. Forty miles from Montgomery, all signs of police protection vanished. When the bus reached the city, an eerie silence met the disembarking passengers—no one was to be seen. Then the mob appeared. Armed with baseball bats and lead pipes, some one hundred racists attacked the riders. Seigenthaler, who had driven ahead of the riders, was beaten until he lost consciousness. The police arrived only after twenty minutes of unchecked brutality.

The bloodied riders sought sanctuary with families in Montgomery. On May 22, at the First Baptist Church, a mass meeting supported the students. King had flown into Montgomery to speak at the rally, but his words were punctuated with gunshots and tear gas. A mob had formed outside the church, and it was, for the moment, contained only by U.S. Marshals that President Kennedy had ordered in from Maxwell Air Force Base. It was clear that the mob would soon overwhelm the outnumbered lawmen. King called Robert Kennedy from the church and predicted that without more help, the racists would soon storm the church. As eager to avoid bloodshed as Kennedy, Patterson declared martial law and sent in the Alabama National Guard. By morning the mob had disappeared.

Two days later, the buses rolled out of Montgomery, headed toward Mississippi with the full protection of the National Guard. As soon as the riders reached Jackson, they were arrested. Robert Kennedy had made a deal—their arrest had been traded for their physical protection in Jackson. The riders each received sixty-day sentences in maximum security prisons, but that hardly stopped the protests. More and more riders came into Mississippi—by summer's end, three hundred students were in Mississippi jails. Other activists followed, and then entertainment celebrities, all of whom brought media attention on the situation. The Kennedys now had no choice. On September 22, 1961, the ICC ruled that passengers on interstate carriers would be seated without regard to race, and it banned segregated terminals.

The Kennedys had now learned that the civil rights movement *they* faced was not the one faced by Eisenhower. This movement broached no compromise with either side; was racially integrated; brought new, young, volunteers into the South; and had moved into a no-man's land between King's call for non-violence and the realization that violence not only moved human hearts, but also got great television coverage. In an attempt to advance its original racial agenda, the administration encouraged SNCC and CORE to work for voter registration in the South. The Voter Education Project, funded largely by entertainer and activist Harry Belafonte, was spearheaded by SNCC member Bob Moses, a teacher from New York who held a master's degree in philosophy from Harvard. Moses came to Mississippi in the fall of 1961 to attempt to register the black citizenry to vote. In so doing, he put himself and those who accompanied him in the middle of the devil's den. Since 1954, Mississippi had de facto been run by the Citizen's Council, a statewide organization dedicated to both the separation of the races and the political emasculation of blacks. Not averse to open shows of violence, the Citizen's Council made Mississippi the most dangerous state in the nation for any type of social reformer. Moses himself was arrested on numerous occasions and severely beaten while accompanying blacks as they attempted to register. His volunteer driver was found in a parking lot with a single, fatal gunshot wound to his head. Yet Moses, the quiet activist, persisted outside the glare of the spotlight. Also working in Mississippi was Medgar Evers, the NAACP field representative. A World War II veteran, Evers worked as tirelessly as Moses to register black voters. He also spearheaded a June 1963 economic boycott of the city of Jackson that led to mass demonstrations and arrests. As gregarious as Moses was reserved, Evers became the public face of black resistance in Mississippi and a constant target of white threats.

As King tried to regain control of his nonviolent movement, he gravitated toward another student protest, sparked by the success and notoriety of the Freedom Rides. In November 1961, students from traditionally black Albany State College in Albany, Georgia, free for their Thanksgiving break, tried to enter the white waiting room of the town's bus station—a right that had been won for them by the Freedom Riders and guaranteed them earlier that year by the ICC. Nevertheless, five of the students were jailed, leading to a mass protest and the imprisonment of 267 black youths. The ICC did not intervene. Coming to Albany after the incarcerations, King engineered a protest in which he too was jailed. However, in a deal cut between King and the local authorities, he was set free after only forty-eight hours, leaving many of the students still in jail. King's early release in front of the television cameras infuriated many of the young participants in the Albany Movement. Angry at what they saw to be King's grandstanding at the expense of their own battle commitment, they not-so-privately began to refer to King as "De Lawd." The schism between King and the youthful activists was widening by the day.

The nation did not follow the Albany Movement as it had followed the brutality against the Freedom Riders. Albany had engendered no newsworthy confrontation; it was a failure, and the cameras rarely tracked a failure. Moreover, the nation had been riveted that summer by the Berlin Crisis, and issues of cold war national security were getting more attention in late 1961 and early 1962 than the civil rights movement in the South. That would change in the fall of 1962, when the nation's eyes once again looked south, as another quiet activist confronted racism in full view of the cameras.

On September 25, 1962, James Meredith entered the Woolfolk Building at the University of Mississippi and attempted, with counsel from Medgar Evers and supported by an order issued through the Fifth Circuit Court, to register as an on-campus (living in a dormitory) full-time student. Meredith was physically blocked from registering by Ross Barnett, who had been governor of Mississippi since 1959, thanks to the support of the Citizen's Council. Barnett espoused a political theory that had seen its most famous articulation in 1832 by John C. Calhoun; in his response to the passage of a high federal tariff that he believed would cripple southern agriculture, Calhoun argued that the state had the right to "interpose" its authority between the federal government and the state, negating a federal law that was not in the interest of the state. Barnett did not cut the figure of a political theorist, but his shouting of "interposition" to the cameras gave him an air of legitimacy and forced the Kennedys to attempt to broker a compromise that would admit Meredith without angering either the terrorist mob or southern conservative Democrats. Those attempts stumbled in and out of the public eye. When Meredith first attempted to register, Barnett turned him away personally. Five days later, accompanied by a Justice Department official, federal officials, and a hoard of television cameras that broadcast the confrontation live, Barnett again blocked the door.

That weekend, while most of the campus was out of town for a football game, the president acted. Meredith was simply spirited into a dorm, without having formally registered for classes. That night, trying to avert another violent confrontation like Little Rock, Kennedy spoke to the nation, announcing that Meredith was on campus and "This is as it should be." As Kennedy spoke, rioting exploded on the campus as a mob stormed Meredith's dorm. The rioting lasted all night, and Kennedy's actions bordered on the indecisive. He originally sent in U.S. Marshals, and 160 of them were hurt. The next day, Kennedy mobilized 23,000 troops, which finally quelled the riot. When it was over, two were dead, Meredith was registered, and Ole Miss became but another symbol of southern intransigence against the onslaught of civil rights.

It was easy at the end of 1962 to argue that the civil rights movement in the South had reached its high-water mark. The gains of the Freedom Riders were largely ignored by a southern population no more willing to desegregate their bus stations than they had been their schools. King had failed in Albany. While Meredith was now a college student, Kennedy had looked inept at Ole Miss. Moses and Evers toiled in virtual anonymity in Mississippi and had yet to make a significant impact on that state's voting rolls. And the administration, stung by Ole Miss and empowered by that fall's Cuban Missile Crisis, saw the cold war as infinitely more pressing than the moral war being waged in the South. The movement's slogan for the following year—"Free by '63" (noting that on January 1, 1863, the nation would celebrate the one-hundred-year anniversary of the Emancipation Proclamation)—rang hollow. King knew he needed an immediate victory, or his influence on the civil rights movement would most likely be over.

The city to which King turned his sights was so violent that the blacks who lived there called it "Bomb-ingham." The largest city in Alabama, built upon a burgeoning steel industry, Birmingham was completely segregated and completely controlled by Bull Connor, who boasted that before one inch of that city would be segregated "blood would run in the streets." But the city had been embarrassed in front of the nation for its Mother's Day attack on the Freedom Riders. It was also undergoing a civic revolution—thanks to the damage done to its reputation, Connor and his allies had been challenged and defeated at the polls. However, they simply refused to leave office, effectively leaving Birmingham with two governments. If King was going to mount a challenge to segregation in Birmingham, now seemed to be the time.

King's campaign was planned not just to desegregate Birmingham, but, as he had done in Montgomery, to showcase its segregation to the world. The campaign began on April 3, with the arrest of twenty-one sit-in demonstrators at the city's segregated lunch counters. King was disappointed with the small number of arrests, but a fear of Connor's jail was both understandable and justified. For his part, Connor wanted to send in state troops to rout the demonstrators. However, a cadre of Birmingham businessmen said no-they believed that if they could broker a deal with King, as had been done in Albany, the campaign would die of its own weight. As important was the fact that to this point, the press had not been kind to King's campaign, and there was no indication of any White House intervention on the horizon. Indeed, the White House was in public opposition to the campaign, noting that white reformers were trying to oust Connor and they deserved a chance to make their electoral victory work.

King decided that jail for himself was the only way to jump-start the campaign. He was arrested with his chief lieutenant, Ralph Abernathy, on Good Friday, April 12. They were kept in isolation, with no mattresses or linen—King rested on the metal bed slats. Once he was incarcerated, several of Birmingham's white ministers went to the press and demanded that King stop his campaign. Stung by this criticism from an unexpected quarter, King responded by secretly penning what would become known as his "Letter from a Birmingham Jail." It was drafted in the margins of his newspapers, and later on pieces of contraband stationary, and was smuggled out for typing. The final document ran about twenty typed pages, comprising thirteen long, often rambling paragraphs. Nevertheless, it would, upon its publication, become both an explanation for, and a rationalization of, his movement:

> You deplore the demonstrations that are presently taking place in Birmingham. But your statement, I am sorry to say, fails to express a similar concern for the conditions that brought the demonstrations into being . . . you may well ask "why direct action? Why sitins, marches, and so forth? Isn't negotiation a better path?" You are quite right in your call for negotiation. Indeed, this is the very purpose of direct action. Nonviolent direct action seeks to create such a crisis and foster such a tension that a community that has constantly refused to negotiate is forced to confront the issue. It seeks to so dramatize the issue that it can no longer be ignored.

King and Abernathy were bonded out after nine days; they found a campaign that was, like Albany, about to fail. Thus, one of the most fateful decisions of the entire civil rights movement was made—the decision to use elementary and high school students in the next march in Birmingham. The risks of such a strategy were incalculably high—there was absolutely no question that some of these youngsters would be hurt and possibly killed when they faced Connor's police. But the entire civil rights movement was at a crossroads; in King's eyes, there could be no noncombatants.

On Thursday May 2, the students marched. By the end of the day, seven hundred children had been arrested. On May 3, they marched again, one thousand strong. They were met by special high-pressure water hoses; the force from those hoses lifted marchers right off the ground and sent their helpless bodies tumbling through the streets or smashing into trees, cars, or buildings. They were also met by the most heinous symbol of the campaign—Connor's K-9 units. In perhaps the most famous film footage of the entire movement, the American and international public, watching the nightly news while trying to digest their dinners, saw seventy-pound German Shepherds ripping into the flesh of terrified young marchers. By Monday, May 6, twenty-five hundred demonstrators had been arrested, some two thousand of them children. The mauling of the "Children's Crusade" was the last straw. Some two hundred sympathy protests broke out all over the country, and the Birmingham businessmen demanded a settlement. Robert Kennedy sent Burke Marshall to negotiate the terms of that truce—it led, on May 10, to a desegregation agreement signed some weeks later with King and the SCLC.

King felt the immediate wrath of the chastened Birmingham racists—who firebombed the motel where he was staying, as well as his brother's home. Not waiting for more bloodshed, Kennedy sent thirty thousand troops to Alabama and encamped them just outside Birmingham. This decision would be crucial in the next crisis—once again over the admission of black students to a state segregated college.

George Wallace would build for himself a surprisingly progressive record as governor of Alabama. He eventually built fourteen junior colleges and fifteen new trade schools and started a new $100 million school construction program. But his power base was traditional southern racism. After being defeated in the 1959 gubernatorial race by a Klan-supported candidate, Wallace vowed never to be "out-niggered again." In his successful 1962 run for the office, Wallace promised that rather than see any of the state's colleges integrated, he would place his body in the school's entranceway and physically block their access.

In June 1963, Wallace had his chance to make good on this rather extraordinary campaign promise. The early scenario was much like that of Ole Miss; a court ordered that two black students, James Hood and Vivian Malone, be admitted to the University of Alabama in Tuscaloosa, and mobs were beginning to form. But two variables were quite different from those that existed a year before. First, unlike Ross Barnett, Wallace had dreams of national office and thus had reason not to have a campus massacre on his gubernatorial résumé. And second, there were already thirty thousand troops in Alabama—some fifty miles away in Birmingham; if the president decided it was necessary, there would be no delay in meeting mob violence with military action.

Thus, an elaborate charade was choreographed between Wallace and the White House. First, officials set up a podium in a doorway at the university and alerted the media. Then, Wallace went to the podium, stiff and erect, like a short traffic cop, and Assistant Attorney General Nicholas deB. Katzenbach, assistant attorney general, went to the podium and read a proclamation

from President Kennedy. ("They will remain on this campus. They will register today. They will go to school tomorrow.") Katzenbach then went back
to his car, got Vivian Malone, and walked her to her dorm; federal officials
escorted Hood to his dorm. After a lunch break, Wallace appeared back at
the podium, where National Guardsman Henry Graham announced that it
was his "sad duty to ask you to step aside." Wallace then read a statement ("I
am returning to Montgomery to continue working for constitutional government to benefit all Alabamians—black and white"), and then he stepped
aside. The faux-standoff was over. There was no bloodshed, both the Kennedy administration and Wallace had their say on television, and the University of Alabama formally admitted its first two black students.

The bloodless end to the registration crisis in Tuscaloosa seems to have
ennobled Kennedy. On June 11 he addressed the nation: "Now the time
has come for this nation to fulfill its promise. The events in Birmingham
and elsewhere have so increased the cries for equality that no city or state or
legislative body can prudently choose to ignore them. . . . We face, therefore,
a moral crisis as a country and a people." He also announced that he would
send to Congress a civil rights bill that would, if passed, mandate that all
citizens be able to be served in all public facilities.

That same evening in Mississippi Medgar Evers left his Jackson office
to drive home. Arriving in his driveway, he got out of his car. One shot
rang out, ripping through Evers's back, emerging from his chest, continuing
through his living room window and finally hitting the refrigerator inside
the house where Evers's wife and children had dropped to the floor. Evers
dragged himself to his front door, leaving a trail of his own blood on the
asphalt. His children screamed to him: "Please Daddy, please get up." He
died an hour later.

It is in this light that one must see the August 28, 1963, March on Washington for Jobs and Freedom, and with it, one of the most famous speeches
delivered in human history. The promise of a civil rights bill, and the general ennobling aura of Camelot, gave comfort to the older, more established
members of the movement, who coalesced around the venerable civil rights
organizations—the Brotherhood of Sleeping Car Porters, SCLC, the Urban
League, CORE, and the NAACP. These groups planned an integrated mass
march on Washington, designed to take the movement to a national level for
the first time. But those same groups severely limited the participation of

the more activist youth, particularly those from SNCC, demanding the last-minute editing of John Lewis's speech and, in some cases, not allowing their representatives to speak at all. Denied their moment, those young activists agreed with the assessment of a Muslim minister from Chicago, Malcolm X, when he labeled the march "The Farce on Washington."

King, however, would not be denied his moment. It is a moment that virtually every American has watched, most in its entirety. The peroration of the speech is as familiar to Americans as any words spoken in the nation's history. It was masterfully delivered, with the cadence of a Baptist preacher, to an audience on the Washington Mall too large for the Parks Department to measure, but tallied by some observers at 250,000:

> And so even though we face the difficulties of today and tomorrow, I still have a dream. It is a dream deeply rooted in the American dream. . . .
>
> I have a dream that one day on the red hills of Georgia, the sons of former slaves and the sons of former slave owners will be able to sit down together at the table of brotherhood.
>
> I have a dream that one day even the state of Mississippi, a state sweltering with the heat of injustice, sweltering with the heat of oppression, will be transformed into an oasis of freedom and justice.
>
> I have a dream that my four little children will one day live in a nation where they will not be judged by the color of their skin but by the content of their character. . . .

King's dream, however, was a dream deferred. Three weeks after his speech, on September 15, a bomb exploded at Birmingham's Sixteenth Street Baptist Church, killing four young girls. Despite the movement's local victories in the South, despite the public relations success of the March on Washington, much had not changed since the Montgomery bus boycott. The young activists knew this, and they had had enough of King. It would soon be their turn.

As SNCC was becoming less and less enamored of both King and his brand of movement, their eyes and ears turned to the North, where they heard a new voice—one more attuned to who they had become.

In the 1930s, an unemployed Detroit auto worker named Elijah Poole changed his name to Elijah Muhammad and founded the Nation of Islam.

A quasi–black nationalist, quasi-religious, quasi–street corner hustler movement, the Nation of Islam preached a new, strident view of blacks in American society. To Elijah Muhammad, the white man had descended from blacks, the white man *was* the devil incarnate, and generations of blacks had been duped into worshiping a lily-white God that did not exist. The Nation of Islam, soon rechristened in the white press as the "Black Muslims," also preached the worship of Allah, who they believed was black, and elevated Elijah Muhammad as Allah's prophet on earth.

On their own, the religious views of the Black Muslims would not have been enough of an appeal to impoverished northern blacks. However, Elijah Muhammad mixed these doctrines with a demand for a stoic lifestyle. The Black Muslim was required to give up his surname (seen as the name given him by the slave master), all forms of flashy dress, alcohol, drugs, pork, straightened ("conked") hair, and promiscuity. Many Black Muslims, particularly those who had been convicts, testified that this new lifestyle had saved them from continued personal ruin. The Nation of Islam also supported small black businesses, opened mosques, and promoted literacy and health programs in cities across the North and Midwest. Theirs was a harsh lifestyle, but it was made to order for those seriously trying to escape the horrors of ghetto life.

The most influential convert to the Nation of Islam was Malcolm Little. Born in Omaha, Nebraska, in 1925, Little's father was a strong and outspoken supporter of Marcus Garvey's Back-to-Africa movement. As a result, he was taken from his home by Klansmen, beaten, and tossed in front of a speeding train. The lynching of his father, and the rapid mental degeneration of his mother, embittered young Malcolm. Sent to Boston to live in a series of foster homes and then with a half-sister, he fell into a life of crime, taking turns at running numbers, pimping, and drug sales. Arrested for burglary in 1946, Malcolm was sentenced to eight to ten years in the Massachusetts State Prison at Charlestown. In prison, Malcolm was converted to the Nation of Islam by a fellow inmate; he dropped his surname and took the name Malcolm X—the "X" demonstrating that he would never know his true ancestry. In one of the most famous passages in modern American literature, Malcolm wrote in his *Autobiography* of learning to read in prison by memorizing the dictionary.

Upon his release from jail in 1952, Malcolm worked hard within the Nation as it expanded its mosques and business in several northern cities.

He quickly developed into a public minister of great force. As mesmerizing an orator as Elijah Muhammad was dull and boring, his dynamism on the stump led to his appointment in 1954 as the minister of the Nation's Harlem mosque. By the turn of the decade, he was the Nation's chief spokesman. As had the preachers of the southern movement, Malcolm used the colloquial in his tirades against white mistreatment of the "so-called American Negro" ("We didn't land at Plymouth Rock. Plymouth Rock landed on us"). But as preached by Malcolm, the message of the Nation of Islam became more overtly political. Malcolm detested integration, and all those—white or black—who supported it. He believed that the leaders of the civil rights movements in the South and their white liberal compatriots were more interested in maintaining their status within white society than they were in helping poor blacks better their lot. Malcolm also argued that blacks *themselves* should stand up to whites and not accept either the white man's or the white liberal's solutions as being binding on their fate. When he spoke, Malcolm affected a menacing posture and enjoyed goading white audiences with thinly veiled threats—such as his often-used line that blacks would achieve equality not with nonviolence, but by "any means necessary." When asked by an interviewer if this meant that he was teaching hate, Malcolm replied: "No . . . truth."

His was an appealing message for ghetto youth itching for action. It was equally appealing to those young people in the southern movement who had become disenchanted with King. Where King had come to *mean* the nonviolent movement, Malcolm X had come to *mean* activism. But Malcolm's popularity had become a threat to the preeminence of Elijah Muhammad in the Nation. When on December 1, 1963, Malcolm publicly characterized the assassination of John F. Kennedy as an example of the "chickens coming home to roost," Elijah Muhammad utilized the violent reaction against his statement to suspend him from preaching for three months. Stunned by the censure, Malcolm used that time to investigate more fully both the Nation and himself. After corroborating rumors that Elijah Muhammad had fathered several illegitimate children, and after further exploring the Muslim faith and learning where it diverged with that of the Nation of Islam, Malcolm decided to leave the Nation. In March 1964 he announced that he was forming two groups—the Muslim Mosque, Inc., and the Organization of Afro-American Unity—organizations that preached a more traditional form of Islam and Black Nationalism. Malcolm began to draw even more young people away from the orbit of the southern movement.

To many observers in late 1963, the assassination of Kennedy, who was treated as an icon by large portions of the black community from the moment of his death, and the accession of a southerner, Lyndon Johnson, meant the end of any federal support for civil rights. It would take years of distance from the tragedy in Dallas, and the national grieving that followed, for blacks to see how little Kennedy had advanced the movement—his foot-dragging during Oxford and Birmingham would not be fully known to historians for years. As Johnson took over, one part of Kennedy's legacy remained on the docket. During his last months in office, Kennedy had called for a civil rights bill. But it was sitting in congressional committee at the time of his death, and it is arguable that, even had he lived, Kennedy would have been just as unable to secure the passage of *that* bill as he had been with his other domestic legislation.

Had Johnson not inherited a civil rights bill from Kennedy, it is indeed doubtful that he would have initiated the measure. But the bill had become a part of the Camelot legacy, a part that Johnson could not ignore. Plus, there were political advantages to Johnson securing a quick passage of the bill. As soon as he took office, Johnson was knee-deep in the presidential election campaign of 1964. Distrusted as a southerner by northern liberals and black voters nationwide, Johnson could go a long way toward winning their support by winning a civil rights bill.

The way would not be easy. As Senate debate began on March 30, 1964, the same conservative southern democrats who had stood in the way of much of Kennedy's legislation now filibustered Johnson's civil rights bill. This procedural crisis played directly into Johnson's specialty—unscrambling the world's most powerful legislature. Through an alliance that looked unlikely to outsiders but was perfectly logical to those who knew the two men—Johnson and Republican minority leader Everett Dirksen—the fifty-four-day filibuster was broken on June 10, as the Senate voted cloture on a civil rights measure for the first time in American history. Johnson signed the bill on July 2.

The Civil Rights Act of 1964 was clearly the most far-reaching civil rights legislation in the country's history. Yet to achieve passage, Johnson and Dirksen compromised much of its original language away. Thus, it is as important to see what was *not* included in the bill, as to analyze what *was*.

This bill abolished unequal voting registration requirements, but it did *not* abolish literacy tests, those examinations given at both the federal and state levels that had, since the late nineteenth century, been used in the South to deny African Americans their right to vote. It gave the attorney general additional power to protect citizenry against discrimination and segregation in voting, education, and the use of public facilities, but it *exempted* "private" facilities from these protections. Indeed, the bill "encouraged" the desegregation of schools, but it specifically did not endorse busing as a way to achieve that balance. It did establish a federal Equal Employment Opportunity Commission (EEOC), and it did require the elimination of discrimination in federally assisted programs, or federal funds to these programs could be terminated. It was a landmark piece of legislation, but it was hardly the death-knell for either discrimination or segregation in the nation. It was, in short, a bill that Johnson could get passed. He could now campaign as a civil rights hero.

Martin Luther King attended the White House signing of the Civil Rights Act. Malcolm X, however, was singularly unimpressed. In April 1964, at the height of the filibuster of the civil rights bill, he made a speech in Cleveland. In it, Malcolm articulated a view of the black future that contrasted sharply with King's "Dream" of less than a year earlier:[1]

> Now in speaking like this, it doesn't mean that we're anti-white, but it does mean we're anti-exploitation, we're anti-degradation, we're anti-oppression. And if the white man doesn't want us to be anti-him, let him stop oppressing and exploiting and degrading us. . . . If we don't do something real soon, I think you'll have to agree that we're going to be forced either to use the ballot or the bullet in 1964 . . . and now we have the type of black man on the scene in America today who just doesn't intend to turn the other cheek any longer. . . . I don't see any American dream; I see an American nightmare.

The events of the summer of 1964 brought the choice that Malcolm demanded of America into sharp relief. In June, Bob Moses proclaimed it to be "Freedom Summer" in Mississippi. He proposed that volunteers pour

---

1. Malcolm X, "The Ballot or the Bullet," excerpted in *Takin' It to the Streets: A Sixties Reader,* ed. Alexander Bloom and Wini Breines, 138–40 (New York: Oxford Univ. Press, 1995).

into Mississippi and teach at "Freedom Schools," concurrently educating the poor and exposing the problems of the state to the rest of the country. They would also help Moses continue his work in registering black voters. College students from all over the nation trekked to the campus of the Western College for Women in Oxford, Ohio, for training. For these white, affluent kids, most of whom had been affected by press coverage of the southern movement, it was a civil rights boot camp that brought to mind the training given the Nashville sit-in protestors only four years earlier. In the best tradition of nonviolent confrontation, students were taught the appropriate—and safest— way to take a beating and to be arrested, and how to deal with the press.

The first three recruits to go from Ohio to Mississippi were Michael ("Mickey") Schwerner and Andrew Goodman—both whites from New York—and James Cheney, a black from Mississippi. They had gone ahead on June 20 to investigate the burning of a church that the students planned to use as a base of operations—later evidence would show that the fire was a ruse set by white racists to draw a small group of students to Mississippi before the main body of students arrived. Two days after their departure, the police found their torched car, just outside Philadelphia, Mississippi. The search for Schwerner, Goodman, and Cheney lasted the entire month of July. Indeed, Johnson signed the Civil Rights Act of 1964 on July 2, as the search went into its second week.

If the terrorists' plan had been to use a kidnapping to scare off the other students, it didn't work. By early July, thousands of students had descended on Mississippi; there had been close to one thousand arrested and scores of them were beaten. In the words of the title of a 1989 movie on the events of 1964, it was truly "Mississippi Burning." Despite the terror tactics, forty-one Freedom Schools were opened across the state. The students also got more than sixty thousand blacks to register as members of the Mississippi Freedom Democratic Party (MFDP), with the goal of sending an alternate slate of delegates to the Democratic National Convention in Atlantic City that August.

On August 4, acting on a tip from an FBI informant imbedded in the Klan, the brutalized bodies of the three civil rights workers were found in an earthen dam near Philadelphia. While the conspirators could not be tried at that time for federal murder charges, several of them would eventually be convicted, and serve jail sentences, for violating Cheney, Schwerner, and Goodman's civil rights.

The next month, sixty-eight delegates from the MFDP, sixty-four black and four white, went to Atlantic City to attend the Democratic National Convention. They announced that they represented the true demographic of Mississippi Democrats and, as such, should be seated as the legitimate delegation from that state, not the competing all-white delegation. The dispute went before the party's Credentials Committee, and the testimony before that committee was televised. In one of the most emotional speeches of the entire civil rights movement, MFDP delegate Fannie Lou Hamer made a case that would be forgotten by no one who either heard it or viewed it. Hamer described her attempts to register to vote in her hometown of Ruleville, Mississippi, which led to harassment (the owner of the plantation on which she worked informed her that if she didn't withdraw her name from registration, "You might have to go, because we are not ready for that in Mississippi"), an arrest, a beating ("I was beat by the first negro until he was exhausted, and I was holding my hands behind me at that time on my left side because I suffered from polio when I was six years old"), and time in jail ("After I was placed in the cell I began to hear sounds of licks and screams . . . and I could hear somebody say, 'Can you say, yes sir, nigger? Can you say yes, sir?' . . . They beat her, I don't know how long"). She closed her testimony to the stunned audience: "All this on account we want to register, to become first-class citizens, and if the Freedom Democratic Party is not seated now, I question America."

However, few Americans actually heard or saw Hamer. Not wanting there to be any glitches at the convention that was about to nominate him for his own term as president, Johnson demanded and received national airtime for a White House speech, thus effectively cutting off the airing of the testimony from the committee. The president then used Minnesota senator Hubert Humphrey to broker a deal with the feuding Mississippians. The MFDP would get two seats at large, and the all-white delegation would be seated in its entirety if they swore loyalty to the national ticket (for his efforts, Humphrey was chosen as Johnson's running mate) and agreed that future delegations would not be segregated. Neither side accepted the compromise, and the MFDP was never seated.

Young activists in the movement, while publicly praising the courage of Hamer and her MFDP colleagues, had nevertheless become further separated from the southern movement. To them, the fact that 1964 ended with King being awarded the Nobel Peace Prize and being named *Time*'s "Man of the Year" was little short of ironic. Indeed, when juxtaposed with the February 21, 1965, assassination of Malcolm X by three members of the Nation of Islam while he was delivering a speech in Harlem's Audubon Ballroom, the young activists felt betrayed—King collected awards, while their new hero had given his life. The young were ready to abandon King. He sorely needed a victory.

SNCC had been working for more than a year to register voters in Selma, Alabama. It was clearly a place that needed attention: in 1965, in Dallas County, Alabama, where Selma was the county seat, only three hundred of the fifteen thousand blacks of voting age were registered to vote. By 1965, SNCC had run out of money, and it turned to King's SCLC for help.

There were many reasons for King to oblige SNCC, not the least of which was the fact that despite his Nobel Prize, he was being seen by many as being out of touch with the desires of the activists in the movement. A victory would quiet those critics, and Selma offered a reasonable chance for success. As had been the case in Birmingham, Selma offered to the press not one, but two Simon Legree characters—a sheriff in Jim Clarke who, like Bull Connor, was absolutely certain to lash out when cornered, and a mayor in Joe Smitherman, who was a public-relations gift to the movement (telling the press that he blamed all the problems in Selma on outside agitators, especially "Martin Luther Coon, I mean King"). In mid-January 1965, King brought the movement to Selma.

The campaign began with the arrest of a black teacher, Amelia Boynton. When her colleagues marched on the city courthouse in protest, Clarke initially showed uncharacteristic reserve, refusing to arrest the marchers as they had both expected and desired. After a church meeting to plan a second march, the protesters returned to the courthouse. This time, Reverend C. T. Vivian confronted Clarke in front of a television camera, lecturing him, haranguing him, and finally comparing Clarke to Hitler. The sheriff had had enough. He struck at Vivian, arrested the minister, and used his billy club to clear away the newsmen.

Vivian's arrest sparked several weeks of protests. King himself was briefly jailed on February 1. On February 18, the campaign was shocked by the murder in nearby Marion, Alabama, of Jimmy Lee Jackson, a black teen who was trying to protect his mother from the advances of racist thugs. In response to Jackson's death, King proposed a march from Selma to Montgomery, the state capital. SNCC opposed the strategy, particularly when it was learned that King would be preaching in Atlanta on the day of the event, but John Lewis broke with his organization and agreed to lead the march. Governor George Wallace vowed that it would never happen.

The protest began on Sunday March 7 at the Brown Chapel AME and snaked through the city, toward the main exit from the city, the imposing, arching Edmund Pettus Bridge that crossed the Alabama River and would take the marchers out of Selma. As the line approached the bridge, they saw no police. Then as they reached the bridge, they saw a phalanx of Clarke's police on the other side. In a new, grotesque twist, the import of which was about to be made clear, many of them were on horseback and many more were wearing gas masks.

Clarke addressed the marchers: "This march will not continue. . . . I've got nothing further to say to you." The marchers froze in their tracks. The throng of police began to walk slowly toward the demonstrators. Then the attack commenced. The police lunged into the marchers, flailing their night-sticks and shooting teargas into their midst. They chased and beat the protestors back to Brown Chapel, which now reeked with the smell of teargas and had become a makeshift hospital. An ABC television video truck recorded the event; that evening, the networks broke into their prime-time lineup to show the scenes of what had already been labeled "Bloody Sunday."

SNCC wanted revenge; SCLC responded by putting out a call for more marchers. Thanks to the television broadcast, reinforcements poured into Selma. Noticeable were the white clerics, particularly the nuns, who traveled alongside the students and celebrities. All of the campaigners expected King to proclaim that the march would go on. But a federal judge in Montgomery had granted an injunction against the march, and King had never disobeyed a federal order. Regardless, SNCC wanted King to march.

Few in Selma had time to notice that on Monday, March 8, the day after "Bloody Sunday," the first American ground troops waded ashore in South Vietnam.

On Tuesday, March 9, it seemed that King had decided to disobey the court. He led a march of some two thousand protestors, all of whom assumed they were on their way to Montgomery, on the same route to the Pettus Bridge. When they reached the bridge, the same police, once again in riot gear with gas masks, were waiting for them. Using virtually the same language as he had two days before, Clarke stopped the marchers. Once again the marchers froze and knelt to pray. Then, to the amazement of everyone, King turned the line around and returned to Brown Chapel. Stunned and livid with anger, SNCC activists began to mock King openly, singing the spiritual "Ain't Going to Turn Us Around" with obvious contempt.

King had óbeyed the court order, but it wasn't long before events took on a life of their own. That evening, James Reeb, a white minister from Boston, was clubbed to death outside a restaurant by white terrorists (his attackers would later be acquitted by an all-white jury). As the murder received national press coverage, the protests spread to other cities. Once again, pressure was put on King to mount a march to Montgomery. Johnson met in Washington with George Wallace, but the cagey governor managed to escape the Oval Office without giving a promise to protect the marchers. In an attempt to quell future bloodshed, Johnson addressed a joint session of Congress on the evening of March 15, demanded a voting rights bill, and, in his deepest southern drawl, invoked the words of the movement when he promised his audience "We *shall* overcome." SNCC, which had moved its base of operations to Montgomery, turned a deaf ear to the president. James Forman spoke for many of his SNCC colleagues when he proclaimed, "If we can't sit at the table, let's knock the fucking legs off." Events were pushing toward a march; King lost his legal cover when the federal judge reversed himself and declared the protestors had a legal and constitutional right to march.

On March 21, the third march to Montgomery began. Estimates placed the number of marchers as high as twenty-five thousand; the line was once again headed by King. This time, there was no confrontation at the Pettus Bridge—Johnson had federalized the Alabama National Guard to protect the marchers; two thousand soldiers of the United States Army and nineteen hundred members of the Alabama National Guard protected the marchers. They made the fifty-four mile march in four days. In Montgomery, on March 25, King spoke on the steps of the state Capitol in words that echoed his speech from the Lincoln Memorial: "The end we seek is a society at peace with itself, a society that can live with its conscience."

Campaign organizers proclaimed a victory. The march, after all, had gone on. And the march had been directly responsible for forcing the government's hand and earning a major legislative victory. On August 6, Johnson signed the Voting Rights Act of 1965, which ended literacy tests and gave the attorney general the power to appoint federal examiners to supervise voter registration in any state that discriminated politically. When joined with the passage of the Twenty-Fourth Amendment, which outlawed the poll tax, barriers to voting had, indeed, been shredded.

Yet, the cost to the movement was dear. The March from Selma to Montgomery had not only cost hundreds of wounded within the movement ranks, as well as the life of Jim Reeb, but it had also cost the life of Viola Liuzzo, a Detroit housewife who was stopped and shot by white terrorists after picking up a black marcher in her car and giving him a ride following King's speech in Montgomery. As important for the second half of the decade, there were now, in effect, two civil rights movements. SNCC and King would work together, begrudgingly, one more time in 1966. But after Selma it was clear that it was not King's Southern Moderates who held the future. Indeed, SNCC's leaders were about to replace King as the face of the civil rights movement, as that movement lurched north, to attack racism in the ghettos that had welcomed Malcolm X.

On August 11, two weeks after the end of the Selma to Montgomery march, one of those ghettos in East Los Angeles would explode as the civil rights movement entered a new place—one much less concerned with the ballot than with the bullet.

Recommended Reading

The greatest work on the civil rights movements of the 1960s, as well as the greatest biography I have ever read, is Taylor Branch's three-volume *America in the King Years*. Each volume—*Parting the Waters, 1954–1963* (New York: Simon and Schuster, 1988), *Pillar of Fire, 1963–1965* (New York: Simon and Schuster, 1998), and *At Canaan's Edge, 1965–1968* (New York: Simon and Schuster, 2006)—is a masterpiece of American historical writing. For both the generalist and the specialist, begin your study of the movement with these volumes; in all your reading on the subject you will find none better. The interested student is also encouraged to view (cautiously, as with all documentaries) "Eyes on the Prize: America's Civil Rights Years," produced by the Public Broadcasting System in 1986.

4

"We'll Have the Opportunity to Move Upward"

The Great Society of Lyndon B. Johnson

EACH MAN WHO HAS SUCCEEDED to the American presidency from the vice presidency upon the death of his predecessor is, for a period of time at least, overshadowed by the memory of his predecessor. It is thus a Herculean task that confronts the new president. While propriety as well as political common sense dictate that the new leader should pay homage to his fallen predecessor both loud and often, there comes a point where, if he wishes to succeed with his own agenda, the new president must separate himself from the past.

On the surface, it seemed in November 1963 that Lyndon B. Johnson, a man whose presidential ambitions had long been known, faced an impossible task in this regard. Following his assassination, John F. Kennedy had been deified in the minds of the American people—his youth, vigor, and charisma were now seen as the presidential standard. Indeed, most contemporary observers considered Johnson the anti-Kennedy. He was too coarse in manner for those who had inhabited (or briefly visited) Camelot; they saw him, at best, as a Texas curiosity who could never measure up to the expectations set by Kennedy's charisma. Matching this rather elitist disdain was the visceral hatred with which a large portion of the American people regarded Johnson by 1966, largely over his conduct of the Vietnam War. It is the Kennedy myth in reverse.

We can come closer to a fuller historical understanding of the importance of the Johnson presidency when considering that Johnson was the anti-Kennedy in another significant respect. Unlike Kennedy, who had been bored senseless during his fourteen-year career as a legislator, Johnson had both loved and mastered the legislative process. Indeed, Johnson's coarse, combative personality made him the perfect type of executive for advancing a legislative program. In the first months of his presidency, he shrewdly used the nation's grief to gain passage of those bills that Kennedy could not. Then, following a landslide election mandate in 1964, Johnson put on a legislative tour de force—a two-year clinic in how to advance a president's legislative agenda. What he would label his "Great Society" was a series of laws that went far beyond the liberalism of any of his twentieth-century Democratic predecessors. It was also devastatingly expensive, with bills for his programs coming due decades after Johnson had left the White House. The Great Society was, and remains today, liberalism's finest legislative moment.

Johnson's upbringing put him on a par with the economically disadvantaged that, despite his stories of being affected by poverty in West Virginia during the 1960 primary, Kennedy could never have understood. Born in 1908 in the hill country of Western Texas, Johnson knew a prairie upbringing that, while not poverty-stricken, did not include such luxuries as a home with electricity or running water. Yet Johnson's parents fought through their hardscrabble existence to teach their son the value of an education. His mother, Rebekah, was raised by her father to both value and master intellectual pursuits—he taught her to read and taught her mathematics, and she would graduate from Baylor College before marrying and becoming a housewife. Johnson's father, Samuel, became a cattle trader, cotton dealer, and real estate broker, as well as a Texas politician of some significance—he served five terms in the Texas legislature beginning in 1904. Rebekah saw in her son the makings of the teacher she could have been; Sam saw in him the makings of the politician that he was. They were both right, and young Lyndon would pursue both careers.

The Johnson family moved from their farm on the Pedernales River to nearby Johnson City so that their son could obtain formal schooling. Lyndon graduated high school in 1924, the president of a graduating class of seven. Unsure of his future, he spent the better part of the next three years in search of himself—taking a trip with two childhood friends to California, doing roadwork for the county, and even working as an elevator operator. In 1927, sick of the monotony of manual labor, Johnson enrolled in Southwest State

Teacher's College in San Marcos. He graduated in 1930, part of the labor force that now faced the Great Depression. But luckier than most, Johnson got a job, teaching debate at Sam Houston High School in Houston, Texas.

Throughout his public life, Johnson introduced himself to crowds as a former teacher. But teaching would not long hold his ambitions. While at Southwest State, Johnson had participated in his first campaign—he had managed a candidate for state railroad commissioner. In 1931, acting on the recommendation of a mutual friend from that campaign, Johnson interviewed for the position of secretary in the Washington office of Richard Kleberg, the congressman from Texas's Fourteenth District, a position that Kleberg gave to Johnson. Traditionally this had been an anonymous position. Johnson, however, used the fact that Kleberg was detached and largely uninterested in legislative affairs, meshed it with his own personal ambition, and turned the job into one of real influence and power. His energy and workaholism brought him to the attention of the New Dealers, who saw in Johnson the ability to get things done that would otherwise seem implausible. In 1935, Johnson was appointed Texas director of the National Youth Administration, the New Deal agency designed to provide professional training and part-time employment for the nation's youth. While in this position, Johnson arranged schooling and training for some twenty thousand Texans, making his program a model for the nation. It was his springboard to national politics—in 1937, Johnson was elected to the U.S. House of Representatives from the Tenth District in Texas, after running a campaign that stressed his support for Roosevelt and the New Deal.

In the House, Johnson was both a Roosevelt pet and a consistent New Dealer. Roosevelt was famously quoted as saying "That's the kind of man I could have been if I hadn't had a Harvard education," and he told political operative Tommy Corcoran to "be nice to this boy." For his part, Johnson was shoveling New Deal money back into Texas in an attempt to shore up his political fortune with that state's conservative power base. In 1941, Johnson tried to move into the Senate but was defeated by W. Lee "Pappy" O'Daniel, losing by 1,311 out of some 600,000 votes cast. Roosevelt, who had learned all about voting irregularities while traveling the maze of New York politics, later chided his protégé for not sitting on the ballot boxes during the final tally. But because he had been able to keep his seat in the House, Johnson was still representing his district in 1941 when the Japanese attacked Pearl Harbor. Johnson was the first member of Congress to enlist in the armed forces; he flew one mission in the Southwest Pacific theater of operations, survived a crash landing in Australia, and earned the Silver Star for gallantry in action. In 1942, along with all other members of Congress in uniform, Johnson was recalled to Washington by Roosevelt. As a decorated veteran, Johnson had a leg up in the 1948 Senate race. Winning—some have claimed stealing—a razor-thin election victory of 87 votes (he would be dubbed "Landslide Lyndon" by friends and enemies alike), Johnson joined a class of Senate freshmen in 1949 that would make a substantial impact on American politics for the next three decades—it included Hubert Humphrey, Eugene McCarthy, Estes Kefauver, and Paul Douglas.

Johnson's race to the pinnacle of legislative power was meteoric, unprecedented, and—given his prodigious knowledge of the workings of Congress—not surprising. In his first term in the Senate, he continued to shovel money back to Texas. He also showed himself particularly adroit at bridging the gaps between his party's liberal and conservative wings. Winning party leadership was his goal more than was the creation of legislation, and in 1955, after only one term of service in the Senate, Johnson was elected the majority leader. Teaming himself with another wily Texan, Speaker of the House Sam Rayburn, Johnson became *the* legislative force with which the Eisenhower administration had to contend. Immediately recognizing that a blanket opposition of the administration's programs would earn for him the title of obstructionist, Johnson demanded that his Democratic legions view each piece of legislation on its merits. This strategy allowed Johnson to take much of the credit for many administration initiatives, most notably a 1957 Civil Rights Act that Johnson had to amend severely in order to secure its passage.

Johnson overrated the political value of his rise to pwer in the Senate, however. In 1960, convinced that his experience and skill would ultimately separate him from Kennedy, Johnson refused to campaign publicly for the nomination. As a result, he lost ground to his opponent and opened the door for his natural southern constituency to abandon him for the presumptive winner, claiming behind closed doors that Johnson had sold out the South on the Civil Rights bill. A furious Johnson, feeling betrayed by those whose loyalties he had assiduously courted as majority leader, could only watch in disgust as the Kennedy juggernaut won for the part-time senator the prize that Johnson dearly wanted.

It was not a surprise to insiders that Kennedy offered Johnson the second spot on the ticket in July 1960. Kennedy could not win the election unless he was able to win the South, and of the very few southern leaders with any national exposure, Johnson was one of only a handful who might be acceptable to the party's northern liberal wing. A more interesting question is why Johnson *accepted* the nomination. The decision clearly stood the chance of hurting him in Texas, where the Democrats were in the minority and under constant pressure from conservative business interests. Moreover, the possibility of enduring a second-class servitude to Jack Kennedy, whom he privately referred to as "the Boy," could not have been appealing to Johnson. The "why" of Johnson's decision has never been adequately resolved by historians, but of all the scenarios discussed, the one that resonates the most with Johnson's character and ambitions is the story that links his acceptance to his party loyalty: that at the convention, Sam Rayburn cornered Johnson and demanded that he accept Kennedy's offer, asking his fellow Texan, "Do you want to be responsible for Dick Nixon being elected president?"

Johnson endured no more or less abuse and neglect in his three years as Kennedy's vice president than had any of his predecessors. He was not frozen out of meetings—quite the contrary; taking Eisenhower's working relationship with Nixon as his model, Kennedy included Johnson in most policy discussions and, like Nixon, used him as his representative around the world (as we will see, Johnson's report to Kennedy on Vietnam played a significant role in Kennedy's decision to send the Green Berets to that country). Johnson was also entrusted with the space program, a high-profile and high-priority administration initiative that Johnson not only handled brilliantly but also used to shovel money into the Texas economy, virtually rebuilding the city of Houston. Johnson's advice was not, then, completely ignored, as legend would have it. However, he found Kennedy tentative, and, until the Cuban Missile Crisis, too easily swayed by his advisors. For his part, Kennedy treated Johnson with respect but did not rein in his closest advisors, particularly Robert Kennedy, who treated the vice president with thinly veiled contempt. Johnson knew that his value to the Kennedys lay only in his ability to help carry the South. Just before his death, Kennedy put an end to the newspaper rumors of a rift between him and his vice president, announcing that Johnson would definitely be his running mate in 1964.

In the hours and days immediately following the murder of John Kennedy, as the nation reeled in shock and Kennedy advisors began to circle around their fallen leader, Lyndon Johnson was the paragon of patience, good political decision making, and calm. Playing completely against character,

Johnson kept a low profile, allowing the extended Kennedy family to command the stage during the funeral. The new president's public speeches were short, yet he made his presence known to the bureaucracy in an endless series of meetings with congressional, state, and military leaders. Indeed, Johnson's instant transition to the presidency has been universally judged as being, for that moment in time, perfect. But for those who had served Kennedy, their grief—and, soon, their politics—would not allow them to accept Johnson as anything but a crude usurper, a Texas holding pattern before Bobby Kennedy reclaimed the throne. Johnson, however, had no plans to serve as a one-year caretaker president.

Lyndon Johnson is quoted as saying, "John F. Kennedy was a bit too conservative for my tastes." Johnson envisioned a set of domestic policies that was so sweeping it would not only dwarf anything accomplished by Kennedy but, more important, would rival Franklin D. Roosevelt's New Deal. To Johnson, the New Deal was the first part of an unfinished liberal dogma. He firmly believed that none of his predecessors had done enough to protect and advance the social welfare and economic welfare of the American people. For the poor boy from the Pedernales, government had entered into a contract with its citizenry—it should *guarantee* each American a minimum standard of living; *guarantee* them the opportunity to advance above and beyond that minimum; and *guarantee* them an opportunity to succeed. This was Johnson's Great Society—it was the New Deal on steroids.

Johnson came out of the gate quickly, hoping to dispose of all leftover Kennedy legislation by the 1964 presidential election. By February 1964, Johnson had won passage of Kennedy's proposed tax cut. By July, he had signed into law the first meaningful civil rights act since Reconstruction. It was a bill that had also been proposed by Kennedy, and, like the tax cut, a bill that had been languishing in committee at the time of Kennedy's death (see chapter 3). For most leaders, who faced reelection in a matter of months, the passage of these two controversial measures—plus the personal success of holding the country together in a time of unparalleled trauma—would be enough of a record on which to campaign. Not so Lyndon Johnson. On May 22, 1964, in a speech at the University of Michigan, Johnson announced his vision:

In your time we have the opportunity to move not only toward the rich
society and the powerful society, but upward to the Great Society.

The Great Society rests on abundance and liberty for all. It demands an end to poverty and racial injustice, to which we are totally committed in our time. But that is just the beginning.

The Great Society is a place where every child can find knowledge to enrich his mind and enlarge his talents . . . it is a place where man can renew contact with nature . . . it is a place where men are more concerned with the quality of their goals than the quantity of their goods . . . it is a challenge constantly renewed, beckoning us toward a destiny where the meaning of our lives matches the marvelous products of our labor.

Johnson wasted no time in attacking what he believed to be the key domestic problem in America—the issue on which all domestic challenges, including civil rights, hinged—Johnson did not wait for his own elected term before he declared war on American poverty.

As with so many issues that faced him, before his death Kennedy had been measuring the problem of poverty in America. He had been personally affected by the sight of the poverty in Appalachia during the 1960 campaign; he had been intellectually affected by sociologist Michael Harrington's 1962 book, *The Other America: Poverty in the United States,* argued that there were, in essence, two nations in America—the one identified by John Kenneth Galbraith in his 1958 best-seller, *The Affluent Society,* and another nation, whose citizens led a life of despair:

The United States in the sixties contains an affluent society within its borders. Millions and tens of millions enjoy the highest standard of life the world has ever known. . . . At the same time, the United States contains an underdeveloped nation, a culture of poverty. Its inhabitants . . . are beyond history, beyond progress, sunk in a paralyzing, maiming routine. . . . [Change] can be done if there is a comprehensive program that attacks the culture of poverty at every one of its strong points. But who will carry out this campaign? There is only one institution in the society capable of acting to abolish poverty. That is the Federal Government.

By November 1963, Kennedy and his chief economic advisor, Walter Heller, both of whom had been profoundly affected by Harrington's book, had only begun to discuss a legislative plan to combat poverty; Johnson jumped at the chance to make it his signature. He was clear with his advisors: what would become known as the War on Poverty was "my kind of program."

Shrewdly choosing R. Sargent Shriver, a Kennedy in-law and former director of the Peace Corps, to develop and run the program, Johnson developed what was, in retrospect, a modestly funded set of programs (hamstrung by his recently passed tax cut, one set of writers estimates that Johnson's poverty programs were originally funded at $947.5 million, one-tenth the level of Roosevelt's Works Progress Administration). The plan was to attack the *culture* of poverty, without creating the boondoggle of a vast government handout. Thus Johnson's programs, together included in the Economic Opportunity Act of 1964, concentrated on job creation, not on welfare checks. The Office of Economic Opportunity (OEO) provided modest grants to community agencies in poverty-stricken neighborhoods. Those local governments were then responsible for spending that money, not the federal government. The program also created the Job Corps (occupational training for unemployed teenagers) and Volunteers in Service to America (VISTA), an inner-city volunteer organization modeled on Kennedy's Peace Corps. Yet the OEO was not full-bore federal government intrusion in American's economic lives; the part of the War on Poverty that most represented "welfare"—the Food Stamp Act—was funded by both the states and the federal government and begun in 1965 with little flourish. Also, Community Action Programs (CAPS) were created to give much of the responsibility for change to the community.

The potential problem of the costs of such programs, modest though they were by comparative standards, was lost in the blather of the 1964 presidential contest. The Republicans could not agree on a centrist candidate who could oppose Johnson by painting him as a spendthrift liberal. Instead, the party chose doctrinaire conservative Barry Goldwater as its standard-bearer. To his philosophical credit and future political detriment, the Arizona senator went head-on into the wind, his campaign being an uncompromising attack against civil rights, Great Society spending, and, perhaps most devastating, a thinly veiled promise that a Goldwater presidency would use nuclear weapons to end the war in Vietnam. An honorable, thoughtful public servant, Goldwater was nonetheless too easy a target for Johnson, who painted his opponent as little less than a lunatic. (The Goldwater campaign slogan was "In your heart you know he's right"; Democrats countered with "In your guts you know he's nuts.") Johnson won with 61 percent of the popular vote—at that point, the biggest presidential landslide in American history. The Democrats also won solid majorities in both houses of Congress.

Johnson now had his own presidency by landslide and had the votes in Congress to do his bidding. Where his 1964 legislation can be seen as a moderate package designed to finish Kennedy's legacy, the legislation of 1965–66 was all Johnson's, and it took the idea of the activist state to stratospheric heights. It was the high-water mark of American liberalism; it would be Lyndon Johnson's Hundred Days.

An expert legislator, Johnson knew that even with a Democratic majority in Congress, his honeymoon with Capitol Hill would not last. In early 1965, Johnson charged 135 task forces to develop policies and sent a blizzard of legislation to Congress—a startling sixty-five messages by July. By year's end, Johnson had begun to address every area that he had outlined in his "Great Society" address of only one year before. His highest priority—S1 and HR1—was to fix the nation's sagging health-care system, one that was now, thanks to medical advances since World War II, responsible for caring for an increasingly aging population. Medicare—basic hospitalization, rest home care, and home care benefits for those Americans over the age of sixty-five—was passed over the objections of the American Medical Association (AMA), which thought that government intervention into health care would put a ceiling on their profits. A rider attached to that bill—what became known as Medicaid—was a program that shared basic health-care costs for the poor between federal and state governments. These were bills that Harry Truman had tried to get passed, and failed; within two years of their passage, seventeen million Americans were using them.

Johnson also brought the power of the federal government to bear on the crisis of education that had been caused by the titanic influx of baby-boom students into the system since the 1950s. Strained past their breaking point, the physical plants of American schools were deteriorating, and many urban schools were no longer able to provide their students with the barest of classroom necessities. The Elementary and Secondary Schools Act (ESEA) of 1965 opened the federal coffers to school districts—$1 billion in original aid would be increased to $6 billion by 1968. The Higher Education Act of 1965 did much the same for the nation's colleges, guaranteeing an initial $3.9 billion in federal support for loans to help college students. It is safe to say that were it not for the initiations of Lyndon Johnson, the vast majority of young people reading this book would not be doing so in a college classroom.

Health care and education reform remain the best known of the Great Society initiatives. They were, however, the proverbial tip of the iceberg.

Johnson established the National Endowment for the Humanities to provide federal funding for the arts; Head Start, a program to assist poor preschool children; and a new cabinet-level agency, the Department of Housing and Urban Development (HUD), to insert the federal government into the development of the nation's festering urban areas.

The Great Society also attacked the effects of what had been a particularly casual use of the environment. Historian Douglas Miller suggests that at the turn of the decade, Americans, with less than 6 percent of the world's population, consumed 40 percent of the world's resources annually. And it could easily be said that American's were uncaring consumers—they had casually polluted both water and air and had unwittingly unleashed the possibility of a nuclear fallout that stood to destroy both terra and atmosphere.

As with other movements of the decade, it can be said that the environmental movement began with a book. Written by famed naturalist Rachel Carson and released in September 1962, *Silent Spring* highlighted the destructive effects of pesticides such as dichlorodiphenyltrichloroethane (DDT) on animals, the environment, and humans. She also charged the chemical companies with lying to the public about what their pesticides could do; in this, Carson fit the mold of those sixties activists who were protesting against all kinds of corporate abuses. The book took its title from the title of its chapter on what pesticides did to birds. Her writing was both evocative and heart-wrenching:

> There was once a town in the heart of America where all life seemed to live in harmony with its surroundings. . . . Then a strange blight crept over the area and everything began to change. . . . There was a strange stillness. . . . The few birds seen anywhere were moribund; they trembled violently and could not fly. It was a spring without voices. On the mornings that had once throbbed with the dawn chorus of scores of bird voices there was now no sound; only silence lay over the fields and woods and marsh.

A masterpiece of analytical writing and one of the most influential books of the twentieth century, *Silent Spring* not only led to the banning of DDT, it also sparked an increased public awareness of environmental issues.

The environment was never a high priority for Kennedy, but in the Johnson administration it often took center stage. This was largely due to the effective lobbying of two Democratic party leaders. Edmund Muskie, the junior senator from Maine, was dubbed "Mr. Clean" by his colleagues for his relentless support of environmental reforms. Stewart L. Udall of Arizona, named secretary of the interior by Kennedy in 1961, kept that job throughout the entirety of the Kennedy and Johnson administrations. Together, Muskie and Udall formed an effective team, lobbying Johnson for environmental reforms that, given his rural Texas background and pressure from his environmentally conscious wife, first lady Claudia "Lady Bird" Johnson, he was already inclined to accept. Their most notable successes were the Clean Water Acts of 1964 and 1965, the Motor Vehicle Air Pollution Control Act, and the Air Quality Act of 1967. Cornerstones of Great Society legislation, the bills provided for the first national standards for, and tests of, drinking water and air quality.

As with other areas of reform in the 1960s, young activists were not satisfied with what they believed to be narrow legislative reforms. On the environment, they pointed to a growing amount of smog, a noxious chemical compound caused when sunlight hit various pollutants in the air, that hovered over the largest of the world's cities (in 1966, in New York City alone, 166 deaths were attributed to the adverse affects of smog). They also pointed to a rise in water pollution despite Johnson's environmental legislation. Activists also began to protest the development of nuclear power, virtually unregulated at the time, and the all-too-obvious dumping of nuclear waste in residential areas (also unregulated).

After Johnson had left office, the actions of the environmental activists also led to a different kind of legislative response. In September 1969, Wisconsin senator Gaylord Nelson advocated a national teach-in on environmental issues; in so doing, he referenced the teach-ins utilized less than five years earlier by the antiwar movement. This call for a teach-in led to an astounding protest on April 22, 1970—the first nationwide Earth Day. Some twenty million Americans participated in a day designed to bring environmental issues to the fore. A resounding success, it was the largest demonstration in favor of any issue to that point in American history. Nonpartisan and nonconfrontational, Earth Day stands as the only protest generated during the 1960s that continues to be celebrated each year in contemporary America.

The costs for the Great Society were astronomical. Johnson was warned by his economic advisors that continued support for his Great Society programs, when coupled with his spending on the war in Vietnam, would lead to severe budget deficits unless accompanied by a tax cut. Always at full throttle, Johnson refused to back off his domestic reforms and refused to take the political castor oil of a tax cut. The Great Society was, in his words, his "beautiful woman"—he would stick with her to the bitter end.

As Johnson fostered an activist presidency, his contemporary, Chief Justice Earl Warren, fostered an activist Supreme Court. As it was for the Great Society and its vast array of enacted, statutory laws, the second half of the 1960s witnessed the apex of liberal jurisprudence—constitutional law—in the nation's history.

Since Dwight Eisenhower's 1953 appointment of Warren—a former governor of California, Republican nominee for the vice presidency, and candidate for the presidency—the court had take a decided—and quite unexpected—lurch to the Left. In the first decade of Warren's tenure, the court had infuriated conservatives by ordering the desegregation of public schools, albeit with the vague timetable of "all deliberate speed" (*Brown v. Board of Education of Topeka, Kansas I and II,* 1954 and 1955); had flown in the face of the McCarthy witch hunt by overturning the convictions of convicted Communist Party activists (*Yates v. U.S.,* 1957); had upheld the traditional position of church versus state by outlawing prayer in public schools (*Engel v. Vitale,* 1962); had attacked the institutional racism of the apportionment of legislative districts by ruling that boundary lines must be rational and not drawn to disenfranchise citizens (*Baker v. Carr,* 1962); and had declared that to be obscene, a work must be "utterly without redeeming social value" (*Memoirs v. Massachusetts,* 1964). These and many other cases would be enough to confirm a liberal legacy for the Warren Court. But in 1964–69, the court would further that legacy, leading some historians to include the Warren Court as an integral part of Lyndon Johnson's Great Society.

As the Johnson administration attempted to economically aid the poor and dispossessed, the Warren Court granted them unprecedented constitutional protection. Clarence Gideon was convicted of breaking and entering a Florida pool hall. During his trial, poverty-stricken, Gideon could not afford a lawyer. He requested a lawyer, and the judge refused. After his conviction, Gideon wrote his own petition to the Supreme Court—and its eloquence led to its acceptance. In *Gideon v. Wainwright* (1965), the court unanimously reversed Gideon's conviction; a guarantee of counsel, regardless of the defendant's ability to pay that counsel's fee, was a constitutional right under the Sixth Amendment, as applied to the states by the due process clause of the

Fourteenth Amendment. In 1963, Ernesto Arturo Miranda was arrested in Arizona and charged with kidnapping and rape, even though he could not positively be identified by the victim. Miranda confessed to the crimes but did so without receiving the benefit of legal counsel. Thus, Miranda was unaware of his Fifth and Sixth Amendment rights, as well as the right to counsel that had been won under *Gideon*. The Supreme Court used *Miranda v. Arizona* (1966) to declare that "coercion can be mental, as well as physical"; thus the Fifth Amendment demanded that police had to inform all suspects of their constitutional rights at the time of their arrest.

The Warren Court used a case emanating from the civil rights movement to strike one of the most important First Amendment blows for freedom of the press in the nation's history. In March 1960, the Committee to Defend Martin Luther King and the Struggle for Freedom in the South ran a full-page ad in the *New York Times,* listing names of southern officials who had opposed the movement, and claimed that those listed were trying to "demoralize Negro Americans and weaken their will to struggle." In an innovative move, Alabama governor John Patterson engineered a $500,000 libel suit against the *Times* and all those who had paid for the ad, in the name of Montgomery Police Commissioner L. B. Sullivan (one of the officials mentioned in the ad). The suit charged specific falsehoods in the ad (for one example, protestors had not sung "My Country 'Tis of Thee" at a protest as the ad claimed, but rather the national anthem), and that the ad had wrongfully portrayed them as "violators of the Constitution." To no one's surprise, the state court found for the plaintiffs. The case threatened to bankrupt the civil rights movement in a sea of legal debts, but an equally compelling issue soon emerged—could a statement made in public be made libelous by inconsequential errors such as those in the ad? If so, no public figure would be safe from public harassment. When argued before the Supreme Court, the $500,000 fate of signatories of the ad took a back seat to a debate over the definition of libel. In *New York Times Co. v. Sullivan* (1964), the court dramatically expanded the First Amendment protection of the press, ruling that "erroneous statement is inevitable in free debate; and even those false statements must be protected." Plaintiffs in libel actions now had to prove "actual malice"—that those who spoke falsehood against public figures had to *know* that it was false, or the statement was not libelous and the media in which it was published or broadcast was not guilty of libel.

In another case that would become a fundamental precedent for one of the most important cases in the court's history, the Warren Court went far beyond the original intent of the framers and defined an American civil liberty that had long been assumed but was nowhere written down. A Connecticut law passed in 1879 held that disseminating information about birth control options, or prescribing or purchasing birth control, was a crime. To force a test case of the law, the executive director and medical director of the Planned Parenthood League of Connecticut prescribed a vaginal diaphragm for a married woman. They were arrested. As in *Sullivan,* the Warren Court used the test case to make a broader statement than simply ruling on the constitutionality of the facts. In the case of *Griswold v. Connecticut* (1965), birth control took a backseat to a woman's right to privacy—a right nowhere specifically articulated in the constitution or in statutory or case law. Justice William O. Douglas, the court's leading progressive thinker, argued for a 7–2 majority that the First Amendment demanded that all knowledge—in this case, information on birth control—be made available to its citizens. But Douglas also argued that the First Amendment "has a penumbra where privacy is protected from government intrusion," a penumbra that created "zones of privacy." It would be *Griswold* that would form the key precedent in the attack on state restrictions on abortions when in *Roe v. Wade* (1973) those laws were severely circumscribed, as the Court cited a woman's fundamental right to privacy as covering her reproductive choices.

One case seemed, however, to engulf all issues and choices of the decade. On December 11, 1965, after attending a peace march in Washington, a group of teenagers and their parents met at the Des Moines, Iowa, home of Dr. William and Margaret Eckhardt. The discussion centered on how this group might support one of the key motivations for the march—support for Senator Robert F. Kennedy's call for an extension of the upcoming Christmas truce in Vietnam so that genuine peace negotiations might begin. They decided that the public-school and college-aged children in the group would wear black armbands to their classes in support of peace talks and in mourning for those lost in Vietnam. Although members of Students for a Democratic Society (SDS) were present at the meeting, there was no organized support from the group. Indeed, the young people were encouraged to make their own individual decisions. News of the meeting traveled quickly, and principals of the affected schools decided that such a protest—which in their mind held the possibility of widespread disruption—would not be permitted. Nevertheless, on December 16 and 17 a number of students wore armbands to school. Christopher Eckhardt and John Tinker, two fifteen-year-old high school sophomores, and John's sister Mary Beth, a thirteen-year-old eighth grader at Warren Harding Junior High School, were among those students. All three children came from families who had traditions of social activism; each of them faced a varying amount of reaction to their symbolic protest—a football player tried to rip the armband off Christopher's jacket, and he was told by an administrator that he was "too young to have opinions"; Mary Beth was sent home with a suspension notice; her brother John was simply sent home.

The parents of the disciplined students faced many well-attended, tension-packed meetings of the Des Moines school board. In the words of one member, the board believed that the armbands presented a "potentially disturbing element in our schools"; for her part, Mary Beth wore her armband to one of the meetings. The final decision of a badly split board was that while the armbands *could* be worn by students if they were mourning, the wearing of any symbol that criticized the United States government was forbidden. Lawyers for the Iowa Civil Liberties Union, which had been advising the families since the original protests, prepared for a court fight. At issue would be a definition of a high school student's First Amendment rights: Was the wearing of an armband protected under freedom of speech? And even if so, what role did the government have in balancing that freedom with the state's legitimate right to protect its citizens—in this case, public school students—from an atmosphere of disruption?

Throughout the slow climb through the judicial system of what would be named *Tinker v. Des Moines,* better known in the press as "The Armband Case," the Vietnam War escalated both in the number of soldiers killed and the effect on the American psyche. The headline of the *Des Moines Register* on the day that the students' trial began read, "A Lot of Dead Marines." *Tinker* thus took on a different, more pressing meaning in the national imagination—as were their college contemporaries, these three secondary school students had stood up to power and were now fighting for their constitutional right to do so. If high school students won, their actions would validate many of the tactics of the student and antiwar movements, tactics that were now on the front page of the life of every American. The stakes could not be higher—as Mary Beth Tinker told a reporter who asked her if she would ever wear another armband: "I'm not sure if I would wear one or not, but I'd like to be able to."

Not surprisingly, the lower courts ruled against the students. The judge for the U.S. District Court for the Southern District of Iowa ruled on September 1, 1966, that while an armband *was* symbolic speech and *was* protected by the First Amendment, those protections were not absolute. The judge ruled that the state had a duty to protect a "disciplined atmosphere" in the schools and should set aside disciplinary actions only if the school officials acted "unreasonably"—a situation that the judge did not find to have occurred in the armband case. After the Eighth Circuit Court upheld the District Court's ruling, the Eckhardts and Tinkers took their case to the Supreme Court.

Clearly, the Warren Court was a court that would largely be friendly to the students' case. The question would be whether or not a majority could be found that would support the contention made by the students that the wearing of armbands posed no great risk to the high school population. The direction of the decision could be gleaned from the tone of the November 12, 1968, oral argument before the Court. Justice Thurgood Marshall asked the lawyer for the school board how many total students had worn armbands. When the chagrinned lawyer responded that there were seven such students, Marshall feigned shock: "Seven out of 18,000? And the school board was advised that seven students wearing armbands were disrupting 18,000? Am I correct?" He was.

When the court's 7–2 decision in *Tinker v. Des Moines* was read from the bench on February 24, 1969, no amount of ambiguity could be found. Justice Abe Fortas—a former advisor to Lyndon Johnson, lawyer for Clarence Gideon in the famous 1965 case, and an architect of much of the Great Society legislation—wrote the majority opinion. In that opinion lay one of the sharpest statements in favor of a broad reading of the First Amendment rights to free expression: "It can hardly be argued that . . . students or teachers shed their constitutional rights to freedom of speech or expression at the schoolhouse gate." The court ruled that the armbands were, indeed, symbolic speech, and that the freedom to express one's views in a school setting where the classroom was a "marketplace of ideas," could not be abridged, unless it "markedly and substantially interfere[d] with the requirements of appropriate discipline in the operation of the school"—something that had clearly not happened in Des Moines. As Fortas acidly wrote, "state-operated schools may not be enclaves of totalitarianism."

The government activism of the Johnson years was hardly met with universal praise. The Warren Court was pilloried throughout America as being too activist. Warren himself was burned in effigy, and roadside billboards called for his impeachment. Warren's Court continued its activist approach to jurisprudence, protected by the life tenure afforded federal judges. Johnson, however, had no such protection. His Great Society came to a screeching halt, even before the end of his term in office. Chief among the reasons was the War in Vietnam, which was an additional burden to the American treasury. His foray into urban renewal—the physical improvement and reshaping of America's cities that was a natural outgrowth of the War on Poverty—cost even more money and earned the Great Society even more enemies from localities than had either his fight against poverty or his education reform. This program came under even more criticism in the summer of 1967, when racial tension exploded in the streets of cities that had supposedly been improved. The Housing and Urban Development Act of 1968 and the New Communities Act of 1968—both reactions to the criticism of the previous year—guaranteed with public funds any private entrepreneurial investments in the improvement of urban areas. It was an attempt to infuse America's cities with new thinking, but by 1968 Johnson simply did not have the money he was promising. Republicans soon were able to tag Johnson with the "spendthrift liberal" label that they could not pin on him in 1964. Add to this the criticism that was heaped on Johnson, as critics charged him with having hijacked the true purpose of the American government—to assist with, rather than provide for, the welfare of the American people. The Great Society programs had also become a bureaucratic nightmare—there were so many of them, residing in often competing governmental offices, that they were difficult to administer under the best of circumstances, not to mention wartime.

By 1968, Johnson's policies had come under attack from all corners of the political spectrum. But they were law. And short of an ultraconservative president or Congress who damned-the-torpedoes and repealed these massive outlays of financial aid to the American voter (which, by the way, did not ever happen), Johnson's legislative accomplishments would remain intact. They never were fully appreciated by his nation, however. Johnson knew that, ruefully observing that "I wish the public had seen the task of ending poverty the same way they saw the task of getting to the moon." This was liberalism's greatest moment—the old-style liberalism, that is, that advocated for an activist federal government and outlays of federal monies to guarantee the welfare of its people. By 1968, that liberalism was under attack, as was Johnson, and a new group of younger Americans called themselves "liberal." Disenchanted with the war and the pace of civil rights, these new younger reformers ignored the gains of Johnson and, instead, tried to change the world.

Recommended Reading

Bigger than life, Lyndon Johnson has inspired several multivolume biographies. The most detailed, Robert A. Caro, *The Years of Lyndon Johnson* (3 vols., New York: Knopf, 1982–2002) is incomplete, taking Johnson's life through to 1960. The most thorough and balanced is Robert Dallek's two-volume set, *Lone Star Rising: Lyndon Johnson and His Times, 1908–1960* (New York: Oxford Univ. Press, 1991) and *Flawed Giant: Lyndon Johnson and His Times* (New York: Oxford Univ. Press, 1998). The best one-volume biography of Johnson is Dallek's condensation of his two-volume work, *Lyndon Johnson: Portrait of a President* (New York: Oxford Univ. Press, 2005). A valuable survey of the Johnson presidency, while detailed, is Vaughn Davis Bornet, *The Presidency of Lyndon B. Johnson* (Lawrence: Univ. Press of Kansas, 1984). John A. Andrew, *Lyndon Johnson and the Great Society* (Chicago: Ivan R. Dee, 1998) is the best starting point; more analytical (and ultimately critical) is Irwin Unger, *The Best Intentions: The Triumph and Future of the Great Society under Kennedy, Johnson, and Nixon* (New York: Doubleday, 1996). A useful compendium of documents, along with a good short survey, can be found in Bruce J. Schulman, *Lyndon B. Johnson and American Liberalism*, 2d ed. (Boston: Bedford–St. Martin's, 2007). For conservative opposition to the Great Society, consult Mary C. Brennan, *Turning Right in the Sixties: The Conservative Capture of the GOP* (Chapel Hill: Univ. of North Carolina Press, 1995). On the Supreme Court during this period, consult relevant chapters of Michael Les Benedict, *The Blessings of Liberty*, rev. ed. (New York: Wadsworth, 2005), and John W. Johnson, *The Struggle for Student Rights: Tinker v. Des Moines and the 1960s* (Lawrence: Univ. Press of Kansas, 1997).

5

"As American as Cherry Pie"

Civil Rights, 1965–1969

A NEW PHASE of the American civil rights movement began with a DWI.

On Wednesday, August 11, 1965, only five days after Lyndon Johnson had signed the Voting Rights Act, Ronald Frye was celebrating his discharge from the Air Force by doing some midday drinking with his brother. Frye's car was clearly moving erratically when it was pulled over to the side of the road by the California Highway Patrol just outside the city limits of Los Angeles. What began as a simple stop for drinking and driving soon escalated into a full-blown neighborhood confrontation. Frye's mother, who had run to the scene, was screaming at both her sons for being so stupid and was immediately arrested; Frye's brother refused a police order to follow the truck that towed away his brother's car, shrieking at the police "Go ahead, kill me." As the arrests grew even more confrontational, the crowd of onlookers grew. The arresting officers brandished shotguns and billy clubs, and all three Fryes sustained injuries. The crowd, by then numbering around fifteen hundred, began to pelt the now reinforced police with rocks. The rocks found their targets, and soon the mob turned its artillery on civilian cars and shop windows. The police withdrew, leaving the rioters to wreak havoc on a cordoned-off neighborhood known as Watts.

The riots continued into the next day, leaving some seventy-five people injured. Los Angeles mayor Sam Yorty and his chief of police, William Parker, believed that the worst was over. But on Friday evening, crowds gathered again near the original site of Frye's arrest, and once again they exploded into a spree of rioting that eventually covered an area of 46.5 square miles. Sixteen thousand national guardsmen had arrived in Watts before the riots dispersed three days later. Thirty-four were dead, four thousand arrested, one thousand injured, and there had been $35 million in property damage, with 250 buildings burned to the ground. The rioters stood back to observe their handiwork and chanted "Burn, Baby, Burn," and "Get Whitey." Parker publicly blamed the Black Muslims for the carnage, and on Tuesday, August 17, about one hundred police officers shot up a nearby Nation of Islam mosque and arrested the inhabitants for conspiracy and attempted murder.

For his part, Martin Luther King had resisted the temptation to fly to Watts immediately after the riots. He only did so when he learned that Reverend Billy Graham had surveyed the smoking city from a helicopter. When he arrived in Watts on Wednesday, August 18, the day after the destruction of the Muslim mosque, he faced the pent-up anger of the American ghetto. When he tried to speak, his black audience shouted him down with "Get out of here, Dr. King." And when King tried to argue that all Americans should attack the problems by joining hands, a man interrupted King and interjected, "And *burn*."

It was the beginning of three years of what the press soon dubbed the "long hot summers" of northern urban destruction. Historian Douglas Miller estimates that between 1965 and 1968 there were close to three hundred race riots in American cities, involving close to a half-million blacks. Riots occurred in Cleveland, Dayton, Milwaukee, Rochester, Tampa, Boston, Newark, Buffalo, Wilmington, and San Francisco. Scenes of urban Armageddon became a staple of the nightly television news—as footage from the jungles of Vietnam was becoming just as ubiquitous.

By far, the worst riot occurred in Detroit in the summer of 1967. On Sunday, July 23, a routine raid on five illegal nightclubs ("blind pigs") led to an explosion of violence and arson. Twelve hours after the bust, the city was burning, and the response was largely in the hands of seven thousand national guardsmen who had no training in riot control. Within twenty-four hours, there were twelve dead, two of whom had died in fires. Michigan governor George Romney pleaded with Johnson to send in federal troops; fearing an even greater escalation, Johnson dragged his feet. But the rioting escalated, and the president soon had no choice. By Monday, forty-seven hundred paratroopers had arrived in Detroit with orders to carry only unloaded weapons; they were largely ineffectual in the next three days of rampage. Ultimately forty-three people died, only one of whom was a military fatality, and some seventy-two hundred had been arrested. Property destruction was incalculable.

It does not take a trained sociologist to see why the cities were blowing up. The biggest issue was housing. Since the post–World War II flight of the white middle class to the suburbs, the housing they left behind had become dilapidated and their inhabitants more and more desperate. The appalling condition of inner-city housing can hardly be exaggerated. Federal money earmarked for urban renewal rarely made it to the source of the problem. Moreover, there was no escape. In the city itself, the best apartments went to whites, thanks to a number of shady real estate practices. Any call for "open housing" fell on the deaf ears of all white city administrators, and restrictive covenants and overt racism kept all but the richest blacks (which is to say a few to none) from moving into an all-white neighborhood. The de facto segregation of the northern cities led directly to the de facto segregation of the schools, with whites refusing to bus their children to integrated inner-city schools and instead enrolling them in (just as segregated) suburban or private schools. Not surprisingly, the inner-city schools paled in comparison to their all-white counterparts.

Disparities in the police force contributed to the volatility of the situation. In Detroit, for example, the force was 95 percent white, and tension between police and the black residents had long been an issue. The failure of urban renewal was also key—in many cities new expressways either cut older black neighborhoods in half (Detroit) or displaced a black neighborhood altogether (Syracuse). Black unemployment in the cities ran at 30 percent (with a national average in 1966 of 3.8 percent); 40 percent of blacks in the cities lived below the poverty line (with a national average of about 15 percent). Congestion, filth, rising drug use, and corruption all conspired to make the inner city virtually uninhabitable.

When faced with crises in the northern cities, Lyndon Johnson attempted to use the Great Society motif of spending federal money to help the situation. He assumed that social programs, funded by the federal government in the same manner as his administration had dealt with education and health care reform, would defuse the evils in urban America. This assumption was wrong on a number of fronts. First, Johnson no longer had enough money to make it work; a lack of funds strangled War on Poverty programs, as Johnson diverted more and more federal money to fight the war in Vietnam.

Second, the bureaucratic nightmare that was the Great Society had become so difficult to manage that what little money there was for social action often did not make it to the urban poor who so desperately needed it. Third, even when funded well and administered adequately, many of the social programs simply did not address the core issues of urban life that needed to be solved if the cities were going to recover. Take, for example, the Job Corps. Based upon one of Johnson's favorite New Deal programs, the Works Progress Administration (WPA), the Job Corps took disadvantaged youths out of the cities, put them in a dormitory-style environment, and taught them ostensibly marketable skills like auto mechanics and carpentry. But the "camps" had a level of discipline far beyond what any urban youngster had ever experienced. Mix that with a high rate of homesickness and runaways heading back to the city, and the Job Corps fell short of its full potential. Simply put, all the money in the world could not solve a problem with roots as deep as modern urban poverty.

Searching for solutions, Johnson looked to the intellectuals within his administration. Harvard-trained New Yorker Daniel Patrick Moynihan never lacked for self–assurance regarding his intellectual conclusions. In a 1965 report entitled *The Negro Family: The Case for National Action,* generated from his position as assistant secretary of labor, Moynihan argued that the root cause of the "social pathology" in the American ghetto was instability in the black family, particularly the high number of black families that existed without a live-in father. He further argued that this situation was an inevitable product of the legacy of slavery. Moynihan concluded that until the basic problem of the black family was addressed, no amount of federal money would be effective in dealing with the problem of poverty and injustice in the inner city:

> What then is that problem? We feel the answer is clear enough. Three centuries of injustice have brought about deep-seated structural distortions in the life of the Negro American. At this point, the present tangle of pathology is capable of perpetuating itself without assistance from the white world. The cycle can be broken only if these distortions are set right. In a word, a national effort towards the problems of Negro Americans must be directed towards the question of family structure. The object should be to strengthen the Negro family so as to enable it to raise and support its members as do other families. After that, how this group of Americans

chooses to run its affairs, take advantage of its opportunities, or fail to do so, is none of the nation's business.

Johnson bought into this analysis and articulated it in a June 4, 1965, commencement address at traditionally black Howard University in Washington, D.C. In a speech entitled "To Fulfill These Rights," Johnson first defended his Great Society, as he argued that poverty was a cause of racial injustice, and that "We are trying to attack these evils through our poverty program, through our education program, through our medical care and our other health programs, and a dozen more of the Great Society programs that are aimed at the root causes of this poverty. We will increase, and we will accelerate, and we will broaden this attack in years to come until this most enduring of foes finally yields to our unyielding will." But then Johnson went further. His second cause of racial inequality was "the devastating heritage of long years of slavery; and a century of oppression, hatred, and injustice." Black poverty was thus different from white poverty, and it needed to be dealt with differently. For Johnson, that meant isolating a cultural factor.

Perhaps most important—its influence radiating to every part of life—is the breakdown of the Negro family structure. For this, most of all, white America must accept responsibility. It flows from centuries of oppression and persecution of the Negro man. It flows from the long years of degradation and discrimination, which have attacked his dignity and assaulted his ability to produce for his family.

This, too, is not pleasant to look upon. But it must be faced by those whose serious intent is to improve the life of all Americans.

Only a minority—less than half—of all Negro children reach the age of 18 having lived all their lives with both of their parents. At this moment, tonight, little less than two-thirds are at home with both of their parents. Probably a majority of all Negro children receive federally aided public assistance sometime during their childhood.

The family is the cornerstone of our society. More than any other force it shapes the attitude, the hopes, the ambitions, and the values of the child. And when the family collapses it is the children that are usually damaged. When it happens on a massive scale the community itself is crippled.

So, unless we work to strengthen the family, to create conditions under which most parents will stay together—all the rest: schools, and playgrounds, and public assistance and private concern, will never be enough to cut completely the circle of despair and deprivation.

Johnson's speech, and Moynihan's report, leaked to the press that summer, set off a firestorm of disapproval from the black community (Moynihan would be eased out of the administration as a result). To blacks, Johnson offered more of the same—money thrown at the problem, and, thanks to Vietnam, not enough money at that. But their disapproval ran deeper, as they concluded that Johnson and Moynihan's basic assumptions about urban poverty were innately racist—if only black families could look alike, and be structured like a white family, all would be well.

Following the Detroit riots, Johnson made no attempt to articulate another solution to the problem. Instead, the president, who was now bunkered in the White House over Vietnam, passed the problem on to a presidential commission, chaired by Illinois governor Otto Kerner. The blue-ribbon panel interviewed widely in twenty cities, and their conclusions stunned the Johnson administration. To the Kerner Commission, the underlying problem in the cities was "white racism." The commission argued, in one of the most famous phrases of the late 1960s, that "our nation is moving toward two societies, one black, one white, separate and unequal." By placing the blame for the racial violence in the North squarely on the shoulders of white America, the Kerner Commission made it difficult for any politician who depended on white votes, no matter how liberal, to support the report. Moreover, the commission's solution to the problem—a massive federally supported jobs program, federally supported housing developments, and a "national system of income supplementation"—might have been in the spirit of the Great Society, but it was too expensive in a wartime economy even to consider. After the usual platitudes, Johnson ignored the report. He would leave office defeated by the northern ghetto just as he was defeated in Vietnam, never finding the answer to the question he asked of an aide: "What do they want?"

Martin Luther King had no more of a solution than did Lyndon Johnson. Watts had driven King north; following his humiliating experience there, he searched for an opportunity to try nonviolent techniques in a large urban environment. King wanted nothing less than to declare war on slums, to make segregated, filthy, dangerous ghettoes a functioning part of an "open city." However, the choice of Chicago for the campaign—the "Chicago

Freedom Movement" of 1965–66—proved to be unfortunate. Although none could debate the squalor of the ghetto on the south side of the Windy City, King soon found that he was completely out of his element, unable either to control or to respond to events with the alacrity that he had done in the South (Albany excluded). In Mayor Richard J. Daley, King was denied the perfect foil that he had found in Patterson, Connor, Wallace, and Smitherman. The czar of a massive political machine, Daley was easily one step ahead of King. Indeed, every time the movement pointed out a specific slum for media attention, Daley sent in a team to fix it.

After six months of this cat-and-mouse game, King attempted to force the issue. On July 10, 1966, five thousand campaigners held a rally at Soldier Field. They marched downtown to City Hall, where King taped a list of demands to the door. Daley met with King the next day; the meeting produced nothing. The following day, Chicago detonated. The cause had nothing to do with King's campaign. Overzealous city officials turned off fire hydrants that had been opened by youngsters sweltering in the city's brutal summer heat. The action touched off a four-day spree of rioting that left four dead and Daley publicly blaming King. Following the riots, the campaign shifted direction and moved out into Chicago's de facto segregated suburbs. Over several days, marchers met a shower of eggs, bottles, rocks, bricks, and cherry bombs. When a brick hit a white nun who was marching, sending her to the pavement, a shout went up from the racists: "We got another one." King himself was sent reeling to the ground, hit in the forehead with a rock.

King and his staff were quick to tell the media that in the suburbs, they had met a level of racist response that transcended anything they had seen in the South. That claim, however, was campaign rhetoric for the consumption of the press. For all the pain inflicted on the Chicago marchers, one need only remember the buses burning behind the bloodied Freedom Riders, or the dogs ripping the flesh of the child marchers in Birmingham, or the list of missing and lynched in Mississippi, to be able to dismiss this observation as hyperbole. Regardless, King was beaten down and more than ready to settle and leave Chicago. But the young activists in King's ranks had been along the road from Selma to Montgomery, and they were ready for another fight. Jesse Jackson, a young student at Chicago Theological Seminary, was passionate about leading a new march into the suburb of Cicero, where the racial tension was so acute that no unaccompanied black felt safe.

King refused to sanction the march; instead, he brokered an armistice. On August 26, both sides signed a ten-point agreement—the city vaguely agreed to enforce existing housing laws, and King agreed to end his marches. The activists in his ranks, however, paid no attention to the terms of the agreement. On September 4, 250 marchers, led by Jackson, entered Cicero, only to be pelted with assorted missiles. In a departure from King's nonviolent motif, these marchers stunned the racists by catching the missiles in midair, and hurling them back at their attackers.

King left Chicago as he had left Watts, having made no appreciable progress and further exposing the split in his movement. As he pondered his next move, the young activists who had come to see him as an outdated anachronism tried their hand.

To the leadership of the Student Nonviolent Coordinating Committee, the attempt of the Mississippi Freedom Democratic Party (MFDP) to gain recognition by the national Democratic Party, described in chapter 3, had failed because it had tried to work within the white system and had ultimately been betrayed and swallowed whole by that system. Thus, in spring 1966, SNCC began its own voting drive in Lowndes County, Alabama. As their political vehicle, they formed their *own* political party—the Lowndes County Freedom Organization (LCFO). In direct contrast to the regular Democratic Party in Alabama, which had chosen for its symbol a rooster labeled "White Supremacy," LCFO chose for its symbol a black panther. This, according to SNCC leader Stokely Carmichael, was an animal that slowly retreated from an enemy, inch by inch, until it ultimately sprang to the attack. In a door-to-door campaign reminiscent of Bob Moses's voter drives in Mississippi, the LCFO registered hundreds of new voters for the May 3, 1966, primary. In that primary, nine hundred new voters stunned white residents by showing up at the polls and voting for the Black Panther candidates. None, of course, was elected, but LCFO's show of success led to a coup within SNCC. Eleven days after the primary, Carmichael defeated the incumbent, a moderate student leader and veteran of the Freedom Rides, John Lewis, for the presidency of SNCC. The organization, which had begun as an arm of the southern nonviolent movement, was now firmly in the control of the activists.

In the spring of 1966, the militants of SNCC and the moderates who followed King would be thrust together in one final campaign. James Meredith had released his memoir of the 1962 crisis at the University of

Mississippi, entitled *Three Years in Mississippi*. The book, however, met with poor reviews and lackluster sales. Perhaps as a result, Meredith announced that he was going to hold a one-man "March Against Fear," taking him on a 220-mile trek beginning in Memphis, Tennessee, and ending in Oxford, Mississippi. On the second day of the march, just after Meredith had crossed the state line into Mississippi, a white terrorist hiding on the side of the road shot him three times with a twelve-gauge shotgun. After visiting Meredith in the hospital, Carmichael and King, who was at the same time in the midst of the Chicago Freedom Movement, decided to keep the march alive.

Now flush with reinforcements from all arms of the civil rights movement, including SNCC, the march would follow Meredith's route directly into the heart of Mississippi, where James Cheney, Andrew Goodman, and Mickey Schwerner had been assassinated only a year before—and with absolutely no protection from federal troops. Thus, what was now dubbed the "Meredith March" was tenser and potentially more lethal than had been the previous march to Selma. As the racists threw bricks and taunted the marchers, Carmichael and the SNCC activists called for a direct, violent retaliation, thus exposing dissonance in the movement. King and his more moderate supporters demanded a continued adherence to a nonviolent response. On June 16, Carmichael and several others were arrested trying to pitch tents for the marchers near Greenwood, Mississippi. That night, Carmichael's pent-up anger at King exploded. At a meeting of the marchers, he shouted: "This is the 27th time I have been arrested, and I ain't going to jail no more." Then, jabbing his finger in the air, he began to chant with the crowd, "We want Black Power! We want Black Power!"

In 1967, Carmichael and Charles Hamilton, then a professor of political science at Roosevelt University (Chicago), wrote *Black Power: The Politics of Liberation*.[1] In it, they offered an intellectual assessment of the idea of Black Power. They began by arguing that blacks in America constituted a captured colony, held in place by institutional racism—or colonialism. They saw those members of the black elite who joined the white power structure as "captive" black leaders beholden to the white power structure, reflecting a common part of colonial rule. Thus they saw integration as simply "despi-

---

1. Quotations and summary in this section are taken from the second edition (New York: Vintage Books, 1992), passim.

cable." Once blacks stopped "playing colonial politics"; once blacks stopped *allowing* themselves to be assimilated into the white power structure, thus reinforcing racism; once blacks stopped believing in the panacea of forming coalitions with whites—then and only then would blacks be "liberated." That liberation—that freedom was Black Power.

To Carmichael and Hamilton, "the time is long overdue for the black community to redefine *itself.*" This redefinition could not come through any co-opting of white society or politics. They believed that blacks must work from within, learn as much as possible about their true African roots, and define themselves as a people separate from the white man. This Pan-Africanism was an important part of the emerging Black Power movement. To Carmichael and Hamilton, the link between America and Africa was more than just a cultural one—wearing dashikis, learning African music, and the like. Indeed, Black Power argued that the freedom of blacks in America was inexorably tied to the freedom of blacks in Africa. Indeed, in 1967, Carmichael, now known as Kwame Ture, organized the All African People's Revolutionary Party and moved to the People's Revolutionary Republic of Guinea in 1968.

Thus, Black Power as an intellectual argument did not necessarily mean a Garvey-like exodus of blacks to Africa, in an attempt to separate the races physically. Nor did it mean that blacks would separate themselves by killing all their opponents in the racial blood bath that many whites feared. Black Power meant that blacks would stop *allowing* themselves to be assimilated into white society; they would do so by closing ranks, and, as a group, just say no. This clearly meant a final rejection of those leaders like King who preached a non-violent cheek-turning (Carmichael and Hamilton: "There has been only a civil rights movement whose tone of voice was adapted to an audience of middle-class whites"). It also means that if violence was brought upon those blacks who refused to assimilate, then violence would be returned (Carmichael and Hamilton: "Rampaging white mobs and white night-riders must be made to understand that their days of free head-whipping are over"). But most important, it meant that once separated from the colonial oppression of whites in American, blacks would become self-empowered. It would be the Black Panthers who would put this idea of self-empowerment into gritty practice.

In October 1966, in a direct response to the Watts riots, two students at Oakland City College (California), Huey Newton and Bobby Seale, formed the

Black Panther Party for Self Defense. Although they appropriated the symbol of the Lowndes County Freedom Organization, theirs was anything but a political party. At its heart a community action group, the Black Panthers took the core idea of Black Power—liberation through separation—and developed a bill of indictment against white America. In a remarkable manifesto, "What We Want, What We Believe," the Panthers cited the Declaration of Independence of the United States ("We hold these truths to be self-evident, that all men are created equal . . ."), and then listed their "Ten Demands":

> 1. We want freedom. . . .
>
> 2. . . . We want full employment. . . .
>
> 3. . . . We want an end to the robbery by the CAPITALIST of our black community. . . .
>
> 4. . . . Decent housing. . . .
>
> 5. Education that exposed the true nature of this decadent American society. . . .
>
> 6. We want all black men to be exempt from military service.
>
> 7. We want an immediate end to POLICE BRUTALITY and MUR-DER of black people. . . .
>
> 8. We want freedom for all black men held in . . . prisons and jails. . . .
>
> 9. . . . We want all black people when brought to trial to be tried in court by a jury of their peer group . . . black communities. . . .
>
> 10. . . . We want . . . a United Nations plebiscite to be held throughout the black colony in which only black colonial subjects will be allowed to participate. . . .

Largely an economic document that addressed the injustices of ghetto life, "What We Want" also shows a theoretical kinship with Carmichael and Hamilton's theory of Black Power (see point 10's labeling of the ghetto as a black colony). Yet this document was neither a list of blind threats nor a utopian panacea. The Panthers literally put their money where their mouths were. They provided food, alternate housing, schools (emphasizing African history), and shelters for blacks. This community action, as well as the Panthers' emphasis on black pride, mirrored many of the tactics and philosophies of the Black Muslims. However, the Panthers went beyond the Muslims in their overt use of militaristic force in order to protect blacks. In point 7 of "What We Want," they were explicit: "The Second Amendment to the Constitution of the United Sates gives us a right to bear arms. We therefore believe that all black people should arm themselves for self-defense." Wearing army fatigues and berets and openly carrying loaded firearms, the Panthers organized self-defense groups and made it clear that if attacked, they would respond in kind. That there would eventually be violence, both by and against the Panthers, was a foregone conclusion. In October 1967, a clash between police and Panthers left one cop killed, another wounded, and Huey Newton shot in the stomach and charged with murder. In April 1968, during another gun battle, one Panther was killed and several other Panthers and police wounded.

It is clear in hindsight that the community action programs, while attractive, popular, and helpful, were not the Black Panthers' main reason for being. The Panthers' program made it clear that to them, violence had become an acceptable method of campaigning for black civil rights. As H. Rap Brown, Carmichael's more violent successor as head of SNCC, so eloquently put it: "Violence is as American as cherry pie." Brown told his audiences to "get some guns."

The movement for civil rights for African Americans helped to fuel the fires of similar desires for freedom and equality that were burning in other minority groups. For the most part, these new civil rights movements would not come to full fruition until the 1970s; however, their roots were in the activism of the second half of the 1960s.

The Latino movement had the deepest roots in the 1960s. In California's San Joaquin Valley, a labor movement had begun in the late 1950s to direct attention to the plight of Mexican-American immigrant farm workers in the area, most of whom earned less than subsistence wages for handpicking fruits and vegetables under brutal conditions. Unprotected by their employers from the chemical agents that fed the crop, and unprotected by the government from unfair labor practices, the workers turned to Cesar Chavez, a charismatic community advocate and a former migrant farm worker, to give voice to their concerns. A devout Roman Catholic and a close disciple of King's nonviolent theories, in 1962 Chavez formed the United Farm Workers (UFW), and in 1965 he announced a "Huelga!"—strike—against southern California grape growers. The strike soon transcended its economic roots and morphed into a demonstration of ethnic pride dubbed "La Causa." In the spirit of Birmingham and Selma, many entertainment celebrities and liberal politicians, led by Senator Robert F. Kennedy,[2] visited Chavez and gave their open support to his movement. Shrewdly building on this support, in 1966 Chavez announced a nationwide boycott of table grapes grown in southern California. The boycott grabbed national headlines, and by the end of the decade most California grape growers had recognized the UFW.

It was, however, in the unleashing of a Latino ethnic pride that "La Causa" had its most lasting legacy. Strongly affected by both Chavez and by the Black Power movement, young Chicano youth began to distance themselves from the white society that they felt had appropriated their Latino identity in order to suppress the race. The emergence of a Chicano racial identity, one that encompassed all Latinos, was articulated as "La Raza"—The Race. It caught on across the country, from the migrant workers of the West and Southwest, to those of Puerto Rican heritage who lived in the barrios of the large cities. The first Chicano National Conference, held in Denver in 1969, released a manifesto, "El Plan Espirtual de Aztlán," that included many of the same things that had been set out in the ten-point program of the Black Panthers, including the right of self-defense against "the occupying force of the oppressors." Chicano youth formed the Mexican-American Youth Organization (MAYO), and in East Los Angeles David Sanchez formed the "Brown Berets," modeled closely on the Black Panthers.

Native Americans needed no prodding from any civil rights group to find their cultural anger. Centuries of attempted physical genocide at the hands of empowered Euroamericans had led to a virtual disappearance of the native population—from eighteen million at the time of the European invasion to a mere four hundred thousand by 1950. The decade immediately following World War II saw a deliberate attempt at cultural genocide, and the Truman and Eisenhower administrations moved to sever all links between the federal government and the leftover native population. The government created a commission that would pay Indians who had made claim to any federal land. This ended any further relationship between the newly flush Indian and the federal government, but the government did not properly prepare

---

2. After Lyndon Johnson refused to consider Kennedy as his running mate in 1964, Kennedy ran for the U.S. Senate seat for New York. He won the seat, easily defeating Kenneth Keating.

those who took the money for assimilation into life off the reservation. The claim money was quickly spent, or appropriated by unscrupulous investors. And all too few could retreat to the reservation after this experience because the government moved to end reservations altogether. In a policy known as "termination," the federal government in the 1950s passed laws ending the special status of the tribes on the reservations ("Home Rule"), thus subjecting them to the same law and extending to them the same privileges of any United States citizen. While on the surface termination seemed to be egalitarian, its real purpose was to end any financial assistance that the federal government had previously given to the tribes and to end the expensive (and guilt-laden) reservation system. Both effects were in evidence by the 1960s, leading to a sense of urgency in Indian enclaves that rivaled any ghetto, barrio, or southern shantytown for its filth and squalor.

In 1960 and 1961, representatives of sixty-seven tribes met first in Denver, and then Gallup, New Mexico. They drew up what would be their post-termination manifesto, the "Declaration of Purposes." In it, they argued that as a group they "strongly oppos[ed] the termination of federal trusteeship over the Indians," and that when it came to creating new laws governing the relationship between the tribes and the federal government, "we consider rules based on Indian thinking as being sufficient." This reiteration of an Indian ethnic pride was all but ignored by the Kennedy administration. Johnson dealt with the situation by including Native Americans in his War on Poverty; but the National Council on Indian Opportunity soon was as underfunded as was the rest of his Great Society, further angering those Native Americans whom it was supposed to help.

The "Red Power" movement arose out of these frustrations. In Minnesota, young activists formed "Border Patrols," arming themselves in much the same manner as the Black Panthers so as to protect Indian neighborhoods and rural enclaves from perceived abuses at the hands of both the local residents and the police. Three of these patrollers, Clyde Bellecourt, Dennis Banks, and George Mitchell, organized the American Indian Movement (AIM) in the summer of 1968. Later that year, activist Indians clashed with representatives of Washington State over fishing rights that had been ceded to them by previous treaties. In 1969, many of the same activists occupied the vacant federal penitentiary on Alcatraz Island, off the coast of San Francisco, holding it for nineteen months.

The climactic conflict, fittingly held at Wounded Knee, South Dakota, the site of the 1890 massacre that ended the period of tribal extermination known as the "Plains Wars," was almost five years in the future, as was the creation of a new reservation system, renewed fights over home rule, and debates over taxation, gambling, and assimilation. While they could not be foretold in the 1969, their base was clearly in the renewed activism of that decade.

The public declaration of ethnic and racial pride was a significant part of the civil rights activism of the second half of the decade: "Say it loud . . . I'm Black and I'm Proud" . . . "Red Power" . . . "Brown Power." Identity politics was emerging. But for one group, identity politics was impossible. It was, after all, illegal in all fifty states in the 1960s to *be* gay.

Throughout American history, gay Americans had been routinely discriminated against. In the 1950s, however, gays became a special target of the McCarthyites—the assumption was that people with something in their background that they needed to hide would be easy targets for the communists. American homophobia thus became quite public, with police sweeps of neighborhoods, bars, and beaches. The early 1960s in New York City featured an organized campaign to shut down the gay bars; police routinely used plants to entrap the clientele and lead patrons into mass arrests. While there were isolated protests against these abuses, there was little or no organized response from the gay community. There were virtually no lawsuits—since being gay was unlawful, the police had not violated anyone's civil rights. The only gay organization, the Mattachine Society founded in 1950, largely operated underground and argued that gays should adopt a heterosexual lifestyle and attempt to blend into straight society.

It is not surprising that the explosion that now seems so inevitable happened in New York's Greenwich Village, a haven for homosexuals, lesbians, and transgenders, as well as a neighborhood made famous by the presence of bohemian artists such as the Beats. The Stonewall Inn, located at 53 Christopher Street, was of a kind with other gay bars in the area—filthy, mob owned, and in general cahoots with the local police, who would usually tip off management just before a raid in return for a payoff. However, on Saturday, June 28, 1969, at 1:20 A.M., a surprise police raid happened at the Stonewall. Normally, the police would line up the patrons, check IDs, and release all but the transvestites and drag queens; those released would go home. But on this evening, the liberated patrons refused to leave Christopher Street. Instead, they milled about, gesturing and shouting obscenities at the police, their numbers quickly growing until they reached an estimated one thousand people. When a transvestite who had been hit with a billy club while being arrested turned to the crowd and yelled "Why don't you *do* something," it was like setting off a time bomb. Garbage, rocks, bricks, bottles, and coins (the protestors screamed that they wanted to "pay off" the police) all became flying weapons. When the first night of violence had ended, thirteen people had been arrested, four police officers and a score of patrons had been hurt, and the inside of the Stonewall had been trashed. But this was not to be just one random act of violence. For three more evenings, protestors returned to Christopher Street and clashed with the police. For the first time, the chant of "Gay Power" could be heard above the fray.

The Stonewall Riots literally put gay pride on the front page—each of the major metropolitan dailies covered the story. Moreover, it was the event that sparked movement. Within weeks, activists formed the Gay Liberation Front, and by year's end they established the Gay Activists Alliance. On June 28, 1970—the first anniversary of Stonewall—New York City hosted its first Gay Pride parade. Its motto was "Out of the closets and into the streets"; marchers carried banners like the one that read, "Hey Mom—Me Too!"

Gay power was hardly a national movement at the end of the 1960s. No gay civil rights bills were passed; fights over gay marriage and rights of gays in the workplace were three decades in the future. Indeed, it would take AIDS to nationalize the movement. Nevertheless, Gay Pride was of a piece with the activism of the late 1960s, as young members of social and ethnic minorities stood up—in most cases for the first time—and demanded their share of the American Dream.

Recommended Reading

The reader is referred to the recommendations at the end of chapter 3 as being applicable here. Added to that must be the reading of one of the most important books of the decade, Stokely Carmichael (Kwame Ture) and Charles V. Hamilton, *Black Power: The Politics of Liberation* (New York: Vintage Books, 1967). On Latino activism, see Susan Ferriss and Ricardo Sandoval, *The Fight in the Fields: Cesar Chavez and the Farmworkers Movement* (New York: Mariner Books, 1998); for Native American activism, see James J. Rawls, *Chief Red Fox Is Dead: A History of Native Americans since 1945* (Fort Worth: Harcourt Brace, 1996); for gay activism, see David Carter, *Stonewall: The Riots That Sparked the Gay Revolution* (New York: St. Martin's Press, 2005).

6

"Bodies upon the Gears"

The New Left and the New Feminism

ON MAY 12, 1964, Syracuse University's *Daily Orange* announced that a demonstration would take a place that day during the university's annual review of its Reserve Officer Training Corps (ROTC) cadets, "involving an "informal group of students who have in common the belief that there are alternatives to compulsory conscription, and that military training is not compatible with the pursuit of knowledge in a free society." As the review began, protestors waved signs saying "Don't Teach War at College," "Will Your Children Be Active or Radioactive?" and "The Study of War Is Not a Liberal Art." Campus security had told the protesters to remain on the north side of the quad, off the reviewing field, during the ceremonies. *The Daily Orange* reported that despite such warnings, picketers had entered the center of the quad and followed the withdrawing troops past the reviewing stand where the chancellor was standing. James Overgaard, an employee of the library and a former Syracuse student, was marching at the rear of the line. As he passed university chancellor William P. Tolley, the chancellor rushed down from the reviewing stand and yelled at Overgaard to get off the grass; one report had Tolley shouting, "Get off the field, you bums." After Overgaard refused to budge, Tolley struck him with his cane. Overgaard was treated at a local hospital for a bruise but did not press charges. In fact, he was quoted as saying that "I would like to make it clear that I harbor no

Portions of this chapter were taken from John Robert Greene with Karrie A. Baron, *Syracuse University: The Tolley Years, 1942–1969*, 37-38, 201–2, 221–22. © 1996. Reprinted with permission of Syracuse Univ. Press.

personal animosity towards the chancellor. There were strong feelings on both sides—only the methods were different."

It is important to understand that what would become the student movement of the 1960s was, in very large part, a movement not just against the forces of the far right, but also against a liberalism that was first espoused in the 1930s and sharpened in the succeeding decades into a philosophy that was as repellant to the students as was conservatism.

The challenge of the Great Depression was originally faced by Republican conservatives, led by president Herbert Hoover, who argued quite vociferously that the government should *not* intervene in the public sector to help business and should *not* give public monies to individual unemployed citizens to help them weather tough times. This philosophy of "American individualism" argued that direct government intervention—"welfare"—would help citizens in the short run, but would actually hurt them in the long run by destroying their self-esteem. Franklin Roosevelt rejected individualism as a philosophy and, in so doing, remade American liberalism. To Roosevelt, the government *existed* to promote the *complete* social welfare of the citizenry. Thus, Roosevelt expanded both the size and scope of the federal government, as his New Deal created jobs, spent money on relief, and, eventually, prepared the United States for a war against fascism. All told, the greatest legacy of the New Deal was this expansion of government—one that was impossible to reverse.

In the postwar period, these New Deal liberals, who remained in power and influence during the Truman administration, added to the requirements of liberalism their avowed anticommunism. This began with Harry S. Truman himself, who held a nonintellectual, knee-jerk reaction disgust for the Soviets. (When writing a senator, Truman was blunt about his feelings: "I want you to understand very distinctly that you cannot trust them"). George Kennan, a former ambassador to the Soviet Union and influential Truman intimate, seconded this distrust when he wrote to the secretary of state in 1949: "Whoever, peering in from the comfortable distance of the bourgeois-liberal world, views Stalin as just another successful political leader . . . has failed to grasp the cataclysmic horror of modern totalitarianism." The Truman administration translated this distrust into actions and policies while it attempted to remake the health care system, reform education, and take small steps toward civil rights, at the same time inflaming the cold war. Truman's financial support of the French in Indochina, discussed in more detail in the next chapter, certainly fits into this category. The conservatism of Dwight Eisenhower challenged, but did not attempt to erase, the big-government view of dealing with American society; the most spirited conflicts between the parties between 1953 and 1961 were over the budget, and how much money would be allotted to social programs as compared to defense spending But Eisenhower conservatives *and* New Deal liberals agreed on a strident anticommunism. They largely supported the administration's efforts to contain communism around the world and voiced no opposition to the administration's actions in Vietnam. Thus, by 1961, both New Deal liberals and Republican conservatives were ready to take steps to squash communism wherever they found it.

On the surface, John F. Kennedy offered the hope of a new type of liberalism. His youth led many to conclude that he would break significantly with the past; the tone of his inaugural address suggested that he would do so immediately. But while Kennedy called for self-sacrifice and service to country that January morning, his rhetoric also laid down a challenge— some analysts have labeled it a direct threat—to the Soviet bloc: "Let every nation know . . . that we shall pay any price, bear any burden, meet any hardship, support any friend, oppose any foe, to assure the survival and success of liberty." By the end of his second year in office, Kennedy had invaded Cuba, brought the world to the brink of war with the Soviet Union, and showed all the signs of approving a deeper U.S. military involvement in Vietnam— all while being no more successful on either social welfare legislation or civil rights than Truman had been. Kennedy was, arguably, no different from the New Deal liberals who had preceded him.

As noted in chapter 1, progressive thinkers had begun to challenge the ideas of New Deal liberalism during the 1950s. Leading the charge was sociologist C. Wright Mills. A burly Texan who rode his motorcycle to teach his classes at Columbia University, Mills became an intellectual mentor for those who were beginning to rethink the ideas of traditional liberalism. In *The Power Elite* (1956), Mills argued that America had become militarized and centralized, to the point that its democratic ideals had been compromised. When defining the elite that he felt ran America, Mills wrote:

> What Jacob Burckhardt said of "great men," most Americans might well say of their elite: "They are all that we are not." . . . Within American society, major national power now resides in the economic, the political,

and the military domains. Other institutions seem off to the side of modern history, and, on occasion, duly subordinated to these. No family is as directly powerful in national affairs as any major corporation; no church is as directly powerful in the external biographies of young men in America today as the military establishment; no college is as powerful in the shaping of momentous events as the National Security Council.[1]

Mills maintained that a new liberalism—what he, and others, termed a "New Left," would challenge the power elite of both traditional conservatism and New Deal liberalism that controlled postwar America. Mills also predicted that the direct challenge to this culture would come from the newly energized youth attending America's colleges and universities. In his influential essay "Notes on the New Left," published in *New Left Review* in 1960, he argued that "the meanings of left and right are now liquidated," and that the young intellectuals would now step into the power vacuum: "Who is it that is getting fed up? Who is it that is getting disgusted with what Marx called 'all that old crap?' Who is it that is thinking and acting in radical ways? All over the world—in the bloc, and in between—the answer is the same: it is the young intelligentsia."

While influential in his own right, Mills was a part of a late-1950s intellectual trend away from the ideas of New Deal liberalism—what he now termed the "Old Left." In history, the University of Wisconsin's William Appleman Williams's *Tragedy of American Diplomacy* (1959) argued that America had always been an imperialist nation. Williams, whose work will be discussed more in the next chapter, founded *Studies on the Left* in 1959 with several of his students. This journal and Irving Howe's *Dissent* became two of the leading academic voices of what I would term "New Progressive" thought. These publications were joined by the iconoclastic *Village Voice*, an underground newspaper founded in 1955 in New York City by a group led by writer Norman Mailer.

The New Progressivism had many roots; it is too simple to claim, as do many historians, that it was a natural outgrowth of the civil rights movement of the second half of the 1950s. However, the energy of that movement stoked the fire of the New Progressivism, and many of their early writings showed their support of that movement. But this New Progressivism transcended

1. A body within the Executive Office that gives national security and defense advice to the president of the United States.

one social cause or political label. Seeing themselves not as solely rights activists, and certainly not simply as "Democrats," these New Progressives held a critical view of America that went to the core of the national experience—to them, as to those of their literary contemporaries with whom they shared a kindred soul—America had become "beat."

Yet the views of the New Progressives would have remained in the 1960s what it was in the 1950s—a small, vocal school of criticism found on the fringes of contemporary intellectual thought—had it not been for their ideas being adopted wholesale by a newly vocal group of intellectuals, heretofore not serious players in the history of American intellectual and political thought—American college students.

The Servicemen's Readjustment Act of 1944—better known as the GI Bill of Rights—provided one free year of college for each ninety days of service and one additional month of paid education for each month of service up to forty-eight months. Veterans would receive free books, full payment of their student fees, and a living allowance of $50 a month for lodging with an additional $25 for each dependent. The legislation was incredibly popular; 83 percent of the public was in favor of educational assistance for returning vets. However, the War Department did not believe that many men would take advantage of the offer. In 1944 a War Department survey estimated that 1,280,000 men intended to go back to school after the war.

The War Department was wrong. Between 1945 and 1950, some 2.3 million students used the GI Bill. Between the spring of 1946 and the spring of 1950, veterans made up anywhere from 33 to 50 percent of all matriculated college students. It seems fair to conclude that most of the veterans who took advantage of these new benefits—most of whom were males between the ages of twenty-three and thirty who had seen combat—would never have been able to get a college education without the GI Bill.

Having fought at Normandy and Anzio, returning veterans found no meaning in some college traditions—beanies, hazing, and Greek life. While they continued to demonstrate the respect for authority that had been expected of them in the armed services, they passed on a sense of reality to the eighteen-year-olds sitting next to them in the classroom. They represented a new type of student—one that began to question the very foundation upon which the traditional American university had been built.

At that same moment, however, a new type of university was being born of the postwar period. In his 1963 book *The Uses of a University,* University of California president Clark Kerr looked at his own institution and found that it had changed profoundly since the war. He noted that its evolution had created an organization that operated at a budget of half a billion dollars serving forty thousand people, "brought departments into universities, and still new departments; institutes and ever more institutes; created vast research libraries; [and] turned the philosopher on his log into a researcher in his laboratory or the library stacks." He noted the creation of university presses, research centers, and graduate schools, and he singled out the development of extension programs. His university was now, to use Kerr's terms, the "multiversity." He compared it to a small state or city, with "fractionalized power" that must be governed. But, Kerr warned, there was no longer a consensus as to who would govern this conglomeration. He observed that a faculty and student body who were affected by the ideas of the New Progressives were now lobbying for a role in the governance of the multiversity along with the administration, and suggested that to guide the institution through the landmines to come, the president of the multiversity must not be a "giant" as of old, ruling autocratically from on high, but a "mediator" whose job was to find "peace within the student body, the faculty, the trustees; and peace between them and among them."

It was precisely this growth that made Kerr's California, Tolley's Syracuse University, Grayson Kirk's Columbia University, and dozens of other multiversities that had modernized and diversified in the 1950s such perfect targets for the faculty and student uprisings of the 1960s. A newly engaged student and faculty body, freed from the shackles of McCarthyism, grew to see the multiversity as an impersonal machine that had lost touch with its humanistic roots. They would now demand that it become proactive in dealing with questions of human rights and political issues that had become important since the 1950s.

The multiversity, of course, would have none of this. They all applied the doctrine of *in loco parentis* ("in place of the parent") to both their students and their faculty. Students were not treated as chattel, but neither were they treated as peers with whom administrators would negotiate. Administrators defended the unwritten Rule Number One—that attendance at a university was not a right, but a privilege.

Despite the tone of future television documentaries, and the often wildly hagiographic reminiscences of the principals, the students who adopted the point of view of the New Progressives were always in the minority on college campuses between 1960 and 1965—a microscopic minority. They were far outnumbered by their more conservative, normally politically apathetic colleagues, who attended college for the same reasons that teenagers had always attended college and still do: to get a good job, to enjoy the last phases of an adolescent social life, and—for some—to better their minds. Yet those few who adopted Mills's moniker and called themselves the student "New Left" were a unique breed. There had never before been a group like them in American history. Their time as a group of intellectual thinkers would be brief—about five years, from 1960 to 1965—and following their downfall no other such group of young intellectuals has emerged.

Certainly the times in which they lived and were educated played a part in their uniqueness. Many of the New Left's leaders came from families steeped in the ideals of the New Progressives; as a result, the students felt no need or desire to "blend in" to their new college environment. Once on campus, they found (often they consciously sought out) a cohort of younger faculty, New Progressives themselves, who had become disgusted with both the intellectual witch-hunt of the McCarthyites and the noblesse oblige attitude of the college they attended. This faculty was ready to teach and mentor these young intellectuals in a progressive manner—even if it meant bucking the traditional academic system.

Both student and faculty progressives were deeply and irrevocably shaped by the southern civil rights movement. They also knew they were a part of an international youth movement, as in 1960 alone student demonstrations had broken out in Japan, Korea, Venezuela, Turkey, and Great Britain. Indeed, many of them played a role in that crusade, most notably in Bob Moses's voter registration campaigns in Mississippi. These students were incredibly sophisticated writers, and, as we will see, better organized than any student group before or since. Yet it is important to note that the issue of the war in Vietnam did *not* bind the early New Left. The student New Left and the movement against the war—both on college campuses and nationally—were originally two separate things. The New Left was active on college campuses by 1960; the antiwar movement did not catch fire until about 1965. When they converged in about 1966, both groups would suffer for it. Put another way, the target of the early student New Left was never the war—it was always American democracy as a whole.

The epicenter of the student New Left was the group Students for a Democratic Society. Formed in 1960 out of the shards of several student groups from the 1950s, SDS had as its original plan nothing less than offering new alternatives to an American society that they saw as increasingly decrepit and self-serving. Greatly influenced as a group by the writings of Mills, SDS believed that America was no longer a democracy, and that they, the young intelligentsia of Mills mind, were in a unique position to change that world. There were very few of them—an estimate suggests that in mid-1960, there were only 8 SDS chapters on college campuses boasting a total membership of about 250. The chapter at the University of Michigan in Ann Arbor was the most vigorous, sending several representatives to the South in fall 1961 to work with SNCC during the Freedom Rides. The president of Michigan SDS, Al Haber, was the son of a prominent economist and labor arbitrator; his home had been a bastion of New Progressive thinking, and his own organizational skills led to the convening of a major Human Rights Conference in 1960. In December 1961, in order to face the issue of the small numbers in its membership, the national executive committee of SDS was moved to write an organizing tool for the organization. It was not surprising that it turned to an Ann Arbor student to write the first draft; it was also not surprising that they turned to one of Haber's star recruits.

Tom Hayden grew up in Royal Oaks, Michigan. Unlike Haber, his roots were not in the New Progressivism; Hayden's father was an accountant, and his mother a librarian. At the University of Michigan he became the editor of the *Daily*. In that role he attended the 1960 Democratic Convention in Los Angeles that nominated John F. Kennedy; while there, he interviewed Martin Luther King. For Hayden, C. Wright Mills was little less than a hero; it was his work that inspired Hayden and his first wife, Casey, both SDS members, to go south to work with SNCC. For his efforts, Hayden was arrested in Georgia and Mississippi, spending time in the same jails from which many blacks had disappeared. Like King, Hayden smuggled letters out of jail that were published in the North. His writing was wordy and acidic, but at the same time thoughtful and penetrating. He was the logical member to draft the recruiting tool for SDS. However, his first attempt tipped the scales at close to seventy pages. Some sixty members of SDS, during a retreat in Port Huron, Michigan, June 11–15, 1962, debated and amended Hayden's draft, until it became a forty-page, single-spaced manifesto.

What became known as the Port Huron Statement was not widely read at the time of its release—Hayden remembered later that it was never marketed and that SDS produced only twenty thousand copies of the statement as a mimeographed pamphlet, copies, selling for thirty-five cents apiece (pieces of it were, however, excerpted in several student newspapers on other campuses). In many ways, it is a difficult read—it is far too long, betrays a clear gender bias toward the young man who controlled its composition, and is written in a particularly pedantic style. Nevertheless, it is of a par with many of the great sociopolitical documents of the 1960s—King's "Letter from a Birmingham Jail," the Bill of Rights of the National Organization of Women; the Black Panther's "What We Want, What We Believe"—for its passion, its progressivism, and most important, for its articulation of a single idea that would take the student New Left into movement.

The Port Huron Statement began with a paean to the preamble to the constitution of the United States: "We are people of this generation, bred in at least modest comfort, housed now in universities, looking uncomfortably to the world we inherit." Noting that while they "might deliberately ignore, or avoid, or fail to feel all other human problems," they could *not* react in this manner to the impact that either the cold war or the civil rights movement had had in their young lives. In America's reaction to these two challenges, Hayden saw paradoxes of power—such as the "superfluous abundance" of the upper classes in the midst of poverty and the blind eye turned to the rising nationalism in the developing world (although Vietnam was not specifically mentioned). Hayden bemoaned the fact, à la Mills (who had died earlier that year of a heart attack), that America had proven ill-equipped to deal with these paradoxes; thus, the Port Huron Statement called for beginning "a search for truly democratic alternatives to the present."

SDS did not find this alternative in their universities (Port Huron Statement: "our professors and administrators sacrifice controversy to public relations . . . passion is called unscholastic"); they certainly did not find any alternatives in the ideas of the Old Left (the statement noted that an explanation of "how we would vote" on an issue meant nothing). Their alternative was devastatingly simple: "As a social system we seek the establishment of a democracy of individual participation." Participatory democracy was grounded in several principles: that "decision-making of basic social consequences be carried on by public groupings," that "positives be seen positively," and that "the political order should serve to clarify problems in a way instrumental to their solution." It was a politics based on individual involvement. It evoked memories of small town meetings and a politics of community.

Hayden contended that participatory democracy was far from utopian, and he was right—it had already been tried with success in Pereclean Athens. But modern America was hardly Ancient Greece, and America had long since followed the advice of James Madison in *Federalist 10* and made representative democracy, not a democracy of individual participation, the government for the sprawling republic. Thus, advocating for participatory democracy in 1960 was eminently impractical. However, what made the Port Huron Statement a truly revolutionary document was this: it called for a return to what SDS saw as a "purer" democracy, one unsullied by the corruption of a politics that elected representatives. Hayden proposed taking the direct pulse of every citizen.

The Port Huron Statement, as a document and as an idea, can be usefully compared to the theories propounded in Stokely Carmichael and Charles Hamilton's *Black Power* (see chapter 5). Both theories fly directly in the face of political realism. Both were written by thoughtful young intellectuals attempting to wrap their minds around key social issues (even if *Black Power* is, in my mind, better written and more accessible to the everyday reader). Where Hayden wanted young white, middle-class youth to shake off the oppression of the academic machine and participate in their own destiny, Carmichael and Hamilton wanted young blacks to shake off the oppression of white colonialism. Both were self-help documents; both documents were revolutionary in nature. Moreover, both theories unleashed powerful forces in American society that put relevant theory into practice.

As they did with *Black Power*, critics charged that the Port Huron Statement did not offer an alternative government to the one that its authors wished to replace. This however, is a false charge—participatory democracy *itself* was the alternative. Other critics noted that the Port Huron Statement did not offer a plan for how the nation would get to participatory democracy. This criticism is valid, but it must be remembered that the Port Huron Statement was originally meant as a recruiting document—the "how" of their revolution was expected to evolve through future discussion. The criticism also sells short an attempt made by SDS to organize northern blacks as an interest group. Christened the Economic Research and Action Project (ERAP) and operating on a $5,000 grant from the United Auto Workers, the program placed SDS members in the ghettoes of several northern cities as community organizers. The goal of ERAP was to show citizens living in the inner city that participatory democracy could work for them—that in union, there was strength. ERAP had small victories over several municipal governments, but by 1965 the funding had run out, and ERAP died of its own weight.

While the changes made by ERAP were minor, the experience proved to SDS that students could, indeed, be agents of social change. In words that could easily have been written by C. Wright Mills, Hayden's Port Huron Statement charged that "the power of students and faculty united is not only potential, it has shown its actuality in the South and in the reform movements of the North." Many students now looked closer to home to effect social change. Once again from the Port Huron Statement: "We must look within the university and act with confidence that we can be powerful."

That power would both be demonstrated and be actively resisted by the multiversity, at Berkeley.

The University of California was in 1960 the largest public university in the nation. The University of California at Berkeley (hereafter, Berkeley) was the largest and most important campus in the system. Covering almost thirteen hundred acres, boasting sixteen colleges and schools, Berkeley was the epitome of what had happened to higher education with the "GI Bulge"; thanks to the GI Bill, its student population had doubled to almost twenty thousand by 1960; by 1973 it would reach thirty thousand. Flush with government and military research contracts, staffed by one of the largest—and most prestigious—faculties in the nation, and simply gargantuan in size, Berkeley was the epitome of what its chancellor, Clark Kerr, had termed the "multiversity."

The student body at Berkeley was no more active than any other campus in the 1950s. Berkeley was hardly a mecca of New Progressive thought; pictures of its students in the late 1950s show the expected groups of conservatively dressed kids, most of whom were active in a thriving Greek system and, like their peers nationwide, had yet to give politics or social action a serious thought. That all changed in May 1960, when a group of Berkeley students went to San Francisco City Hall to protest the presence of the

House Committee on Un-American Activities (HUAC), then holding their notorious hearings there ("Are you now, or have you ever been, a member of the Communist Party?"). The students were stunned when fire hoses were turned on them and they were dragged down the steep granite steps into the arms of the waiting police. A later film produced by HUAC, labeling the students communist dupes, only served as a national recruiting tool for radical students, who now flocked to Berkeley to be a part of the protest scene.

Their numbers were initially small, but the progressive students banded together in an organization they called SLATE (after the slate of candidates they ran in the fall 1960 student elections). Claiming that they did not want "off-campus issues" to pollute the academic environment, Berkeley's administration threw SLATE off campus, only to be forced to renege and restore the group after a surprising number of student and faculty complaints.

Many of these same students spent the summer of 1962 and 1963 working in the South with SNCC, perfecting their organizational skills and hardening their activist passions. In March 1964 a sit-in of several hundred Berkeley students forced San Francisco's Sheraton Hotel to sign an agreement to racially integrate its staff. Following this victory, many students spent the summer of 1964 working in Mississippi, registering voters and teaching in the schools set up during Freedom Summer. By fall 1964, Berkeley had a core of serious, well-trained activists, ready to become the shock troops for the assault of the New Left that had been predicted by Mills and then called for in the Port Huron Statement.

These student activists would be led by Mario Savio. Born in New York City, Savio studied at Manhattan College and Queens College. When his parents moved to Los Angeles in 1963, Savio enrolled at Berkeley, ostensibly to finish his undergraduate degree in philosophy. A born activist, Savio had spent summers in Taxco, Mexico, working with the poor. He had been arrested at the March 1964 Sheraton sit-in, and several months later he went to Mississippi to work in Freedom Summer. Savio and his Berkeley activists were helped by the fact that Chancellor Kerr's administration had a particularly advanced case of noblesse oblige and overreacted to virtually every situation. Faced with the return of the activists to campus in fall 1964, the administration tried to shut down one of their most important communications lifelines. Students soon learned that the administration had banned the setting up of tables on campus property, at the corner of Bancroft and Telegraph Streets, tables that had for years been used by student groups to disseminate information. Expecting compliance, the administration was stunned when the students moved their tables to another location. On September 30, university deans were dispatched to issue disciplinary citations to the offending students; as students were cited, other students took their places, mocking the deans and demanding to be cited as well. As the day ended, hundreds of students descended on Sproul Hall, the administration building. They demanded to be cited, and they cheered Savio, who shouted into a bullhorn, demanding that the students "stand up for freedom." Berkeley initially stood its ground; later that evening, the administration announced that eight of the students cited at the tables had been suspended.

The next day, October 1, the activists began to organize protests in support of the suspended students. One activist, former Berkeley student Jack Weinberg, was arrested and removed to a nearby police patrol car. What followed was one of the most extraordinary scenes of the 1960s. Students quietly, but with absolute resolve, surrounded the car—by nightfall, they were numbered at six thousand. They did not touch the car, but neither the police nor Weinberg could leave the vehicle—for thirty-two hours. In that time, students appropriated a microphone and began to speak from the hood of the car. Treating the car with care (removing their shoes before climbing aboard), students took three-minute turns to say anything—even in opposition to the activists. This time, the protest yielded fruit. Savio and Kerr negotiated an agreement—the demonstration would cease, and a committee would be set up to look at relevant administrative rules. It was, in many ways, the largest sit-in of the decade; it was the birth of Berkeley's Free Speech Movement (FSM).

The FSM transcended any one issue—as the participants said at the time, "it's not about the car." Savio and his cohorts saw the FSM as a crusade to win for students their First Amendment right of free speech and assembly, rights that students all over the country had been denied under the patronizing system of *in loco parentis*. Moreover, the FSM turned out to be participatory democracy in action, as varied groups of student activists at Berkeley—from all parts of the political spectrum—worked together to achieve consensus on how they should proceed against the administration.

Had it stopped there, perhaps the influence of the FSM might have been muted. But once again, Kerr's administration showed its tin ear. In November, the committee announced that the students could have their tables back, but they could not use the tables to advocate unlawful acts. This restriction eliminated all those groups that used direct confrontation as a strategy, an act that Savio castigated as "prior restraint" of ideas. The activists also learned that the students originally suspended for their advocacy at the tables two months earlier had now been expelled.

Enraged, Savio lashed out at the administration. From the steps of Sproul Hall, speaking without either notes or text, he gave a passionate speech against the entire educational system. In so doing, he coined one of the most famous phrases of any public speech given by any activist in the 1960s:

> There comes a time when the operation of the machine becomes so odious, makes you so sick at heart, that you can't take part, you can't even tacitly take part. And you've got to put your bodies upon the gears and upon the wheels, upon the levers, upon all the apparatus and you've got to make it stop. And you've got to indicate to the people who run it, to the people who own it, that unless you're free, the machine will be prevented from working at all.

Immediately following Savio's eloquent diatribe, hundreds of students entered Sproul Hall, completely filling its hallways and effectively shutting the building down. Rather than waiting out the students, Kerr decided to clear the building. He called in the police, who emptied Sproul by forcibly removing the activists, many of whom resisted arrest by using a technique taught to them in Mississippi; they went completely limp, forcing the police to drag them out.

Following the retaking of Sproul Hall, the administration called an all-college meeting at its Greek Theater. Attended by thousands, administrator after administrator—including Kerr—spoke. But when Savio, apparently believing it was his turn to speak, headed to the lectern, he was grabbed by police and dragged off the stage. For the faculty, that was the last straw. They overwhelmingly voted a motion of no confidence in Kerr and in favor of the students. The students soon received, in writing, the rights to both their tables and freedom of speech on campus. Kerr would be fired from his position as chancellor by the Board of Regents in 1967.

The FSM had engineered a civil rights victory no more or less important than that won in Birmingham or Selma. The machine had, indeed, been brought to a halt; participatory democracy among the students was a large part of the reason it happened. Many other campuses saw similar, if smaller, protests (see the incident at Syracuse University related at the beginning of this chapter). The activists soon grew larger in number.

But it would only last a moment. By 1965, the focus of the student movement was changing. No longer directing its indignation against the sins of the multiversity, student activists, now larger in number, began to protest what was in their mind a greater sin. As Tom Hayden would later write, "we could not imagine that Vietnam was just around the corner."

As the student New Left originally articulated its disenchantment with the society bequeathed to them by their parents through its writings and its actions for social justice, so too, at the same time, did women begin to articulate their disenchantment with America's male-orientated society through their writings and their actions.

It is ironic that a president who all too often treated women as sexual chattel created the first executive-level commission dealing exclusively with the issues of women. The Commission on the Status of Women, created in 1961 by John F. Kennedy and chaired by former First Lady Eleanor Roosevelt, was charged with investigating "the story of women's progress in a free democratic society." The commission was historic, but its findings were decidedly traditional. It recommended in October 1963 that the government should lend its support to maintaining the traditional family structure and recommended that government-subsidized programs be created to help women prepare for their roles as housewives and mothers. It also concluded that women needed no further governmental protection, as women's rights were already protected under the Fifth and Fourteenth Amendments. Those who would argue throughout the 1960s that the lot of women was adequately served by the government would point to the narrow conclusions of this commission's report. They would also point to the Civil Rights Act of 1964, whose Title VII mandated that there be no discrimination in the job market on the basis of sex (when he moved to add the word "sex" to those protected by the act, Senator Howard W. Smith (D-VA), a vocal opponent of the bill, quipped, "This bill is so imperfect, what harm will this little amendment do?").

At the same time that the Kennedy Commission report was released, thousands of Americans were reading the most important and influential book—then and now—written by an American author since World War II. Betty Friedan, born in 1921 in Illinois, attended both Smith College and the University of California at Berkeley. Trained as a journalist, Friedan gave up a fellowship at Berkeley after being chided by a boyfriend for accepting money that might help a male fellow, and took up the role of mother and housewife. She also began to freelance, submitting magazine stories that dealt with the role of women in society. She soon became interested in how those magazines, through their articles and advertisements, actually pressured women into accepting the role of housewife as their only acceptable option. She began to interview those housewives; they told her that despite their financial affluence, they felt incomplete. Despite the image of women that they all saw in popular magazines—an image that Friedan the freelance writer had helped to perpetuate—of the happy housewife, content with her time-saving kitchen devices, they were experiencing illness, depression, even thoughts of suicide. One Long Island housewife told Friedan: "I seem to sleep so much. I don't know why I should be so tired. . . . It's not the work. I just don't feel alive."

Friedan's 1963 masterpiece, *The Feminine Mystique,* told a largely unsuspecting America that a crisis, which she dubbed "The Problem That Has No Name," existed in the spirits of the American housewife. The problem was caused by a myth—a mystique—that said that

> the highest value and the only commitment for women is the fulfillment of their own femininity. . . . [T]he new image this mystique gives to American women is the old image: "Occupation: Housewife." The new mystique makes the housewife-mothers, who never had a chance to be anything else, the model for all women.

For Friedan, there was enough blame for the existence of this mystique to go around—women's magazines, Sigmund Freud, Margaret Mead, sex educators, advertisers, and women themselves all received their share of Friedan's scorn. But after laying historical blame, Friedan offered a mystique-bashing solution. Women needed to adopt a "new life plan" to reject the role of the American housewife being her only option. Friedan urged women to seek a higher education that allowed them to train for jobs that were traditionally male bastions and called for government to afford women the same financial help that men had been offered through the GI Bill. For Friedan, this would only happen when the traditional marital roles were redefined, as she called for child care and a new, more nurturing role for men. If, indeed, women were given—or took—these opportunities,

Who knows what women can be when they are finally free to become
themselves? Who knows what women's intelligence will contribute when
it can be nourished without denying love? Who knows of the possibilities
of love when men and women share not only children, home, and garden,
not only fulfillment of their biological roles, but the responsibilities and
passions of the work that creates the human future and the full human
knowledge of who they are? It has barely begun, the search of women
for themselves. But the time is at hand when the voices of the feminine
mystique can no longer drown out the inner voice that is driving women
on to become complete.

This "inner voice" affected young women in a manner little less than
revolutionary. No less than their male counterparts, young women were
caught up in the excitement of both the civil rights movement and the student New Left. In her masterful study of the period, historian Sara Evans
shows how women began to challenge the mystique of the urban housewife
by working in the Freedom Summer, where they worked hand-in-hand with
men as they registered voters and taught in the Freedom Schools. Women
were also a key component of the ERAP experiment, providing a large part
of the shock troops in the northern shelters. In their efforts, they also found
a new type of female role model—activists like Fannie Lou Hamer and Casey
Hayden. They were indeed challenging the constraints of the feminine mystique. The first shots were being fired in what historians would term, after
the virtual invisibility of the feminist movement since women gained the
vote in 1919, "second-wave feminism."

There were, however, limits. Casey Hayden and Mary King noted these
limits in a famous 1965 memo to their SNCC colleagues, entitled "Sex and
Caste." They noted that the "women we've talked to who work in the movement seem to be caught up in a common-law caste system . . . which, at its
worst, uses and exploits women." Women seethed against these restrictions,
but they butted heads with the sexism of their male counterparts in the
movement. For just one example—the most famous—in his rebuttal to "Sex
and Caste," SNCC president Stokely Carmichael quipped that the place for
women in SNCC was "prone." As they returned from battle in the South,
both with the white racists and the sexists in their own organizations, these
young women would little suffer any solutions to the feminine mystique save
full gender equality.

However, these women were part of a dichotomy in second-wave feminism that bore a fascinating parallel to that which had developed in the civil rights movement. While youthful activists began to clamor for full gender equality, another arm of the feminist movement, à la King, was moving decidedly more cautiously. Disappointed with the results of the Kennedy Commission, as well as angered at the ineffectiveness of the Equal Employment Opportunity Commission (EEOC) to enforce the 1964 Civil Rights Act's Title VII adequately, some women began to explore other options. The State Commissions on Women, made up of white middle-class professional women, union activists, and academics, held their third national conference in Washington in June 1966. A motion placed on the floor demanded that the EEOC treat sex discrimination on a par with racial discrimination. The leadership of the conference, however, infuriated the rank and file by announcing that it was not empowered to entertain motions of any kind. Twenty-eight of the delegates, including Betty Friedan, met after the session and in protest formed the National Organization for Women (NOW). In its statement of purpose, drafted at an October 29–30 organizing conference, NOW announced its intention to form a "fully equal partnership of the sexes," and to "bring women into full participation in the mainstream of American society." To do this, they would have to dissolve the ties of the feminine mystique that had bound women: "We do not accept the traditional assumption that a woman has to choose between marriage and motherhood, on the one hand, and serious participation in industry or the professions on the other." To achieve these goals, the focus of NOW became overtly political. Its members lobbied the Johnson administration; worked to pass laws against discrimination in education, employment, and the marketplace; and initiated lawsuits.

In November 1967, NOW wrote and adopted a "Bill of Rights for Women." Its goals were largely political, calling for Congress to "immediately pass the Equal Rights Amendment to the Constitution," insisting that the EEOC enforce Title VII, demanding the passage of laws that protected a woman's job after taking time off for childbirth, calling for an end to barriers that kept women from attaining a higher education, and insisting on job training for poor women. But the final clause of the document hinted at the direction that second-wave feminism was about to take: "We demand . . . the right of women to control their own reproductive lives by removing from the penal code laws limiting access to contraceptive information and devices, and by repealing laws governing abortion."

As a result, many women found NOW's approach too radical. Those who opposed the call for a relaxed view toward abortion left the organization, and formed the Women's Equity Action League (WEAL). They argued that NOW was going too fast and that women should not attempt to deal with the thorny issue of reproduction control. Rather, they felt that feminists should continue to fight legal battles against sex-based discrimination. Others found the NOW approach decidedly restrictive and too political in nature. They saw NOW as a group of professional women whose main goal was not true equality, but rather economic achievement. For this latter group, led by young activists, a more holistic approach to feminist issues was needed—they were ready to step forward with a new, more radical set of demands.

For this cadre of younger feminists, NOW was moving too slowly. They felt that NOW's legalistic approach smacked of the NAACP and SCLC's approach in the civil rights movement, and they pushed to have the feminist cause move faster, arguing that women should demand nothing less than full gender equality. In the words of feminist writer Roxanne Dunbar: "We are damaged—we women. We are damaged, and we have the rights to hate, and have contempt, and to kill, and to scream. But for what? . . . How could we possibly settle for anything remotely less, even a crumb in the meantime less, than total annihilation of a system which systematically destroys half its people." These younger feminists were, in different quarters, initially dubbed "Radical Women" or later as supporters of a vaguely defined concept labeled "Women's Liberation." They placed a woman's private life squarely at the center of their concern, rather than outside the sphere of women's demands, where they believed such concerns had been relegated by NOW. Ti-Grace Atkinson of the radical women's group Redstockings, summarized this view: "Any real change in the status of women would be a fundamental assault on marriage and the family. People would be tied together by love, not legal contraptions. Children would be raised communally; it's just not honest to talk about freedom for women unless you get the child-rearing off their backs." The statement of principles of another radical group, the New York Radical Women, put it even more clearly: "We take the women's side in everything."

The tactics of the radical women were as different from their more moderate NOW sisters as were their demands. They first used "consciousness-raising" sessions that were modeled after the free-form student sessions that had been inspired by the idea of participatory democracy, as well as the open sessions many women had experienced while working in the South. Women—only women—met in small groups for a period of completely unstructured dialogue. From these sessions came a cathartic outpouring of individual experiences and pain, stories of everyday discrimination, tales of the problems of motherhood—mixed with a discussion of sexual politics and the direction of a fast-growing radical movement. From these consciousness-raising sessions came community—there came "sisterhood."

But the radical women had cut their teeth in the civil rights movement, and they would not be content solely with discussing their concerns behind closed doors. They broke with their more moderate sisters in their desire to take feminism to the same ramparts that the civil rights movement had assaulted. The first attack came in September 1968, when some two hundred women picketed the Miss America Pageant in Atlantic City. The event was chosen partially because it provided a perfect target—it featured, by its very definition, women being paraded as sex objects. It was also chosen, in the tested tradition of the civil rights movement, because their protest would be carried on national television. The Atlantic City feminists were nothing if not creative, as they crowned a live sheep the winner of the pageant and tossed various articles of oppression—dishcloths, steno pads, high heels, and bras—into a "Freedom Trash Can."

Contrary to popular myth, no bras were burned in Atlantic City. But the radical women had caught the attention of the media. Throughout 1969, more radical organizations sprang upward, and various tactics and strategies kept the issue of feminism white hot. As the 1970s commenced, second-wave feminism was maturing as a movement, one with moderate and activist wings, that was headed toward the two issues that would challenge the movement to its core and continue to define feminism in the 1970s—the 1973 reintroduction of the Equal Rights Amendment and the decision of the Supreme Court in that same year to legalize abortion.

Recommended Reading and Viewing

To understand fully both the intellectual underpinnings and the intellectual contributions of the student New Left, one must read the two works of C. Wright Mills that influenced their thought: *The Power Elite* (New York: Oxford Univ. Press, 1956) and "Letter to the New Left," *The New Left Review* (Sept.–Oct. 1960). The best history of SDS continues to be Kirkpatrick Sale,

SDS (New York: Vintage Books, 1973). The Port Huron Statement can be found in its entirety several places on the Web. Tom Hayden wrote a particularly thoughtful retrospective with fellow SDS member Dick Flacks, "The Port Huron Statement at 40," *The Nation,* Aug. 5, 2002. See also Hayden's *Reunion: A Memoir* (New York: Random House, 1988). "Berkeley in the 60s" (PBS, 1991) is a useful documentary that interviews many of the students involved. William J. Rorabaugh's *Berkeley at War: The 1960s* (New York: Oxford Univ. Press, 1989) is an excellent treatment not only of the uprisings on that campus, but also of the place of higher education in the 1960s. Betty Friedan, *The Feminine Mystique* (New York: Dell, 1963) stands as the most important book written by an American author since 1945. Sara Evans, *Personal Politics: The Roots of Women's Liberation in the Civil Rights Movement and the New Left* (New York: Vintage Books, 1979) is a superb treatment of its subject.

7

"Waist Deep in the Big Muddy"

Vietnam, 1960–1967

IT CAME UPON US with no attack on American soil, no great proclamations, no declaration of war. The Vietnam War snuck up on the American people, virtually unaware. In 1960, the United States had but a handful of military "advisors" protecting its interests in South Vietnam—the cold war outpost inherited from the French in 1954 and financially supported since that time. In 1961, Kennedy increased the number of military "advisors" to about 3,200. By the time of his assassination, he had committed 18,000 troops to South Vietnam. In January 1966 that number leapt to 25,000. It doubled in July, tripled by January 1966, tripled again by December 1966, and doubled again by December 1967. By 1968, the maximum troop level, there were approximately 536,000 troops "in country"—on the ground and in the air. All told, some 3,000,000 men were sent to Vietnam by Kennedy, Johnson, and, eventually, Richard Nixon. The term used to describe this growth was "escalation"—and it had a frighteningly inevitable quality to it. By mid-decade, it seemed to many Americans, both in and outside of the government, that the war was out of anyone's control; even to the most sincere politician there seemed to be no way out. In the words of folk singer Pete Seeger, the country was "Waist Deep in the Big Muddy." There was a feeling of hopelessness, constriction, suffocation.

The 1960s represent the most destructive period of a war that had its genesis in the 1940s and its final meltdown in the 1970s. Indeed, the Vietnam War *was* America in the 1960s. As with the effect of World War II, but completely unlike the Korean War and all conflicts since, American society in the 1960s was not only affected by the war but completely and unalterably shaped by it. Even the civil rights movement, which redirected the American conscience, did not have as long-lasting an effect on the nation as did its contemporary crisis in Vietnam. First and foremost, the war destroyed more than 58,191 American lives. But it also destroyed Lyndon Johnson's domestic revolution and created a distrust of the presidency that was, to that point, unique in American history. It also balkanized the country's opinion of itself—not into two camps, as some have simplistically offered elsewhere, but into many shades of opinion and suggested solutions, all being loudly heard and seen in the same media that had helped create the civil rights movements. The Vietnam War ultimately destroyed America's place in the world, its faith in its leaders, its faith in governmental institutions, and ultimately, its faith in itself. The Vietnam War was arguably the most important event in the history of the twentieth-century United States.

Kennedy inherited this conflict in 1961, and he attempted to deal with the growing problem by shoving it aside. It was not yet a time when the United States could see Far Eastern policy as anything other than an irritant—its policy was Eurocentric, and its view of the world bipolar. Therefore, Kennedy concentrated (as noted in chapter 2) on the cold war with the Soviet Union, and worried more about World War III breaking out over either Berlin or Cuba. But major foreign policy mistakes in the cold war (the Bay of Pigs, the Geneva Summit, and the creation of the Berlin Wall) soon had the administration searching for victory. In May 1961, Kennedy received reports from both the Joint Chiefs of Staff and the National Security Council (NSC) advocating that he should strengthen America's commitment to South Vietnam. Kennedy sent representatives of both those groups—chairman of the Joint Chiefs General Maxwell Taylor and Walt Rostow of the NSC—on a fact-finding trip to South Vietnam. On their return they argued for a "logistic" task force of some eight thousand "advisors" (Eisenhower had sent eight hundred such advisors) and an increased American financial commitment to the government of Ngo Dinh Diem. Recognizing the fundamental corruption within the Diem regime, several of Kennedy's advisors counseled against this increased aid. Needing both more information and more time, Kennedy dispatched Vice President Lyndon Johnson to Saigon. Whether or not Johnson was joking when he proclaimed Diem the "Winston Churchill of the Far East," in his report to Kennedy, Johnson drew the line in the sand that would become the cornerstone of American policy in Vietnam until 1974: "The fundamental decision . . . is whether we are to attempt to meet the challenge of Communist expansion now in Southeast Asia by a major effort in support of the forces of freedom in the area, or throw in the towel."

Temperamentally incapable of throwing in the towel *anywhere,* in December 1961 Kennedy agreed to increase American financial aid to the Diem government. He also agreed to send U.S. Army Special Forces—the Green Berets—to South Vietnam, ostensibly to train the South Vietnamese regulars. In December, Kennedy sent 3,205 advisors; by the end of 1962 that number had reached 9,000; by the time of Kennedy's death it stood at 18,000. The military strategy during the Kennedy era was later dubbed the "Strategic Hamlet" program. This was a plan to remove the residents of villages thought to be compromised by Vietcong infiltration and resettle them in new villages that were, in actuality, fortified encampments. Ideally, the program was meant to protect the villagers and expose the Vietcong. In reality, the Vietcong found it very easy to infiltrate the new encampments, and the displaced population came to hate the Americans who removed them from their ancestral homes more than they did the Vietcong. The situation was fast becoming lethal; by December 1963, there had been a reported 77 Americans killed in action.

It was soon evident, however, that in the name of protecting a domino, America had committed itself to the protection of a monstrous regime. The intransigent Diem, refusing to toe the American line, began as a mild embarrassment to both Eisenhower and Kennedy. Indeed, Diem took American funding and quickly grafted his share. It was not long before the Diem regime grew from being a private problem among allies to being a public, international embarrassment, triggered by the regime's persecution of Buddhist monks who demanded to be allowed to fly flags to celebrate the birth of Buddha. The largely Catholic government of South Vietnam (a holdover from the French occupation) saw this celebration as a direct threat to its authority, as well as a clash of idolatry—Diem refused to allow Buddhist worship to interfere with the cult of power that he was creating for himself. On May 8, 1963, troops fired into a crowd that was protesting government orders forbidding the celebration of Buddha's birth. One month later, on June 11, a Buddhist monk protested the actions of the government by sitting down in a public square, dousing himself with gasoline, lighting a match, and exploding himself in flames. Diem's sister-in-law, Madame Ngo Dinh

Nhu, publicly laughed off the immolations as "barbeques." But later that month, faced with many more such public immolations, the Diem regime began to round up the monks.

There is some evidence to suggest that Kennedy, the nation's first Roman Catholic president, found the actions of his fellow Catholic to be morally repugnant. There is a greater body of evidence found in the collection of documents on the conduct of the war that would become known as the *Pentagon Papers* to suggest that what was about to transpire was a result of Kennedy's desire for a more malleable puppet in South Vietnam. All attempts to mollify Diem had failed; a State Department cablegram dated August 24, 1963, coldly concluded that "we must face the possibility that Diem *himself* cannot be preserved." U.S. officials had learned of a coup effort being planned by Diem's generals. As Henry Cabot Lodge, then U.S. ambassador to South Vietnam, would cable Secretary of State Dean Rusk on August 29: "We are launched on a course from which there is no respectable turning back: the overthrow of the Diem government. . . . We should proceed to make all-out efforts to get Generals to move promptly." Kennedy's reaction was both unequivocal and deniable, as seen in an October 5, 1963, cable transmitted to Lodge on a secure CIA channel: "President today approved recommendation that no initiation should now be taken to give any active covert encouragement to a coup. There should, however, be urgent covert effort with closest security . . . to identify and build contacts with possible alternative leadership as and when it appears. Essential that this effort be totally secure and fully deniable."

On November 1, the leaders of the coup took Diem and his brother, Ngo Dinh Nhu (Diem's closest political lieutenant and himself an outspoken critic of American actions in Vietnam), into custody. Despite promising safe conduct, the two men were bound, tossed in the back of an armored personnel carrier, riddled with machine-gun fire, and then stabbed with knives until the bodies were beyond recognition. The generals, who now formed a ruling junta for South Vietnam, announced to an unbelieving world that the two men had committed suicide.

Much of the aura around the Camelot Myth comes from the belief that at the time of his death, stung by the assassination of Diem, Kennedy was trying to get the United States out of Vietnam. There is absolutely no evidence of this, and much to support a contrary hypothesis that Kennedy was in the midst of increasing America's troop involvement, had significantly increased funding, and had turned a deaf ear to the assassination of Diem both before and after the event. However, there was, in November 1963, no overt war in Vietnam. There were no U.S. troops on the ground; no corresponding air or naval war; no body bags returning to American shores. *That* would all be part of the complex legacy of Lyndon Johnson.

Like his predecessor, Lyndon Johnson saw the oncoming war in Vietnam in the simplistic good-versus-evil terms of the cold warrior. To Johnson, South Vietnam was an American ally, and was to be defended at all financial and military costs. Publicly, he never had any doubt as to the outcome of the conflict, proclaiming that "America wins the wars she undertakes, make no mistake about it." But unlike Kennedy, who had been largely reactive in Vietnam, Johnson was decidedly proactive. From his second day in office, Johnson made that clear; in a meeting with Lodge, he ordered his ambassador to inform the flimsy military junta in South Vietnam that the United States would continue its support. By the New Year, however, the situation had become even more precarious. The ruling junta had been overthrown by a new faction led by General Nguyen Khanh, and this coup, joined with a perception on the part of North Vietnam's leadership that there was chaos in the United States following the assassination of Kennedy, led the National Liberation Front (NLF) to escalate its activities throughout South Vietnam. In what would eventually be a significant escalation of the conflict, Ho Chi Minh began to plan for the introduction of regular North Vietnamese troops alongside the guerillas of the NLF.

Johnson responded with a three-pronged strategy of his own. First, he increased American aid to the South Vietnamese government to $50 million. Second, he increased the covert war in the region, approving sabotage operations, U-2 flights over both North Vietnam and neighboring Laos and Cambodia, commando raids, kidnapping, and intelligence patrols in the Gulf of Tonkin, all designed to collect intelligence and intimidate the North Vietnamese. But the Joint Chiefs knew that a covert war alone could not win in Vietnam. So third, by the summer of 1964 the administration had begun to develop scenarios for the saturation bombing of North Vietnam. The military presented several plans to Johnson and McNamara, and with each of them the military warned that they probably would not have the desired effects. While the in-house debate raged, Johnson ordered his advisors to keep planning. These discussions were well underway by August 1964, when a chance attack on an American destroyer allowed Johnson to change the face of the war.

On August 1, 1964, while on intelligence patrol in the Gulf of Tonkin (which formed much of the eastern border of North Vietnam), the American destroyer USS *Maddox,* which was conducting electronic surveillance of North Vietnam as part of Johnson's covert war, encountered a North Vietnamese torpedo boat. After a brief engagement, Johnson ordered the destroyer USS *C. Turner Joy,* on patrol nearby, to join the *Maddox.* Three days later, both destroyers reported that they were once again under attack. Information was sketchy as to the level of the North Vietnamese threat, but Johnson authorized the destroyers to defend themselves. Even when conflicting information came in suggesting that the two destroyers had actually *not* been attacked, the administration did not reverse itself. From the steps of the newly dedicated S. I. Newhouse School of Public Communications at Syracuse University, Johnson drew a line on the sand:

> The attacks were deliberate. The attacks were unprovoked. The attacks have been answered. . . . We welcome—and we invite—the scrutiny of all men who seek peace, for peace is the only purpose of the course that America pursues. The Gulf of Tonkin may be distant, but none can be detached about what has happened there. Aggression—deliberate, willful, and systematic aggression—has unmasked its face to the entire world. The world remembers—the world must never forget—that aggression unchallenged is aggression unleashed. We of the United States have not forgotten. That is why we have answered this aggression with action.

The public, of course, knew nothing about the nature of the *Maddox*'s mission. But more important, neither did Congress, which had been told nothing about the covert intelligence operations being carried out in the Gulf of Tonkin. This, however, was nothing new. Since World War II, Congress had refused to interfere with, or even effectively to oversee, American presidents as they placed American military forces in harm's way around the world. In 1950, Harry Truman committed American troops to battle in Korea without a vote from the Congress; Congress did not protest. As a result, Congress effectively abrogated its power under Article I, Section 8, Cl. 11 of the Constitution, which baldly states that "The Congress shall have the power to declare war." In a seminal 1973 book on the growth of the presidential war-making power, Arthur M. Schlesinger, Jr., termed this development the rise of the Imperial Presidency. Schlesinger argued that the 1950 decision of Harry Truman to meet the invasion of South Korea by North Korean forces with American troops without obtaining a declaration of war from Congress constituted the logical, albeit unconstitutional, dénouement of this development. It also paved the way for Eisenhower to send advisors and for Kennedy to send the Green Berets to Vietnam—all without a declaration of war. By August 1964, the power to engage American military power had clearly shifted from Congress to an increasingly imperial White House.

Were Johnson to have retaliated to the clash at the Gulf of Tonkin by immediately sending ground troops to South Vietnam or by bombing the North, he would have met with virtually no opposition on Capitol Hill, even if he made such moves without a formal declaration of war. But Johnson knew that any widening of the American commitment in Vietnam would mean a large number of American casualties; he was not about to bear the complete brunt of such a decision. Ever the master of political realities, Johnson introduced a resolution to the Congress designed both to legitimize his upcoming actions in Vietnam and to give him political cover. The resolution gave the president the power to "take all necessary measures to repel any armed attacks against the forces of the United States and to prevent any further aggression." In a speech to Congress wherein he defended his proposal, Johnson stated, "as I have repeatedly made clear, the United States intends no rashness and seeks no wider war." That was simply not true; moreover, the resolution violated the Constitution in both letter and spirit. Regardless, what became known as the Tonkin Gulf Resolution passed the Senate by a vote of 88–2 and was unanimously passed by the House.

Yet despite being given this unprecedented grant of authority, Johnson would neither send troops to South Vietnam nor start the bombing of the North in the middle of a presidential election. Indeed, throughout the fall campaign his opponent, the Republican senator from Arizona, Barry Goldwater, provided a perfect foil for Johnson, who hoped to maintain the illusion of statesmanship in Vietnam throughout the campaign. In calling for the use of low-yield atomic weapons to expose North Vietnamese supply routes, Goldwater ran afoul of an American public that was still terrified of nuclear annihilation. Most important, he looked like a trigger-happy hawk (which he was not), allowing Johnson to look downright pacifist by comparison.

Yet once Johnson had trounced Goldwater at the polls, receiving the greatest popular mandate to that point in the history of American presidential elections, the internal White House debate over a bombing scenario reignited in earnest. Further instability in the South Vietnamese government gave support to those who argued for immediate bombing. In January 1965, Khanh's government was overthrown by a new military junta, now led by the flamboyant General Nguyen Cao Ky. Believing that the South Vietnamese government was too unstable to save itself, Johnson was now but one provocation away from ordering the bombing.

That provocation came on February 7, 1965, when an NLF attack on a marine base at Pleiku resulted in the death of nine Americans. Five days later, Johnson approved the initiation first of Operation Flaming Dart, then of Operation Rolling Thunder—the saturation bombing of North Vietnam. General William Westmoreland, in command of American forces in South Vietnam, then made the case to the president that American ground troops were needed, ostensibly to guard the bases from which the air war was being launched. One month later, on March 8, Johnson sent the first contingent of American ground troops to South Vietnam.

The *entirety* of the American military establishment—from the president on down through the ranks—believed in the summer of 1965 that there was no possible way that American military might would not prevail in Vietnam. The early strategy, labeled with the ironic tag "the war for victory," reflected this. The original key to the strategy was an air war that inflicted some $600 billion in damage on the North Vietnamese, and, by one analysis, eventually cost the North twenty-eight hundred casualties per month. The results in the field, however, were negligible, and neither the White House nor the military could figure out why the bombing did not completely destroy the enemy.

The reason the enemy was not completely destroyed by the U.S. air war was that the United States never fully understood who its enemy in Vietnam was. Never bothering seriously to learn about the culture of its enemy, the United States worked under the guiding assumption that it was aiding South Vietnam in a fight against a completely different people, a completely different culture—a culture that when seen through cold war eyes was the epitome of the evil of communism. Johnson initially felt that he could simply bomb the North into submission, thus winning the war in quick fashion. But this division of the nation into north and south had been arbitrarily done at

Geneva—the NLF simply ignored this political division and recruited freedom fighters from the *whole* of the country, north and south. What the
United States did not understand was that few Vietnamese, north *or* south,
wanted them there, and that America had become entangled in a war when
it was, in effect, being attacked by the entire Vietnamese people. It was a
scenario where an air war was doomed to failure because it was not bombing
the entire enemy.

Nevertheless, the military establishment attempted to turn the tide with
traditional tactics. When it became clear that the air war was not bringing the enemy to its knees, the strategy gradually morphed into one that
placed more emphasis on the ground troops. In what became known as
"search and destroy," American troops scoured the countryside ("humping
the boonies"), looking to engage an enemy that was difficult to find. The
Joint Chiefs convinced Johnson that for this strategy to work, more and
more troops would be necessary. As more troops came from "the world" to
"Nam," the word "escalation" began to strike an almost obscene chord with
many Americans. Indeed, the troop escalation was so rapid that the military
could not handle it—soldiers began to arrive in Vietnam by commercial jet.
But like the air war, "search and destroy" was also doomed to failure by the
political and cultural realities in Vietnam. It was difficult for the military
to wrap its mind around the fact that *anyone*—even those who lived in the
south—could be the enemy. Thus, pouring more and more American troops
into battle did little to change the situation—they never defeated the enemy,
because they never really understood who the enemy *was*.

Armed with a full understanding of the cultural situation in Vietnam,
but faced with overwhelming opposition numbers, the strategy of both the
North Vietnamese army and the NLF quickly became the same—strike a
defensive posture, wait for the Americans to "find" them, and then engage
them on favorable ground. It was soon obvious that no matter how many
soldiers went to Vietnam, *all* advantages were with the enemy. Well versed
in guerilla warfare, the North Vietnamese were a more nimble enemy. And
having sucked their opponent into fighting on their home turf, they simply
outran the American machine. Body counts—the traditional method for
deciding the victor and the vanquished in battle—meant nothing in this
scenario. The number of Americans killed in action was usually quite a bit
lower than that of their North Vietnamese and NLF opponents. Indeed,
the American people and their government saw the reported kill-rates that

favored America and concluded that they were winning the war. But until the North ran out of soldiers—which it showed no sign of doing—it could drag the war out for a very long time. The "war for victory" had, by 1967, become a "war of attrition" for both sides.

In an attempt to break the logjam, the United States initiated two new strategies, each designed specifically for the type of warfare in which they now found themselves. Since the terrain was making it difficult to find the enemy, Operation Ranch Hand initiated the use of chemical herbicides, dumped from cargo planes onto the jungle below, in hopes that it would destroy the flora and fauna so that the enemy would have less of a hiding place. The herbicides had little impact—the jungle was as defiant as was the enemy. But Operation Ranch Hand had a longer-term effect. The herbicides contained a considerable quantity of dioxin, an extremely toxic chemical. Unaware of this danger, the military often dumped the herbicide directly on the American troops below. The troops made no effort to shield themselves from the chemical shower—indeed, it was so cool in comparison to the oppressively humid temperatures of the jungle that many of the soldiers took off their uniforms and rubbed the cooling liquids all over their bodies. The military used these herbicides—code-named Agents Purple, Pink, Green, and the one with the least amount of dioxin, but the herbicide that became best known to the public, Agent Orange—until 1970. Almost immediately, soldiers exposed to the herbicides began to exhibit a wide range of symptoms, including Hodgkin's disease, non-Hodgkin lymphoma, and chloracne; later, many children of Vietnam veterans exposed to Agent Orange exhibited a variety of birth defects. As veterans pushed to get their illnesses treated, the Pentagon balked, refusing to admit that the herbicides were responsible for the illnesses, thus refusing to pay for any medical treatment. It was not until 1992 that the Department of Defense officially took responsibility for the fact that the above-listed diseases, and others, could have been caused by exposure to the herbicides, and an out of court settlement was reached with Dow Chemical Company and other manufacturers of Agent Orange.

The second strategy, born of the failed "Strategic Hamlet" plan, involved the systematic infiltration of South Vietnamese villages by American troops. Once in place, the troops were charged with "interviewing" the residents and deciding which were Vietcong and which were not. It was an attempt to break through the impasse caused by not being able to ascertain who the true enemy was. Rather than develop techniques designed to ascertain the true affections of a village, torture techniques were widely employed. The brutality of the "interviews" would later be exposed; particularly notorious was Operation PHOENIX, a CIA-led operation that used torture technologies that would later be used in the post–September 11, 2001 War on Terror. This strategy—known as the "Pacification Program"—simply widened the gap between Americans and all Vietnamese and drove more and more southerners into the open arms of the NLF.

Frustration at not being able to identify the enemy led, perhaps inevitably, to abuses and atrocities. The most infamous American atrocity occurred on March 16, 1968. Charlie Company, 1st Battalion, 20th Infantry raided a small village in northeastern South Vietnam, a village that the army had christened "Pinkville" because of the color used to identify it on their maps; the locals knew the village as My Lai. Charlie Company had been briefed to expect a high concentration of Vietcong resistance in the village. Instead they found elderly men, women, and children. Later reports claimed that Second Lieutenant William Calley, commander of the operation, ordered his men to round up the civilians in the center of the village, told his second in command "I want them dead," then stood back and started shooting. Charlie Company followed suit. Civilians were shot as they attempted to flee; other were led to a mass grave and executed. The killing did not stop until a pilot landed his helicopter between Americans and the escaping Vietnamese. Depending on whose figures are believed, between 370 and 540 villagers were murdered by Charlie Company at My Lai.

Why was the United States in Vietnam? This question is absolutely fundamental to an understanding of the country's recent history. The debate raged throughout the second half of the 1960s and continues today, as Americans look to explain and understand their participation in that debacle. Lyndon Johnson never wavered from his belief that the Vietnam War was a classic American attempt to stop the spread of totalitarianism and protect a smaller nation from being fed to the communist menace. Johnson's most articulate and thoughtful defense of his actions came in a speech delivered on April 9, 1965, at Johns Hopkins University:

> Why are we in South Viet-Nam? We are there because we have a promise to keep. . . . Over many years, we have made a national pledge to help South Viet-Nam defend its independence. And I intend to keep that promise. . . .

We are also there because those are great stakes in the balance. Let no one think for a moment that retreat from Viet-Nam would bring an end to conflict. The battle would be renewed in one country and then another. The central lesson of our time is that aggression is never satisfied. . . .

In recent months attacks on South Viet-Nam were stepped up. Thus, it became necessary for us to increase our response and to make attacks by air. . . . We do this to convince the leaders of North Viet-Nam—and all who seek to share their conquest—of a very simple fact: We will not be defeated. We will not grow tired. We will not withdraw.

Johnson's speech was a more comprehensive treatment of Eisenhower's domino theory—we *had* to be in Vietnam; we had no choice, as Americans, but to stand up to communist aggression. In a popular 1971 history of the period, *Coming Apart: An Informal History of America in the 1960s,* historian William O'Neill put this argument more succinctly—the United States was in Vietnam out of habit; since 1945, whenever a nation had looked like it might "fall" to the communists, America went in to save the day.

However, the mid-1960s saw a seismic shift in the ability of the president to use his "bully pulpit" in order to convince the American people that his actions, particularly in foreign policy, were justified. The president had always been criticized for his decisions. The social critics of the 1950s, and even the early intellectuals of the New Left, while both highly critical of Eisenhower and Kennedy, stopped way short of publicly calling them liars. The Vietnam War created a new type of American discourse: those who had come to believe that in virtually every action, their own government was wrong. The first shots of this new criticism were fired by a new generation of diplomatic historians who charged that rather than molding a foreign policy designed to make the world safe for democracy, America had in reality pursued a foreign policy driven by paranoia, imperialism, and capitalism—that since the turn of the century, America had been trying to expand its empire around the world not in the name of democracy, but in the name of naked economic self-interest. One of the first intellectuals to voice this argument was William Appleman Williams of the University of Wisconsin. His *Tragedy of American Diplomacy,* written in 1959 and revised twice before the end of the Vietnam War, was a passionate and blunt criticism of American *intent;* its charge that America simply didn't *care* about other nations, so long as they conformed to its wishes, explained for many why America was in Vietnam, but also *why* it would not extricate itself from the growing disaster:

> [An] idea entertained by many Americans . . . insists that other people can-
> not *really* solve their problems and improve their lives unless they go about
> it in the same way as the United States. This insistence that other people
> ought to copy America contradicts the humanitarian urge to help them and
> the idea that they have the right to make such key decisions for themselves.
> In some cases, the American way of doing things simply does not work for
> other people.

First revised in the wake of the Bay of Pigs debacle, which convinced Williams of both the paucity of American foreign policy in general and the validity of his overall thesis, *Tragedy* signaled the beginning of a new revisionist history—one that did not see the job of the historian to be either the writer of patriotic platitudes nor the collector of facts uncommented upon. Rather, Williams saw the role of the historian as an analyst. He and his disciples in the historical field—Gar Alperovitz, Lloyd Gardner, Walter LaFeber, and Joyce and Gabriel Kolko—attempted to see through the explanations given by government for their actions and allow the evidence to speak to an alternative, often damning, hypothesis—that the government might just be wrong.

It was not just the revisionist historians who were beginning to question the intent of their government. The American mass media also found itself growing into an even more antagonistic role with government. Up to the 1960s the press had not taken its oversight role very seriously. More concerned about perks and access to power than with digging to the truth, many reporters—for all the major news dailies, as well as for radio stations and the embryonic television newscasts—chose to ignore the true intent of their government, and simply print press releases without question. However, as with their brethren in history, the turbulent times of the early 1960s led the media to put a mirror up to the government, and it found the reflection to be inconsistent with past national assumptions.

The first example of this change, discussed earlier in this book, was television's coverage of the civil rights movement. By showing Mamie Till, Bull Connor's savage dogs, and the signs of hope at the Lincoln Memorial, television had begun—with very little editorial commentary save the power of their pictures—to expose its government as racist. The media's coverage of the civil rights movement also helped create a new type of journalist—a "revisionist reporter," if you will. Reporters now stepped into the field of government watchdog. They began to resist age-old strictures and traditions that led the media to self-censor. No longer would reporters blindly accede to White House orders like the one that insisted, for example, that the only pictures to be published of Franklin Roosevelt were to be pictures that did not show him on crutches (if this pact was violated, the offending newspaper or magazine would be shunned by the press). Gone were the days when, as in the Eisenhower years, press conferences edited by the White House would be aired. And soon to be discarded were any limitations on covering the personal lives of governmental officials, as the press had done by not publishing their knowledge of the sexual affairs of both Kennedy and Johnson. Reporters now wanted to get, in the words of one of the most famous radio personalities of the broadcast period, "the rest of the story."

This development of a new media attitude toward government would be accelerated by the Vietnam War. Always hungry for a war to cover, young journalists, many of whom had covered various phases of the civil rights movement, competed with each other to get to cover Vietnam firsthand. When they did, they discovered that the official releases of the military were simply wrong. They had discovered what would soon be dubbed the "credibility gap"—the enormous chasm that existed between official explanations and the truth. Refusing to accept press releases from military command as fact, as had been done in previous wars (fed to the press corps once a day, in what reporters derisively called the "Five O'Clock Follies"), these reporters observed for themselves, "embedding" themselves with platoons and companies in the field *long* before that term was made popular in the Gulf Wars of the next century. They also became stars in their own right—Ward Just of the *Washington Post;* David Halberstam and Neil Sheehan of the *New York Times;* Peter Arnett of Associated Press; Dan Rather of CBS News; freelance writer Michael Herr. It would be Seymour Hersh, another freelance reporter, who in 1969 would break the story of My Lai. Their resourcefulness, along with the willingness of their editors to print and broadcast their stories, led to coverage of the war that soon became harshly critical. They were the vanguard of what a decade later would be called "investigative journalists."

And it turned out that they were right. In June 1967, Secretary of Defense Robert McNamara commissioned a top-secret study of the Vietnam

War. Driven both by his own disenchantment with the war and, according to some later observers, a desire to give his friend Robert Kennedy some ammunition for his upcoming campaign for the presidency, McNamara demanded an "encyclopedic and objective" history of the war, from its French roots to the present. The committee of thirty-six analysts whom McNamara assigned to the project were assured that their work would remain absolutely confidential for their lifetimes, and they were given complete, unfettered access to all Pentagon files, as well as to a great deal of classified CIA material. The report was completed in 1968. The report would be leaked to the press in April 1971 by one of the analysts, Daniel Ellsberg; his actions, and Richard Nixon's failed attempt to restrict the publication of what had been dubbed "The Pentagon Papers," would set in motion a series of events that would lead directly to Nixon's resignation from the presidency in August 1974. But the release of the report—forty-seven book-length volumes, three thousand pages of narrative history, and four thousand pages of documents—instantly proved the investigative reporters to have been right. Indeed, the Pentagon Papers offered incontrovertible evidence that Truman, Eisenhower, Kennedy, and Johnson had lied to press and public about America's involvement in Vietnam. Truman's money . . . Eisenhower's secret covert war . . . Kennedy's complicity in the assassination of the Diems . . . Johnson's lies about the development of Rolling Thunder . . . all were revealed to the American people. The report ended the "quagmire myth"—that the United States was dragged slowly into a war that was not of its own making.

The analytical exercises of the revisionist historians, and the investigative reporting of the war correspondents, created an atmosphere that changed the New Left. Already predisposed to question authority, the students—energized by the civil rights movement, many as participants; educated in many cases by revisionists in their college faculty; steeped in the press reports of the time—began to voice their opposition to the war. That they did so actively, publicly, and often violently, owes much to the concurrent change in the civil rights movement, discussed in chapter 5. As their colleagues in the movement had broken away from what they perceived to be the failed tactics of King and his more moderate followers, so too by 1965 did a significant number of students break away from the more intellectual opposition of SDS and instead confront the government in the streets.

By the spring of 1965, the focus of the student movement had clearly begun to change. Some historians date the change from the March Teach-In at the University of Michigan, the first of many such intellectual debates on the validity of the war that would be held nationwide. Others note the anger that followed Johnson's decision that April to send American troops to the Dominican Republic to quell disturbances there—thus convincing many students that William Appleman Williams was right. In April, SDS sponsored an antiwar march in Washington, D.C., and one of the featured speakers was SNCC's Bob Moses. Clearly, the focus of the New Left was shifting from its original protest against the multiversity to a protest against the war in Vietnam. As SDS shifted to an antiwar focus, it also grew in numbers. By the end of 1965, its national membership was about fifteen thousand—triple what it had been in 1964. It also became less tolerant of those who sat on the sidelines, and the organization as a whole began to use less of the language of thoughtful intellectualism that had been its focus in the early part of the decade. A different voice was coming from SDS—a voice that the casual observer called "radical."

It is telling to note that it was difficult at times to tell if it was an anti*war* movement or an anti*draft* movement. In his seminal 1993 book *Working Class War: American Combat Soldiers and Vietnam,* historian Christian Appy analyzed the Vietnam-era draft, and in so doing put the antiwar movement into a new perspective. Appy showed that the odds of a young man between the ages of eighteen and twenty-six actually getting drafted were quite slim. There were considerably more men exempted from the service than were actually drafted, and student deferments—the legal postponement of military service until a young man completed college[1]—were plentiful. Plentiful, that is, for the middle- and upper-class youth who could afford college in the first place. Appy's data showed that the war was largely fought by youth from blue collar and poor families. Indeed, a full 80 percent of those who served in Vietnam had no better than a high school education. Those who resisted the war were largely those who were comfortable enough to be where the protests began—in college. It is important to note that some went to jail rather than be drafted, and some fled to Canada. But as Appy made clear, the numbers in both these groups was quite small. The vast majority of students who protested the war did so under the cover of an exemption or a deferment. And it would be their presence, and their tactics, that would dramatically change the student New Left.

1. Student deferments originally extended to graduate or professional schools; in the summer of 1968, that deferment ended, and to the end of the war student deferments only applied to undergraduate school.

Oversimplifications of the nature of the antiwar movement abound in the historical literature. Despite the claims of many scholars, the antiwar movement was not a "radicalization" of the student movement—as we have seen, the Port Huron Statement was clearly a radical document, and SDS and the Free Speech Movement advocated radical ideas. Nor can the antiwar movement be explained away as students who had suddenly become "activists." Those many historians who accept this conclusion forget the students in Mississippi and at Sproul Hall. However, an explanation of the nature of these antiwar protests is necessary, since they definitely became something completely different and separate from the "student movement" that had preceded it.

It is more useful, I believe, to see the antiwar movement *as* "movement." The students had seen movement—mass opposition to a moral wrong—begin to work in the realm of civil rights. Indeed, many of them had been part of that effort. Now by 1965, they wanted a "movement" against the war in Vietnam. They began with a concerted effort to get their cause into middle-class living rooms. Using tactics borrowed from the civil rights movement, the antiwar movement took its cause before the cameras. Chanting "Hey, Hey, LBJ—how many kids did you kill today?" by 1966 student protestors were as commonplace on the nightly news as were civil rights protestors. They also adopted the strategy of the civil rights movement to broaden the scope and membership of their ranks. As SCLC accepted SNCC in 1964, SDS now accepted radical groups such as the Maoists and the Radical Youth with the ease that they accepted the political comedians of the Yippie Movement. As the civil rights movement was a confederation of different voices, so too was the antiwar movement a confederation of young voices. And like most confederations—like the civil rights movement—the antiwar movement was unwieldy, unkempt, and eventually fratricidal.

By the summer of 1967, the movement was ready for a wider attempt at organization. At the same moment that the cities burned in what was called the "long, hot summer" of the civil rights movement, and the counterculture was heading to San Francisco for the "summer of love," the antiwar movement launched "Vietnam Summer." Using a sophisticated organization patterned after the Freedom Summer of 1964 and dubbed "The Resistance," the movement went door-to-door nationwide, spreading the antiwar message. As 1967 progressed, it became clear that those in the antiwar movement, like the young activists in both the civil rights movement and the later student movement—openly sought public confrontation. In the fall of that year, the National Mobilization Committee Against the War—the MOBE—was created. An amalgam of students, alumni of the civil rights movement, intellectual liberals, radicals, pacifists, and hangers-on, the MOBE sponsored marches all over the country. In October, it sponsored "Stop the Draft Week," which culminated in the October 21 antiwar march on Washington. Beginning with speeches at the Lincoln Memorial, some thirty thousand marchers crossed the Potomac River to the Pentagon, to be met by federal troops with fully loaded weaponry—it was the first time that federal troops had been in the nation's capital since the Bonus Army Protest of 1928. There, the protestors sang hymns like "Silent Night," and laughed at Yippie leader Abbie Hoffman's spiritual attempt to levitate the building and exorcise it of its demons. The protests so memorably recounted in Norman Mailer's *Armies of the Night* (1968) led to one of the most enduring photos of the sixties—a young protestor delicately placing a flower into the muzzle of a soldier's rifle.

Rather than stop or slow the war in the face of these protests, Johnson attempted to shift public opinion in his direction. He approved Operation CHAOS, a CIA infiltration of the student movement, and used the information gained by agency informants to discredit the movement—most notably through stories planted in the press. He also approved U.S. participation in the peace talks beginning in May 1968 in Paris and agreed that the war should eventually be turned over entirely to the army of the ally—what Richard Nixon would eventually call "Vietnamization"—while at the same time continuing to increase American troop commitment. But Johnson's attempt to sway public opinion failed. Indeed, by 1968 more people were publicly against continued American participation in Vietnam than were for it. As 1968—a presidential election year—neared, the United States was still at war in Vietnam. The war would eventually end—but not in the sixties.

Recommended Reading

The best concise survey of the war, used with great profit in this chapter continues to be George C. Herring, *America's Longest War: The United States and Vietnam, 1950–1975*, 3d ed. (New York: McGraw Hill, 1996). On both the soldiers in the field, and the impact of the draft on both the war and the home front, Christian G. Appy, *Working Class War: American Combat Soldiers and Vietnam* (Chapel Hill: Univ. of North Carolina Press, 1993) is indispensible. In many ways, the most thoughtful and compelling book on the war is a work that combines journalism and a fictional voice—Michael Herr's classic *Dispatches* (New York: Avon, 1978). On the development of the presidential war-making power, the standard is still Arthur M. Schlesinger, *The Imperial Presidency* (Boston: Houghton Mifflin, 1973). The serious student of Vietnam and the rise of the presidential war-making power must also read the Pentagon Papers. The most useful edition is George C. Herring, ed., *The Pentagon Papers* (New York: McGraw Hill, 1993). They are available in their entirety as *The Pentagon Papers: The Defense Department History of United States Decision Making on Vietnam* (Boston: Beacon Press, 1971–72).

8

"What It Is Ain't Exactly Clear"

Sixties Culture, Straight and Counter

NO DECADE IN AMERICAN HISTORY is as defined by its culture as is the 1960s. Indeed, it comes with its own soundtrack—the overwhelming majority of documentaries, movies, and television shows that deal with the decade usually begin with one of the three musical anthems of the decade: The Byrds "Turn, Turn, Turn" (Columbia, 1965: "To everything, turn, turn, turn; there is a season"); Buffalo Springfield's "For What It's Worth" (Atco, 1967: "There's something happening here; what it is ain't exactly clear") or the Youngblood's "Get Together" (RCA, 1967: "Come on people now, smile on your brother, everybody get together, try to love one another right now").

Indeed, sixties culture is still being appropriated. And not only the ubiquitous nature of rock and roll music, with the inevitable remakes of sixties hits, but virtually every area of sixties culture is still visible—in a plethora of posters, buttons, and other collectible paraphernalia; in the many bizarre commercial uses of the peace sign; in the sale of sixties knock-off fashions to teenage hippie wannabes; in the revivals of Broadway plays from the sixties (*Hair* has never gone away, but neither has *The Sound of Music*).

The vast majority of survey texts on the sixties approach the culture of the decade by analyzing that part of the culture that ran against—counter to—the culture of established, or "straight" American culture. The number of chapters on the counterculture that are subtitled "Drugs, Sex, and Rock and Roll" are literally too many to count. This does an injury both to a study of the complexity of the counterculture and to the study of straight culture in the 1960s—the culture that surrounded the overwhelming majority of Americans. This chapter will attempt to redress what I have seen to be an imbalance in the cultural history of the period by looking at sixties culture—straight and counter.

What would become known as the counterculture movement of the 1960s was, indeed, a reaction against the cultural priorities of the postwar generation. As introduced in chapter 1, the children of the Great Depression and World War II wanted as much comfort and luxury as they could afford—and in the immediate postwar period, they could afford quite a bit. This gave rise to what economist John Kenneth Galbraith christened "the affluent society." The white, affluent youth of the 1960s often derisively referred to this culture of their parents as the "straight culture." Despite tales told earlier in this book of the young activists in the South and on college campuses, most young Americans ignored the protests of their brethren (they would later say, many with a smile, that "the sixties passed me by"). Indeed, the vast majority of baby boomers had grown to appreciate the advantages of being affluent. They neither "tuned in, turned on, nor dropped out"—they stayed in college, avoided the drug culture, and, following college, got white-collar jobs. These choices allowed them to enjoy the television, automobiles, suburban life, alcohol, and security that their parents had enjoyed. Parenthetically, as noted in the previous chapter, taking this path allowed them to use the various legal means at their disposal to avoid military service in Vietnam.

Of course, not all Americans were affluent, nor were all Americans white. For most Americans of color, their cultural imperatives would not, in the 1960s, include a life of even casual luxury. We have, at various places in this book, seen evidence of the hard life led by most African, Chicano, and Native Americans—urban and rural—that was in deep contrast to the life of most white baby boomers. The history of an era's popular culture is often a story of the lives of those who have leisure time and how they choose to spend that time. Many Americans of color looked at the "white kids" and repressed a smile—here were kids who had it all, who would never know the life of a sharecropper, life on a reservation, or in a barrio or ghetto, talking about how they "did not trust anyone over thirty," "leaving" their life of luxury to try their hand at being young social workers, or to live life in a commune—if it didn't work out, they could go home to the suburbs. And many did.

But many didn't. It is one of the most important phenomena of the decade of the sixties that many young Americans chose to reject completely the culture of their parents and instead chose a lifestyle that openly, honestly, and in many cases comically, rejected a life of upper-middle-class luxury.

They were few indeed—those who embraced a "hippie" lifestyle were always a tiny minority of the youth of the 1960s. However, it must be noted from the start that it was *much* more than the age—old issue of rebellious youth. Young people have always harbored resentment for the generation that preceded them. But rather than simply being at odds with their parents, and then reconciling to the middle-class lifestyle as they "grew up," hippies saw all straight culture to be harmful to their mental health. They could conceive of only one way of living—in a manner dramatically *opposite* to that of their parents. To do so, they would have to create their *own* culture, one that lived alongside straight culture but was not *of* that culture. It was something that had been attempted only a few times in previous American history—the Mormons and the Shakers come to mind. Hippies would, in a catch phrase of the era, "Do their own thing"—even if that "thing" exposed them to economic hardship, ridicule, and the draft.

This choice did not happen in a vacuum or spring to life as a result of the ecstasy experienced at a Grateful Dead concert in 1964. This younger generation had experienced Birmingham, Selma, Watts, and Vietnam; they had also experienced the rise of the New Left and its often successful criticism of the educational establishment. And in the face of this reality, their parents ran to the middle-class opiates of television sit-coms, swimming pools, and alcohol. This was the world that they were expected to join; for many young people, it was simply more than they could bear. As many of their contemporaries had broken with society over education and race, and as many more would break with it over the war, other youth simply refused to live any longer in a manner that represented any kind of straight culture. They would create, in a term popularized by history professor Theodore Roszak, a "counterculture."

That was the hippie phenomenon. Perhaps the most misunderstood aspect of the entire history of America in the 1960s—defined too often by their dress rather than by their beliefs—being a hippie *meant* living a life that was *counter* to the culture of straight America. Other cultural aspects of the sixties—drugs and sex—fed the hippie movement, but, as we shall see, they also fed straight culture. Other aspects of American culture in the sixties—popular music, movies, and fashion—merely reflected the counterculture, placing its own artistic spin on the movement. But the hippies were singular. They, truly, "dropped out." Indeed; the hippie movement *was* the true counterculture.

The word "hippie" is misleading, invented as it was by a journalist to mean kids who were both in vogue with the "hip" trends of the period and aware of the issues in the larger world around them. By this definition, there were many middle-class children of luxury who were "hip to the scene" of the 1960s. Many of these "hip, swinging guys and chicks" wore the accepted hippie uniform—long hair, beads, ripped jeans, tie-dyed shirts, and the ever-present peace sign. These kids understood, perhaps even empathized with their disillusioned brothers and sisters, but did not leave their colleges or homes to *join* them.

But hair and dress did not a hippie make. Hippiedom was a philosophy; a way of life. In his thoughtful 1967 essay entitled "What Is a Hippie?" Guy Strait, a leading publisher and gay rights activist of the period, put it succinctly: a hippie was one who rejected "everything that is commonly expected of the individual"—traditional fashion trends; the desire to make money and to own property; the need to keep up with the middle-class Joneses. Along the same lines, in his groundbreaking 1970 study of the evolution of the counterculture, *The Greening of America*, Charles B. Reich argued that the philosophy of the counterculture was actually the acceptance of a new stage of human consciousness: "Older people are inclined to think of work, injustice and war, and of the bitter frustrations of life, as the human condition. . . . But to those who have glimpsed the real possibilities of life . . . the prospect of a dreary corporate job, a ranch-house life, or a miserable death in war is utterly intolerable." Thus, the true hippie moved as far away from straight society as he or she could; in their communes, they consciously set out to create an alternative America.

The term "commune" has several different connotations. One, which uses the word as a noun, refers to a place where like-minded people live together, sharing their possessions and the fruits of their labor. The second use of the word is as a verb—the act of being in intimate contact with another, as in "communing with nature." Both uses of the word come into play when describing the hippie lifestyle. Eschewing what they thought to be the trappings of materialism, many young people moved out of their parents' homes, quit their jobs, or dropped out of college. They moved to, or established, one of the many clusters of shared living that were popping up all around the country. Some were established in the heart of large cities, with the communards squatting in abandoned buildings or jamming into low-rent apartments. These formed the foundation of counterculture communities that sprang up in Chicago's Old Town, Atlanta's Peach Street, the Haight-Ashbury district in San Francisco, and the Dupont Circle area of Washington, D.C. Other communes—part of the "back to the land" movement—were established far from the city limits, out in the woods, and far removed from even the most basic of modern conveniences. Among the more famous rural communes were Morning Star and the Hog Farm outside San Francisco, and Magic Forest Farm in Oregon.

No one knows how many people left straight lives to join the counterculture as hippies. One survey suggests that there were over two thousand rural and five thousand urban communes, with about two million Americans accepting the hippie lifestyle in the 1960s. There were most certainly more hippies than the straight press, who treated them as a fringe element, admitted. There were, however, most likely substantially fewer hippies than some contemporary accounts of the decades—which treat every nineteen-year-old in a tie-dyed shirt as a "hippie"—would have us believe. The number of hippies will probably never be known with any accuracy—there was never a census taken of the communes, and by virtue of their lifestyle choice, most hippies did not want to be found anyway. But it is clear that those who went did so with the expressed purpose of both creating and living a completely alternative—countercultural—lifestyle. In both rural and urban communes, daily life was simple—the bounty was shared among all members of the commune; dress was simple and freeing; the group was more important than any one member. Strait observed that for the hippie, this lifestyle represented the ultimate in freedom: "It is very likely that the hippie will go hungry and suffer exposure, and perhaps freak out. But he considers these far less dangerous than the kind of dehumanization society tried to wreak on him before the rebellions. He has escaped from a culture where the machine is God, and men judge each other by mechanical standards of efficiency and usefulness."

This lifestyle was culturally significant; it was also politically revolutionary. One of the most famous of the California communes, the Diggers, argued quite simply that "every brother should have what he needs to do his own thing." This was the pure socialism of Friedrich Engels (not the "communism" of Karl Marx)—it was a complete rejection of capitalism as a unifying social structure.[1] But in the 1960s the media paid no attention

1. Unlike most communes, the Diggers left behind a significant historical archive. See http://www.diggers.org.

to this philosophy (indeed, the media has never paid any attention to this philosophy). Rather, the media concentrated on hippies as freaks, paying attention to the length of their hair and their often comical or extremely well-worn clothes.

Two cultural indicators are traditionally seen as part of the counterculture. Straight culture largely felt that any youth who did drugs and/or argued for or practiced free love was a hippie. Hippies certainly did drugs and had sex. But this stereotype evaded the hypocrisy of the straight culture that the hippies had abandoned. Straights chastised hippies for dropping acid and having open, casual sex, while the straight drug of choice was copious amounts of alcohol and valium, and straight culture used the same birth control pill as the hippies—and probably as frequently. Straight observers winked at this irony; for many young Americans, it was the main reason they had dropped out of straight society—so that they might use drugs and have sex more openly and without the puritanical hypocrisy of their parents. Indeed, this is the key to understanding the role of sex and drugs in the counterculture—it was not *that* they had sex or did drugs that was important, but *why*.

"Make Love, Not War" . . . "Free Love" . . . "Love Is All You Need" . . . slogans and lyrics that adorned the buttons and T-shirts of the decade. Helen Gurley Brown, in her 1962 best-seller *Sex and the Single Girl,* exhorted women to make love whenever "her body wants to"— hardly a new message. The rise of the ideas of Sigmund Freud in the 1920s—most notably his contention that satisfying the sexual id led to better overall mental and physical health—had led to the rise of a youth rebellion that included, among other things, the flapper—a young woman who prided herself on her sexual freedom. The birth control pill, first appearing in 1960, gave an unprecedented number of women—and men—that freedom. Despite the strong puritanical strain in American culture that spoke against such inhibition, by the 1960s Americans—straight and hippie—were ready to "make love, not war."

For many Americans, the sexual revolution fit nicely with their newly acquired life of luxury. Many upwardly mobile professional men adopted a flamboyant lifestyle, living in garishly decorated "bachelor pads" (where the focal piece of furniture in the apartment was a gigantic bed) and focusing their leisure time on the excitement of the sexual conquest. They met—usually in the new "singles bars" that began to pop up in urban areas—young, miniskirted veterans of the sexual revolution, and as ready for a casual relationship as were their temporary suitors. Aided by the tremendous popularity in the 1960s of *Playboy* magazine, which openly argued for the virtues of this lifestyle (what it dubbed "The Playboy Philosophy"), the press gobbled up stories of such decadence and boldly proclaimed a "sexual revolution" in middle-class America.

The reality, however, was that middle-class straight culture had only changed around its youthful fringes. There were as few playboys and "swinging chicks" as there were hippies. Moreover, the "Playboy Philosophy" was integrally mixed with the upwardly mobile lifestyle of affluent America. You experimented with sex, and then settled down into the life for which you had been prepared—spouse, children, and career. The "sexual revolution," then, for these Americans, was a rite of passage, a part of "growing up," to be discarded when puritanical normality was necessary for career and life advancement.

For the hippies it was quite different. Free sex practiced openly, without shame, often publicly and communally, and with no thought of compromising that lifestyle for a career or a traditional, monogamous relationship, was an integral part of the hippie philosophy. Where straight youth had come to equate casual sex with personal freedom, the hippies also equated it with cultural emancipation. Sexual freedom was, for the hippie, a rejection of the straitlaced, puritanical lifestyle of their parents. In the words of author and journalist Paul Krassner, "the arousal of prurient interest is, in and of itself, a socially redeeming act." Sex, then, was a key part of the communal lifestyle—if one was to share everything in the spirit of the commune, then one should share partners as well. Indeed, in some communes, children were raised communally, without formal ties to any one set of "parents." Sex, then, offered as much a societal cleansing as it did an opportunity for individual hedonism.

The "drug culture" can be seen in much the same way as can the "sexual revolution" of the era. Like sex, drug use was hardly a discovery of the 1960s. Indeed, drugs made up a fundamental part of straight culture—as endemic in dorm rooms and board rooms as it was in the commune. However, the drugs of choice in straight society were alcohol and nicotine. Nicotine consumption hit its all-time high in 1963—a per capita consumption of 4,345—but then slowly decreased through the decade as the link between cancer and nicotine was both experimentally proven and made public. Alcohol consumption, however, rose; total American alcohol consumption in

1945 was at its highest point since 1910, and it continued to rise until 1975. The use of these two drugs, then, was so prevalent in the 1960s that the hippies actually found themselves rejecting *these* drugs as part of the lifestyle they had abandoned. As one hippie would write in an underground newspaper of the period: "Dope not Drugs. Alcohol is a drug, pot is dope. Nicotine is a drug, Acid is Dope."

For the hippie, drugs were as consciousness-raising as was free sex. Drug use was seen to expand creative horizons, free the mind, and literally break the bond with straight society. The desired result was not just to get high, but to feel special. Thus, getting drunk or getting stoned on marijuana, which college students—and many of their parents—had been using forever (indeed, one survey suggested that by the end of the decade, 50 percent of the public had tried marijuana, and 60 percent of all college students had tried pot), was not enough. Hippies prided themselves on consciously moving away from the drugs of middle-class choice. They first embraced hashish, a more powerful form of marijuana. Then they embraced lysergic acid diethylamide. Better known as LSD, the drug was a hallucinogen that had been accidentally discovered by a Swiss chemist, tested by the CIA, and publicly touted by former Harvard psychologist Timothy Leary as the spiritual anecdote for a generation. In his 1964 book, Leary described what he believed to be *The Psychedelic Experience:*

> A psychedelic experience is a journey to new realms of consciousness. The scope and content of the experience is limitless, but its characteristic features are the transcendence of verbal concepts, of space-time dimensions, and of the ego or identity. Such experiences of enlarged consciousness can occur in a variety of ways: sensory deprivation, yoga exercises, disciplined meditation, religious or aesthetic ecstasies, or spontaneously. Most recently they have become available to anyone through the ingestion of psychedelic drugs. . . . Of course, the drug does not produce the transcendent experience. It merely acts as a chemical key—it opens the mind.

Many people reported having such a mind-opening "trip," which seemed to yank open their senses. But others reported "bad trips" that led to disorientation, violent physical illness, and a recurrence of the hallucinogenic effect several days after the dosage had been administered—better known as an LSD "flashback."

Granted, more people used LSD than just the communards. Indeed, by the end of the decade it had become the drug of choice for many of the intelligentsia and for many artists. Here was an interesting hypocrisy: many musicians, painters, and writers were dropping acid in order to free their artistic consciousness, so that they might write a book or a rock anthem that might make them rich and famous—a different road to the same materialistic nirvana sought by their parents. But this widespread use of drugs in the 1960s should not blind the historian to the role that drugs played in the *true* counterculture. When joined with a communal lifestyle and free sex, hippies considered drug use to be an important step toward breaking with straight society and achieving the uniqueness of the counterculture itself.

It should also not blind us to its consequences. By the 1970s, for example, the Haight-Ashbury district of San Francisco had evolved from a haven for hippies into a series of storefront drug-shooting galleries. It would be decades before the neighborhood was clean again. It also goes without saying that countless young people suffered serious medical consequences from extended drug use. And one must ask—for what? *Were* minds expanded, universes conquered, and seeds of consciousness successfully sown? Was Timothy Leary right? One can only smile when reading the words of writer Arthur Koestler, who after trying LSD for the first time, told Leary: "This is wonderful, no doubt, but it is fake. . . . I solved the secret of the universe last night, but this morning I forgot what it was."

The straight culture that the hippies rejected also underwent a dramatic change. As with all eras, popular culture in the 1960s kept much from the era that preceded it. But by decade's end, American popular culture showed several dramatic breaks from the past, as the way that most Americans lived had been profoundly affected by the political, social, and economic tremors of the times. Virtually all areas of popular culture were touched by the civil rights movement, the youth and antiwar movements, and the counterculture. Indeed, by the end of the decade, it was clear that the values of the various movements affected what Americans wore and listened to on the radio and watched at the movie theater and on television, in ways that would have been unthinkable to straight society only a few years before. It was never universal, of course—a sizable portion of straight society resisted the changes in the culture around them and would continue to do so well into the 1980s, when a vocal rejection of what they saw to be the corrupt values of the 1960s would become a key component of the conservative revolution, spearheaded by Ronald Reagan. But many members of straight society who did not drop out and join a commune, travel to Mississippi to teach in a Freedom School, or protest at a college campus, nevertheless wore peace signs on chains draped around their neckties and bought every Beatle record immediately upon its release. They were vicariously enjoying the pop culture reflection of the movements of the sixties. To them, and to the millions of others up to the present day who would remember nostalgically the popular culture of the decade, that, in all its manifestations, *was* for them "the sixties."

The study of the fashion of 1960s illustrates these cultural vagaries. Originally, the established popular fashion styles of the decade were inherited from 1950s trends—men in crew cuts, little or no facial hair, deep-colored suits, multicolored casual shirts; women in bouffant hairstyles and knee-length dresses. The Kennedy style glamorized, though it did not significantly alter, these styles—men adopted JFK's narrow-lapel jackets, refused to wear hats, and wore light pastel dress shirts, as well as his midlength haircut; women adopted Jackie's pillbox hats, empire-style evening wear, and European-style bouffant hair.

Not surprisingly, as was the case in the 1950s, fashion trends changed the most, and the most rapidly, for young Americans. By mid-decade, young women's hemlines were skyrocketing above the knee, as "miniskirts," then "micro-miniskirts," and the inevitable "hot pants," came in vogue. By decade's end, pantsuits were worn by many younger women, by some as a part of their breaking from all things feminine; by other in an attempt to emulate male corporate uniforming. Both younger men and younger women wore their hair much longer—to escape the bouffant, women adopted straightening techniques that often took their hair below the waistline. Young men initially gravitated to the Beatles' haircut—a modified "mop-top"—then many simply let their hair grow . . . and grow . . . and grow. Young men and women accessorized their "look" more than in previous decades, with both sexes wearing beads, necklaces, and charms. Both young men and women also adopted the quintessential article of youth protest clothing from the 1950s—blue jeans, which began as part of the uniform for disaffected youth, were worn by young activists in the 1960s to show their solidarity with the workers and the oppressed. It is not accidental that many civil rights workers wore jeans even in the oppressive summer heat.

Many of the fashion trends for young American's in the 1960s began as backhanded protests against the "uptight" conservative dress of their parents; parents returned the favor by citing long hair and the ubiquitous blue jeans as signs of the oncoming apocalypse. But by the decade's end, while straight culture had largely kept its conservative uniforming, particularly in the work force, more and more middle-aged Americans were wearing their hair long, sporting moustaches, experimenting with shorter skirts, or wearing jeans. Moreover, what became known as the "hippie look"—tie-dyed shirts, sandals, torn jeans, love beads—was worn by middle- to upper-class college youth who were many things, but hardly "hippies." Thus, by decade's end, straight society had accepted fashion that had begun in the 1960s as a countercultural protest as part of their popular culture.

Television also mirrored aspects of both popular and countercultural currents, finding by decades end that those currents had blended together. There was no question about either the importance of television, or about its omnipresence—96 percent of American families had at least one television in the home by 1970. Television had begun to challenge the daily newspaper as America's news source of choice. For most of the decade, from 6:30 to 7:00 P.M., an overwhelming majority of viewers watched NBC's *Huntley-Brinkley Report* (with news anchors Chet Huntley and David Brinkley); by 1968, that trend had shifted, and *The CBS Evening News with Walter Cronkite* was the new ratings winner—a position it would keep in American life for over a decade. Indeed, as noted previously, Americans watched the civil rights and youth movements, as well as the Vietnam War, unfold—often in grisly detail—in their living rooms at suppertime.

The entertainment aspect of television remained largely the same for the first part of the decade. As was the case in the 1950s, westerns (*Gunsmoke, The Virginian, Wagon Train, Have Gun Will Travel,* and *Bonanza*) and variety shows (*The Red Skelton Show, Sing Along with Mitch, The Jack Benny Program, The Jackie Gleason Show,* and the undisputed king of variety, Sunday night's *Ed Sullivan Show*) ruled the airwaves. Initially, situation comedies ("sitcoms") kept the 1950s formula intact, featuring the zany antics of a middle-class white (read, "perfect") family. Of this genre, *The Dick Van Dyke Show* ran at the top of the ratings from 1962 to 1966. Other family-oriented sitcoms, notably *The Danny Thomas Show, Lassie, The Patty Duke Show,* and *Bewitched* (if having a witch for a wife can be considered middle-class perfection), were of a piece.

However, television did indeed react to the turbulence of the decade. Even before activism was the norm, Hollywood had changed the sitcom— they kept the perfect family but invented a new, more perfect place for that family to live, quietly insulated from the rest of the world. At the height of the tumult in American cities, an idealized small-town-America was enshrined in sixties television comedy. Leading the way were the gentle folks from Mayberry, North Carolina, who made up the players in the most popular television show of the decade, *The Andy Griffith Show* (running in the top ten of the ratings from 1960 until the show ended its run at number one, in 1968) and its successful spinoffs, *Mayberry, RFD* and *The Gomer Pyle Show*. A twist on this theme was the wildly popular *Beverly Hillbillies,* which satirized the straight society of the 1960s by having a clan of moun- tain folk invade the moneyed sanctuary of Beverly Hills. The *Hillbillies* also spouted successful spinoffs—*Petticoat Junction,* extolling the virtues of a hamlet so small it was identified by its nearby train stop, and *Green Acres,* the inverse plot of *Hillbillies,* which satirized straight society by showing how inept a Park Avenue society couple could be when asked to master the art of truck farming.

Other television shows, just as successful as the small-town sitcoms, showed a much more realistic view of American society. As the social tumult grew in volume, television regained a social conscience that, it can be argued, had not existed since the exposés of Edward R. Murrow in the 1950s. It started gently enough, with a tweaking of the American sitcom family. First, the single-father family appeared (*My Three Sons,* then *Family Affair*), then a show that broke both social and racial barriers, *Julia,* premiered in 1968 with African American Diahann Carroll in the title role of a single, professional (nurse) mother. Though never as highly rated as *Julia,* the drama *I Spy,* which preceded *Julia* to the airwaves by two years, featured an interracial spy team and gained a 1967 Best Actor Emmy for its African American half, comedian Bill Cosby. These shows offered a challenge to social norms; they were also commercial hits, garnering millions in advertising dollars and turning their stars into bona fide celebrities in the straight culture. Thus, much like blue jeans, they can be seen first as kicks in the shins of the established straight culture, and then becoming a part of that establishment.

The Smothers Brothers Comedy Hour, easily the most culturally and polit- ically significant—and controversial—television show of the decade—was in a class by itself. Coming out of the coffeehouse circuit, brothers Tom (on guitar) and Dick (on standup bass) combined folk music with a standup comedy routine that gleefully made fun of the norms of straight society. A hit with younger audiences, in February 1967 the brothers' variety show premiered on CBS. It was originally a rather tame affair, featuring the new comedy styling of Steve Martin and Pat Paulsen and the debut musical performances of Mason Williams and Jennifer Warnes, as well as performances by the Doors; Jefferson Airplane; Peter, Paul and Mary; and Steppenwolf. But the show quickly developed an activist edge, with sketches that lampooned the drug culture, criticized (by name) Lyndon Johnson, and openly called for an end to the war in Vietnam. When folk singer Joan Baez appeared as a guest, she interrupted her musical interlude to call for an end to the draft; her music was aired in the final credits of the show, but her political plea was edited out. The Smothers Brothers were in a constant battle with the network censors to keep their sketch scripts unedited and their guest list unchallenged.

The high-water mark of this fight, indeed, the high-water mark of countercultural television in the 1960s, came on February 25, 1968, when Pete Seeger, despite the virulent protests of the censors, appeared to sing his antiwar anthem "Waist Deep in the Big Muddy." *The Smothers Brothers Comedy Hour* was canceled by CBS on April 4, 1969, despite having won an Emmy that year as Best Variety Show. Despite its critical success, the show was never accepted by the majority of Americans. But it remains an icon of political satire, as well as a case study in the history of American censorship of the mass media. It also influenced a host of other politically themed variety shows, most notably *Rowan and Martin's Laugh-In,* a much tamer version of the *Smothers Brothers,* which featured political satire and sexual innuendoes buried in old-fashioned slapstick.

Motion pictures moved a bit more slowly than television in reflecting the social consciousness of the times. The first half of the decade at the movies was dominated by three genres. First was the spy movie, a direct reflection of the ever-present cold war. Based on the pulp-fiction thriller series by British author and journalist Ian Fleming, the James Bond series was one of the most successful movie franchises of the 1960s (*Dr. No,* 1962; *From Russia With Love,* 1963; *Goldfinger,* 1964), turning its star, Scottish actor Sean Connery, into a worldwide superstar. But the best of this genre was the eerily prescient *Manchurian Candidate* (1962), based on a novel by Richard Condon in which a Korean War prisoner of war is brainwashed, becoming an assassin whenever he sees a Queen of Diamonds while playing solitaire. The botched assassination attempt at the end of the movie made it a industry pariah in the months following the successful assassination of John F. Kennedy; Hollywood lore has it that the film's star, Frank Sinatra, had the movie pulled from wide distribution after November 22, 1963, out of respect for Kennedy. The second genre was the historical epic—a direct holdover from the megaproductions of Cecil B. DeMille in the 1950s (e.g., *The Ten Commandments,* 1956). Epics were incredibly expensive to produce and promote, and as such carried enormous risks. Indeed, *Cleopatra* (1963), starring Elizabeth Taylor and Richard Burton, was a critical and commercial failure—one of the most famous flops in motion picture history. However, two British epics were among the most successful pictures of the decade—*Lawrence of Arabia* (1962) and *Dr. Zhivago* (1965) have been consistently rated among the greatest movies of all time, with *Lawrence of Arabia* winning the Academy Award for Best Picture of 1962. But it was the musical that continued its rule at the box office throughout much of the decade. Indeed, of the ten movies that won the Oscar for Best Picture in the 1960s, four of them were among the greatest musicals in Hollywood history—*West Side Story* (1961); *My Fair Lady* (1964); *The Sound of Music* (1965); and *Oliver!* (1968).

Most motion picture historians explain the direction taken by Hollywood in the early 1960s quite simply—a cold war, then Vietnam-obsessed America craved escapism at the drive-in. That is true enough, but it should not be interpreted to suggest that there were *no* films of social consciousness produced in the early sixties. There was one. Gregory Peck's breathtaking portrayal of southern crusading lawyer Atticus Finch in the screen adaptation of Harper Lee's novel *To Kill a Mockingbird* (1962) stands as one of the greatest screen performances in history. Moreover, the film dramatized the brutality of southern racism in a manner that galvanized audiences, particularly in the North. Indeed, the death of black sharecropper Tom Robinson (not seen on screen) brought lynching into the movie theater just as Americans were following the news of Martin Luther King's attempt to integrate the city of Birmingham. However, as a film of social conscience, *Mockingbird* stood alone . . .

. . . until 1967. In that year, the commanding presence of Sidney Poitier, the big screen's first bona fide African American leading man, exploded onto the screen with two films destined to integrate the cinema and challenge audiences as never before. *In the Heat of the Night* pitted Poitier's Virgil

Tibbs, a cop from Philadelphia, against portly Rod Steiger's Bill Gillespie, a small-town Mississippi sheriff. As the two men struggled to solve a brutal murder, they broke through the barriers of their own racism, exposing the prejudices of both the North and the South in gritty realism (for his performance, Steiger would win the Academy Award for Best Actor). Even more challenging was *Guess Who's Coming to Dinner,* a parable about interracial marriage that set the dapper Poitier, now playing a successful physician, up against screen legends Spencer Tracy and Katharine Hepburn, playing the parents of the girl engaged to Poitier. As in *Heat of the Night,* all concerned confronted their own racial demons (including a smattering of anti-Catholicism). While Hepburn won a Best Actress Oscar for her performance, Poitier turned what was written as a supporting role into an acting tour de force. It was his quiet self-assurance (from *Heat of the Night:* "They call me *Mister* Tibbs") that turned his performances into statements of African American strength—if you will, as noted earlier in this book, artistic statements of Black Power.

Motion pictures saw other influential changes in 1967. Thanks largely to the decline of the rigor of the studio system, new young producers and directors broke with the conventional; sex and violence were beginning to take center stage at the movie theater. The brutal relationship of *Bonnie and Clyde,* as told by producer and star Warren Beatty and director Walter Penn, offered some of the most graphic violence seen to that point on the screen. (An ad for the movie: "They're young. They're in love. They rob banks.") To a public anesthetized by a nightly dose of television bloodshed from Vietnam, the grizzly death-by-ambush of Bonnie Parker and Clyde Barrow—or the brutal treatment of chain gang prisoner Paul Newman in that same year's *Cool Hand Luke*—was small potatoes. The public was also becoming accustomed to sex (more accurately, hints of a sex act, or small amounts of nudity) on the screen. The seduction of a young man by his girlfriend's mother was the key to Mike Nichols's 1967 masterpiece, *The Graduate.* These films would be followed by countless others—1969 was particularly brutal (Peter Fonda's *Easy Rider* and Sam Peckinpah's *Wild Bunch*) and sexy (*Bob and Carol and Ted and Alice* would seem to be self-explanatory). In response to a conservative cry for a restoration of decency, in November 1968 the Motion Picture Association of America unveiled a rating system for motion pictures. Audiences of all ages could be admitted to a G–rated movie; a youngster could see an M-rated movie with parental consent; an R-rated movie could be seen only by patrons over the age of sixteen, and only those over the age of seventeen could enjoy an X-rated film. It is telling that the 1969 Academy Award for Best Picture—*Midnight Cowboy,* the story of a male prostitute and his companion in New York City—bore an X rating.

Of all the pieces of sixties culture, the piece that elicits the most nostalgia is the music. "Sixties music" (known respectfully to today's baby boomers as "oldies") labeled the decade as did no other cultural force. A mix of the political and the danceable, the slick and the rough, the English and the American, popular music (*not* just, as we will see, "rock and roll") did, indeed, define the youth of the sixties as much as did their activism.

The rock and roll rebellion of the 1950s had died by 1960. In 1958, Elvis Presley was drafted, and after he returned from his service, his music had lost its early edge. By the turn of the decade two other raucous careers had been destroyed—Jerry Lee Lewis's by the negative publicity that swirled around him after he married his thirteen-year-old cousin, and Chuck Berry's, as a result of his arrest for transporting a female across state lines for the purpose of prostitution. Their reputations sullied, the rockers were quickly replaced by the teen idols; squeaky-clean white pop artists such as Fabian ("Turn Me Loose," Chancellor Records, 1959), Paul Anka ("Diana," RCA, 1957), and Bobby Vee ("Take Good Care of My Baby," Liberty, 1961) dominated the airwaves at the dawn of the new decade.

Into this artistic vacuum would emerge a revival of folk music—a music of political and social protest that had its roots in the 1930s music of artists like Woody Guthrie, Pete Seeger, and the Weavers. The new folk music troubadours wrote of spirituality and protest, with lyrics that were eminently topical to the day's events. As a result the genre found an audience far beyond the coffeehouses of Greenwich Village. The artistic father of the new folk movement was Bob Dylan, whose synthetic and haunting lyrics were also searing social criticisms. Born in Duluth, Minnesota, Dylan's early dalliance with pop-rock (he provided the hand claps on several Bobby Vee records) would soon disappear, as he crafted songs that yanked American popular music out of the 1950s. A disciple of Woody Guthrie, Dylan wrote and sang with a conscience, rather than with, and about, teenage angst. His "Blowin' in the Wind" (Columbia, 1963) became part of the soundtrack of the civil rights and antiwar movements ("How many deaths will it take 'til he knows that too many people have died? The answer, my friend, is blowin' in the wind . . .") Dylan also earned the respect of the entire music community by walking out of a May 1963 gig at the *Ed Sullivan Show* rather than submit to a censorship of his performance (the CBS television wanted Dylan not to play his "Talkin' John Birch Paranoid Blues," out of fear that the ultraconservative John Birch Society would sue the network). His gravelly voice and asymmetrical harmonica playing endeared him to folk purists. But ever the progressive, his 1965 performance at the Newport Folk Fest drew boos from the crowd because he had committed what for folkies was the cardinal sin—he performed his first set using electrified instruments. He bounced back with his searing "Like a Rolling Stone" (Columbia, 1965), which encapsulated the angst of the youth of the sixties as did no other song of the decade ("How does it feel, to be without a home, like a complete unknown, like a rolling stone?"). "Rolling Stone"—named by more than one poll as the number-one song of the sixties—clearly demonstrated that Dylan was at his best when writing songs of conscience and protest—what he called "finger-pointing songs"—that became identified with the social movements of the sixties.

Dylan was introduced to a wider audience when Peter, Paul, and Mary, a Greenwich Village trio, took his "Blowin' in the Wind" to the number-two position on the pop charts in 1963 (Warner Bros. Records). Joan Baez was as well known to folk music by the 1960s, with two gold albums to her credit. But she would be enshrined into the pantheon of the decade with her haunting performance of the Negro spiritual "We Shall Overcome" at the August 1963 March on Washington—an event that also featured musical performances by Peter, Paul, and Mary and Bob Dylan.

Folk music, then, provided the background music for the protest movements of the early 1960s. But most American teenagers did not "groove" to folk music. Their music of choice—played on small record players with heavy metal needles (styli) that eventually mangled the soft vinyl 45 RPM records they bought for less than a dollar apiece—was a new form of pop-rock. The sound was typified by a group that would become the most commercially successful American recording group in music history. A California family band originally named the Pendletones and then rechristened by their record label, the Beach Boys' sound featured a driving beat, tight four-part harmony, and simple lyrics about cars, girls, and an idealized surfing life that existed only in composer Brian Wilson's imagination. Their 1963 anthem "Surfin' USA" (Capitol) was a decided break with the bland, Vegas-style croonings of the teen idols. Their "Surfer Girl" (Capitol), released later that year, hinted at the sophisticated style into which pop would soon evolve—it also peaked at number seven on the Billboard charts.

In their early career, the Beatles gave even fewer clues as to the influential musicians they would soon become. Recording lightweight pop songs that were highly influenced by both British skiffle and American rockabilly—1963's "Love Me Do," "P.S. I Love You", and the comic "She Loves You" ("Yeah, Yeah, Yeah"; all for Parlophone records) were all million sellers. The British quartet's first two albums were wildly successful both in their own nation and, once introduced overseas in 1964, in America. But the teenage hysteria that followed—"Beatlemania"—was as much about the personalities of the band members (John Lennon, Paul McCartney, George Harrison, and Ringo Starr), which had been carefully molded by their manager, Brian Epstein, as it was about the music. Indeed, Harrison famously quipped that he could play any song on his guitar that he wanted in concert, as the screaming of the prepubescent girls drowned out the music anyway. Nevertheless, the popular success—and sales—of the Beatles eclipsed any other American popular music act (with one exception—Frank Sinatra). Before 1969, they would have twenty number-one songs on the charts, and three others would peak at number two.

But in 1964, no one seriously argued that either the Beach Boys or the Beatles offered anything with their music other than the pleasant diversion that late 1950s rock and roll offered. There were changes around the edges—the production quality of both groups offered a break from the tinny-sounding records of the past (thanks to the engineering and production abilities of Brian Wilson and the Beatles' producer, George Martin); and both groups offered songs that were perfect for the growing medium of AM radio—particularly the Beatles, as Lennon and McCartney were the undisputed masters of writing and scoring a 2:15 song. Aside from that, their music was hardly innovative. In fact, it can be argued that none of their early music was rock and roll at all, if one means music that is gritty, socially relevant, sexually driving, and, in the words of one critic, "music that your parents can't stand to listen to." Indeed, *folk* music was more "rock and roll" than any of the early Beach Boys or Beatles offerings.

Three albums would change all that, and in so doing revolutionize popular music. In late 1965, the Beatles released *Rubber Soul* (Parlophone, Capitol, EMI). While the cut "Michelle" was a sure teenage hand-holding hit, other songs on the album represented a serious break with the pop of the past. "Nowhere Man" ("Doesn't have a point of view; knows not where he's going to. Isn't he a bit like you and me?") and "The Word" ("The Word is Love") were overtly political, but also contained a driving rock beat that tended to mask the challenging nature of Lennon's lyrics. Brian Wilson remembered being tremendously affected by *Rubber Soul,* which was a commercial and critical smash. He set out to create a concept album that matched the Beatles' pioneering style. That album was *Pet Sounds,* released in May 1966 (Capitol). The level of Wilson's studio artistry—he used session musicians, double-tracking, and other techniques—was astounding. "God Only Knows" literally remade the ideal of the popular love song (using, for example, harpsichord and French horn as melodic instruments in the song); it stands as one of the most complex—and beautiful—songs in the annals of American popular music. But the playfully weird "Sloop John B" and the psychedelic "Pet Sounds" broke new ground, taking rock music away from its casual lyrics and its melodic structures into what was then completely unchartered territory. The Beach Boys were never overtly political in their music. But the next album by the Beatles, *Revolver* (Parlophone, Capitol, EMI), combined the studio artistry of George Martin with the ever-more-strident political lyrics of John Lennon, to produce what most contemporary critical polls have christened the number-one album in the history of rock and roll. Released in August 1966, *Revolver* was so complex, delicate, and sophisticated an album that the group never performed any of its tracks live. From the haunting "Eleanor Rigby" ("Ah, look at all the lonely people") to the snotty "Taxman" ("Should 5 percent appear too small; be thankful I don't take it all. 'Cause I'm the Taxman."), Lennon cast himself as the champion of the common man against the powerful—a theme that would resound through the protest rock of the rest of the decade. Two other songs represented the cutting edge of studio magic—the haunting strains of "I'm Only Sleeping" were created by reversing the tape of George Harrison's guitar solo and mixing the altered tape into the song; and the asymmetrical buzzing sitars of "Tomorrow Never Knows" was an LSD-induced studio tour-de-force, as audio tapes were run through tape machines backwards to produce a sound previously unheard on vinyl.

It is tempting to spend pages listing all the bright, controversial, innovative, and (yes) danceable music that was created in the second half of the 1960s—universally seen to be the "golden age" of rock and roll—as everyone has a favorite. But it is accurate to say that *all* the trends of post-1965 rock and roll were spawns of either the folk movement or these three albums.

The Beach Boys' own "Good Vibrations" (Capitol, 1966), Jimi Hendrix's, "Purple Haze" (Track, 1967), Iron Butterfly's "In a Gadda Da Vida" (Atco, 1968), and Jefferson Airplane's "White Rabbit" (RCA, 1967) are but a few examples of psychedelic or acid rock and are a direct linear descendants of "Pet Sounds" and "Tomorrow Never Knows." Protest rock, particularly the music against the war in Vietnam, was started by "Blowin' in the Wind" and "The Word" and was later seen in the work of Barry McGuire, "Eve of Destruction" (Dunhill, 1965), Country Joe and the Fish, "I Feel like I'm Fixin' to Die Rag" (Vanguard, 1967), and Creedence Clearwater Revival, "Fortunate Son" (Fantasy, 1969). And folk-rock, as best typified by the music of the Byrds, was an electric synthesis of the folk tradition backed by the Beatles' beat (indeed, the group's "Mr. Tambourine Man," Columbia, 1965, was written by Bob Dylan).

One genre, however, stands on its own—a genre defined by the name of its label. Motown, a record label founded in Detroit in late 1959 by ex-boxer Berry Gordy, would, at first glance, not be seen to be particularly innovative. Like the early music of the Beatles and the Beach Boys, early releases from the label, while catchy and danceable, offered little more than the time-tested lyrical messages of early teen pop—the travails of young love, set to a soulful groove. The list is endless: Smokey Robinson and the Miracles' "Shop Around" (1960); the Marvelettes' "Please Mr. Postman" (1961); Mary Wells's "My Guy" (1964); and the Temptations' "My Girl" (1964)— all, at face value, straight from the malt shop. But Motown was unique in many ways, not the least of which was that it was the second multimillion-dollar business owned completely by African Americans.[2] The success of the music, then, was mixed with the success of the business itself and with the pride black America took in Gordy's personal business achievement.

As the Motown acts toured to support their releases, the "Motown Revue" did shows in the segregated South. As the acts faced a racism that they had not fully experienced in the North, it sharpened their artistic edge. Several historians have given the revue credit for helping to end desegregation in the South. By the end of the decade, Motown was releasing songs that, while still featuring the signature Motown beat (driven by the label's in-house band, the Funk Brothers) and stellar production values, also spoke about life

---

2. The first were the media holdings (*Jet, Ebony*) of the Johnson Publishing Company.

in poor black America in a way that Americans had not heard before. Best known in this genre were the Supremes' "Love Child" (1968; "Love child, never meant to be; Love child, born in poverty"); and the Temptations' "Papa Was a Rolling Stone" (1969; "And when he died, all he left us was alone") and "Cloud Nine" ("Depressed and downhearted, I took to Cloud Nine"). The label also released several antiwar songs; the most successful—and icon-ic—was Edwin Starr's pulsating 1969 anthem, "War" ("What is it good for? Absolutely nothin'"). As Motown crossed over to white teens with its music and its message, it can truly be said that it was a part of the civil rights move-ment and the integration of American musical art.

Popular music also gave Americans two of the most enduring symbols of the decade. One was billed as a concert of community and caring; the other was undeniably a concert of bloodshed and murder. Readers can take their pick as to which one best symbolizes the decade. Perhaps there is room for both opinions.

In 1967, promoters Michael Lang and Artie Kornfeld developed the idea for a superconcert that would headline all the major rock groups of the moment as well as highlight the artistic endeavors of the countercul-ture. The art never happened. But the Woodstock Music and Art Fair, held outdoors in Bethel, New York, on August 15–17, 1969, was nevertheless one of the most iconic moments of the decade. An audience that had been projected by Lang and Kornfeld to be no more than fifty thousand turned into a swarm of some five hundred thousand people (when asked if he knew how many people were in the audience the night he played, David Crosby of Crosby, Stills, and Nash quipped that the only way to count a crowd that big was "one, two, three . . . many"). They were treated to a concert that featured torrential downpours, awful sanitary conditions, crowds beyond anything ever seen in any musical venue, and terrible music that had been diluted by drugs, poor sound equipment, and the weather.[3]

---

3. Okay . . . of all the performances, the only one that broke new ground was that of Sweetwater, the second act and first band to perform on Friday, August 15. Featuring an inte-grated lineup, Sweetwater offered the piercing vocals of Nancy Nevins and instrumentation that featured flutes, conga, and cello. Their "Motherless Child," arranged as a folk-rock piece (and with a studio recording that opened with Gregorian Chant) was haunting in Bethel, and remains a haunting recording today.

Despite the shrewd production and marketing of the Woodstock motion picture and movie soundtrack (indeed, the soundtrack featured studio cuts that were not played at the concert), the music was never the thing. Woodstock became equated in the popular mind with the counterculture. Those who attended remember sharing their food, drugs, and shelter with total strangers. They would long tell stories of fairgoers helping strangers come down from bad trips, and of the baby who was born on site. They speak of themselves, even today, as members of a temporary "Woodstock Nation," experiencing together, as the famous slogan went, "three days of peace and music."

Of course, it is nonsense to claim that Woodstock represented the counterculture. While a very few stayed near Bethel to make their lives, almost all of the fairgoers went home after the concert—as young people go home after *every* concert. After all, the concert was to make money; indeed, it was the first of thousands of outdoor and stadium rock concerts to come—decidedly *un*counterculture. But in the minds of many fairgoers, Woodstock represented what the counterculture *could* be, if only given a chance by straight society. For many, it became a lost moment of hope as the decade careened to an end.

There was never such a feeling of hope about Altamont. Trying to catch lightning in a bottle for a second time, British rockers The Rolling Stones announced that the last concert of their 1969 American tour would, like Woodstock, be a free one. It would be held at the Altamont Raceway, fifteen miles east of Berkeley, California, on Saturday, December 6, 1969. From the start, it was the anti-Woodstock. The stench of the burning tires from the raceway led one musician to observe that it must be what hell smelled like. To add to the satanic milieu, the Stones' management hired the Hells Angels motorcycle group to provide security for a crowd that was ultimately estimated at three hundred thousand.

The music was no better than at Woodstock, but, even more than Woodstock, the music would ultimately be forgotten. Playing that evening as the concert headliner, the Stones had broken into their signature "Jumpin' Jack Flash" when the Angels stormed the stage, brandishing weapons, pushing members of the audience, and in general flexing their muscles. Lead singer Mick Jagger begged for calm, but it was not to be. Right in front of the stage, Meredith Hunter, an eighteen-year-old black man, was stabbed, beaten with pool cues, and kicked by the Angels until he was dead. No message of peace and love came from Altamont. The concert was seen by many observers to offer a violent end to a violent decade. As one music critic stated: "I won't go to any more of these things."

Recommended Reading

Theodore Roszak, *The Making of a Counterculture: Reflections on the Technocratic Society and Its Youthful Opposition* (New York: Faber and Faber 1968) continues to carry weight in the field; a more recent treatment is Peter Braunstein and Michael William Doyle, eds., *Imagine Nation: The American Counterculture of the 1960s and 1970s* (New York: Routledge, 2001). On the philosophy of the hippies, see the groundbreaking Charles A. Reich, *The Greening of America* (New York: Crown Trade Paperbacks, 1970). Rachel Carson, *Silent Spring* (Boston: Houghton Mifflin, 1962) and Benjamin Kline, *First Along the River: A Brief History of the U.S. Environmental Movement* (New York: Rowman and Littlefield, 2007) should be taken hand in hand when studying the issue. Ed Ward, Geoffrey Stokes, and Ken Tucker, *Rock of Ages: The Rolling Stone History of Rock and Roll* (New York: Rolling Stone Press, 1986) is the best single-volume history of its subject; it is detailed, analytical, and a lot of fun to read. Joel Makower's *Woodstock: The Oral History* (New York: Excelsior, 1989) is both entertaining and useful. Although a textbook, Phyllis G. Tortora and Keith Eubank, *Survey of Historic Costume: A History of Western Dress,* 3d ed. (New York: Fairchild Publishers, 1998) is particularly useful in setting fashion trends in their historical context. There are many good histories of American television, but none better than Eric Barnouw, *Tube of Plenty: The Evolution of American Television,* rev. ed. (New York: Oxford Univ. Press, 1982).

The Limits of Power

To Reform the Sixties

ON JANUARY 23, 1968, the crews from a North Korean submarine chaser and three patrol boats boarded the USS Pueblo off the Korean coast. In the struggle that followed, four of the seventy-five crew members were wounded, one fatally. The North Koreans took the crew hostage, imprisoned them, and took the ship to the nearby port of Wonsan. They charged that the Pueblo was a spy ship that had been conducting intelligence activity inside the twelve-mile international boundary. Bent on humiliation as well as revenge, the North Koreans filmed the ship's commander, Lloyd Bucher, while he was giving a forced confession of his activities as a "spy." After negotiations that lasted for over a year, the Koreans finally set the crew free, claiming a gigantic victory over Western imperialism.

When cornered by a press that had long since stopped taking his pronouncements at face value, Lyndon Johnson admitted only that the *Pueblo* might have "inadvertently drifted" within the twelve-mile limit. In reality, the *Pueblo* was indeed a top-of-the-line spy ship. The Koreans knew all about its activities and were content to let it spy as long as it stayed twelve miles out to sea. It didn't, and the crew paid the price.

The plight of the *Pueblo* gave many Americans their first taste of what *Time* magazine called the "impotence of power." When news of the capture reached American eyes and ears, the reaction was one of amazement. The photograph of Bucher confessing to his North Korean captors was galling,

Selections from John Robert Greene, *The Limits of Power: The Nixon and Ford Administrations,* 1–26. © 1992 are reprinted with the permission of Indiana Univ. Press.

particularly because, as journalist John Hersey later observed, "this was surrender to Mickey Mouse." The United States Navy had to swallow the fact that in order to free the crew it had to release an official apology to North Korea for spying. The cold war mentality of the early 1960s, marked as it was by American arrogance, had received quite a jolt. If the United States could not control the North Koreans, how could it hope to win a victory in Vietnam? Nothing this mortifying had happened in the war against North Vietnam, a war that, according to most reports, the United States was winning.

The reports, however, were wrong. As if by some grotesque design, one week after the *Pueblo* was captured, all hell broke loose in Vietnam. On January 30 some six hundred thousand troops from the North Vietnamese army and Vietcong guerillas celebrated the Vietnamese New Year, Tet, by staging the most startling offensive of the war. The well-coordinated attack was aimed at seven major urban centers in South Vietnam and caught U.S. and South Vietnamese forces completely off guard, even burning American planes on the ground in Da Nang. Once again the enemy's strength had been grossly underestimated. Although American forces eventually repulsed the North Vietnamese, the damage was widespread. The ancient city of Hue was destroyed. Most of the Mekong Delta lay in the hands of the enemy. The United States Embassy in Saigon had been infiltrated and took nearly six hours to recapture. Following Tet, the North Vietnamese Army and the Vietcong both fought with newfound vigor. Nevertheless, Johnson told his military advisors that the attack had been a "complete failure."

Before Tet most Americans were under the impression that the United States was winning the Vietnam War. This was understandable, since that was the picture presented by the military and generally reported in the media. Tet destroyed this illusion. It was said that when newscaster Walter Cronkite heard of the attack, the normally unruffled newscaster snapped, "What the hell is going on? I thought we were winning the war!" If the *Pueblo* represented the feeling of defeat that was creeping into American society in 1968, Tet represented that and more. Americans were slowly coming to the conclusion that the government and the military had deceived them about Vietnam.

Martin Luther King, Jr., had long come to that conclusion. After the failure of the Chicago movement, King had turned his attention to the plight of the nation's poor; he began to lace his sermons with charges that the government's myopia on the war was ruining any chance of success for the administration's War on Poverty. By 1967, a disenchanted King had completely broken with the administration over the war—a furious Johnson ordered that King never again be invited to the White House. On April 4, 1967, King delivered a riveting speech at New York's Riverside Church. In it, he charged that the United States was in the Vietnam War in order to "occupy [Vietnam] as an American colony" and to gain financial profit. King also called the Johnson administration "the greatest purveyor of violence in the world today."

King's opposition to the war fueled his final project—the Poor People's Campaign, launched in early 1968. On April 4, 1968, King was in Memphis, Tennessee, to lend his support to a strike by that city's sanitation workers. That evening, while standing on the second-floor balcony of the Lorraine Motel, King was shot by a sniper; the bullet smashed into his face and lodged in his shoulder. King was pronounced dead one hour later. Riots broke out in virtually every major American city; Stokely Carmichael predicted that white America would "live to cry that she killed Dr. King."

Close on the heels of King's assassination, students at a major American university demonstrated once again that they were more than aware of this deception. Several factors combined to set off a bloody confrontation at Columbia University in New York in April 1968. One issue, Columbia's housing of the Institute of Defense Analysis, a twelve-college think tank used by the U.S. Defense Department, had been a smoldering concern for some time. A second problem had just made its appearance that spring. Columbia owned several buildings in adjacent Harlem, and the school's administration had decided to raze several of them to erect a gymnasium. The two issues fused, with leaders of the campus chapters of SDS and the Afro-American Society banding together on April 23 to march on the administrative offices in Low Library.

The supposedly unified demonstration soon disintegrated into bitter factionalism. The predominately white members of the SDS occupied the library, taking over the office of President Grayson Kirk. Students drank Kirk's liquor, smoked his cigars, rifled his files, and defecated in his wastebasket. When boredom set in they moved to Mathematics Hall. There they were joined by such luminaries as Tom Hayden, an intellectual icon representing what the student movement had meant at its inception. By this point the African American students, who had been pushed out by SDS, moved across campus to Hamilton Hall, the center of the undergraduate college, where they occupied "their own" building. The protestors were by no means unchallenged by their fellow students. A sizable group of athletes, calling themselves "Students Opposing SDS," dubbed the protestors the "Pukes" and organized an effort to cut off the food supply to the occupied buildings.

The protest ended with violence of a kind that had come to be expected in the course of campus confrontations in the late sixties. On the morning of April 25, early enough so that Harlem would still be asleep, President Kirk called in the police. About one thousand answered the call. The black students in Hamilton Hall surrendered peacefully, but the SDS enclaves had to be stormed. The police arrested 700 students and, flailing their nightsticks, injured 148.

The fury of the late sixties seemed particularly apocalyptic to those Americans who had lived through the Great Depression and World War II. In their eyes the deprivations of the thirties had been far worse than the problems of the sixties. And they believed that the national character had been strengthened, not weakened, by those earlier crises. They had brought their land back from the ashes of economic collapse and had been victorious in the struggle to make the world safe from murderous dictators. As their children blithely wore buttons warning that "You Can't Trust Anyone over Thirty," many Americans of the older generation feared that their values were in danger of being permanently displaced.

For some of these Americans, the problem seemed to be that the country had gotten "soft." Protestors should be jailed or drafted, they felt; violence in the streets should be met with an equivalent amount of counterviolence, and the Vietnam War should be ended with a grand, brutal military stroke. Yet these hardliners, called "hawks" by the press, were as much a minority as were the "doves" who hoped for a societal revolution with instant withdrawal from Vietnam. The vast majority of voters occupied the ideological territory between the hawkish far Right and the dovish far Left. They were in the middle, unable to tolerate the solutions proposed by either extreme. Predominately white, members of all economic classes, and politically active, by 1968 Middle Americans had had enough. They longed to replace the climate of welfare, violence, defeat, and deception with leadership that championed the old-fashioned American values of peace, honor, and honesty. As they geared up for the 1968 presidential election, they searched for a candidate who would reform American and end the political experimentation of the sixties.

Richard Nixon would be that candidate. He had ridden the center to victory throughout his career. His political defeats had come after campaigns in which voters of the Middle had abandoned him; his many political victories, both local and national, had come after campaigns designed to court them. No politician on the national scene in 1968 better understood exactly what the Middle wanted than did Nixon. Indeed, by virtue of both his background and the niche that he had cut out for himself in politics since 1952, he was one of them.

Born in 1913 and reared in southern California, young Nixon was exposed to an excess of religion and discipline but not of money or status. Those who remember him emphasize his scholarly nature, his thoughtfulness, and his love of music and reading. The death of Nixon's youngest brother from tuberculosis in 1925 traumatized his father, who threw himself into revivalist religion as a cure; Nixon, however, reacted with the quiet stoicism of his Quaker mother. No one was surprised when this serious young man signed up for prelaw in high school, telling a classmate that he would someday be a politician. A strong pupil who excelled at rhetoric and debate, Nixon was acclaimed the "best all-around student" at graduation. Yet an expensive college was out of the question. Nixon's eldest brother had also contracted tuberculosis, and his care had drained his family's savings. Nixon had dreamed of attending an Ivy League institution, but he had to settle for tiny Whittier College, a local liberal arts school with ties to the Quaker church.

Nixon's career at Whittier was not easy. He commuted to college while still maintaining a rigorous work schedule at the family grocery store. In his junior year his elder brother died. Despite these difficulties, Nixon's classmates remembered him for his hard work. He stayed on the honor list all four years, won election as class president in his senior year, and continued to excel at debate. He did, however, develop one form of noncerebral recreation. Despite his limited physique, Nixon threw himself into football. Only a third-stringer, he nevertheless was remembered by his teammates for the passion he brought to the game. As an adult he would be an astute armchair quarterback, and watching the game became one of his only forms of relaxation.

The Whittier experience also began Nixon's move away from Quakerism. Nixon's most astute biographer, Stephen Ambrose, noted that at Whittier Nixon developed skepticism for the literal word of the Bible. Nixon himself recalled that after taking a course entitled "The Philosophy of Christian Reconstruction," he approached the Bible from a predominantly symbolic point of view. Nevertheless, several of his teachers viewed Nixon's critical mind as first-rate, and he won a full-tuition scholarship of $250 to Duke University Law School in Durham, North Carolina, in 1934.

Duke was the beginning of a new phase in Nixon's life in many ways. There were new sacrifices as the Depression took its toll. To save money Nixon lived for a time in a tool shed with no stove. Nixon found the work of law school surprisingly difficult and had to admit that although he had long excelled at memorizing facts, he had a difficult time analyzing information and synthesizing it in a legal brief. Unnerved but not intimidated by the requirement that all scholarship students keep a B grade average, Nixon bore down so hard that his fellow classmates gave him the nickname "Gloomy Gus." As usual, his hard work paid off. Once again a superior student, he graduated third in his class and made the law review.

Even more important than the formal education that he received at Duke was the fact that the school was in the South. In California Nixon had for the most part been insulated from racial prejudices. Now both of his roommates were southerners, and he lived and studied in a racially segregated city. His attitude toward African Americans did not change; he was appalled at the way they were treated in Durham. Yet despite this introduction to racism, he found much in the quiet southern way of life in the mid-1930s that appealed to him. Indeed, he developed an affection for southerners that few northern or western politicians of the 1960s would share.

After his graduation in 1937 and a brief job search in New York, Nixon returned to Whittier and joined the law firm of Wingert and Brewley. Business was slow. Nixon did some trial work, but the balance of his time was spent doing routine clerking chores. To fill up his time he quickly found his way into local politics. Nixon became a sought-after speaker on the civic-club circuit, had two short-lived candidacies for city attorney and the state assembly, and campaigned for Wendell Willkie in the presidential election of 1940. Nixon also met Thelma "Pat" Ryan, a business education teacher who had recently graduated from the University of Southern California. After a two year courtship, they married in June 1940.

As a Quaker, Nixon could have applied for an exemption from wartime service as a conscientious objector. Yet he could ill afford to do nothing to help the war effort and still entertain thoughts of a political career. In 1942 he moved to Washington and took a job at the Office of Price Administration (OPA), the agency in charge of wartime price controls and rationing. Nixon was an assistant attorney in the Rationing Coordination Section. This experience was as seminal in Nixon's development as Duke had been. Nixon had his first taste of close work with eastern liberal lawyers, for whom he developed an active distaste, and became convinced that the tinkering with the economy that was being done by the New Dealers was wrong. This was also Nixon's first look at government bureaucracy, and the OPA was a red-tape nightmare. In short, he hated it. In August 1942 Nixon volunteered for service in the U.S. Navy.

Biographers have often mocked Nixon's wartime service, which he primarily performed in the South Pacific, with several stateside stops as well. They have sneered at "Nick's Snack Shack," a stand set up by Nixon on Green Island to serve free food to pilots. They have made fun of the stories of his playing poker to while away the boredom. Yet World War II changed Nixon, as it did other young men from small towns who were suddenly seeing the world. He saw active duty, served with distinction, and received a letter of commendation for his efforts. Like John Kennedy, he was a lieutenant (j.g.), commissioned after only two weeks' training. Unlike Kennedy, Nixon did not face any life-or-death decisions for his men, whom he supervised as they loaded and unloaded cargo planes. Nixon, however, did endure constant shelling, did see death (an airplane crash, from which he helped carry away the bodies), and—most important—did grow up. It is of no small import that Nixon made the final break from Quaker pacifist beliefs in order to go on active duty. For Nixon this decision opened a world that would have been denied him had he not compromised his religious beliefs. The man who returned from the South Pacific was better dressed for the bruises of political battle than he had been before he enlisted.

Nixon wasted no time in parlaying his status as a decorated veteran into political capital. The election of 1946 in California's Twelfth Congressional District has a certain legendary quality. There is no question but that Nixon's campaign against Democratic incumbent Jerry Voorhis was dirty. Nixon falsified the voting record of his opponent, understated the number of bills that Voorhis had introduced, and linked him to a labor political action committee that had disowned Voorhis two years earlier. Yet it was the anticommunist tactic that has become the signature of the election. In an outright lie, Nixon's ads declared that Voorhis's "voting record in Congress is more Socialistic and Communist than Democratic." It is clear that the charges were false and that Nixon orchestrated the attack himself. More important, not only was Nixon unbothered by the smear; he later defended it as good politics. What historian Garry Wills would later label the "denigrative method" of politics—the constant hitting of one's opponents with callous charges, be they fact or fiction, so as keep them on the defensive for the entire campaign—was born.

A common mistake made by Nixon observers is to caricature his entire congressional career as nothing more than a six-year chase after communists. In fact, Nixon was one of the more moderate freshmen to enter the Eightieth Congress after the Republican sweep of 1946. In foreign policy Nixon showed a streak of internationalism that was more attuned to the followers of Michigan senator Arthur Vandenberg than it was to the conservative isolationists led by Ohio senator Robert Taft. Nixon strongly supported the Marshall Plan, and as the most junior member of the House Committee on Un-American Activities (HUAC), he led the successful fight *against* a bill to outlaw the Communist Party. He and Karl Mundt of South Dakota responded the following year with a more moderate bill, but it died in Senate committee. When HUAC investigated charges of communist influence in the Screen Actors Guild, Nixon showed little interest in the witch hunt, attending only one of the sessions that grilled the "Hollywood Ten." These relatively temperate stands flew in the face of the innate conservatism of southern California. Nixon, however, was both popular and influential in his district, largely because his constituent service was excellent. He was returned to office in 1948 by a resounding margin.

Yet it was the Hiss case by which Nixon's congressional career—and according to him, his entire career—was ultimately judged. As with most causes célèbres, symbols are more important than facts. Alger Hiss was an urbane, dapper, witty Ivy Leaguer. He had been at the Yalta Conference as a State Department aide, and at the time of his trials he was president of the Carnegie Foundation on World Peace. His adversary was an editor of *Time* magazine, Whittaker Chambers. Earthy, unkempt, yet a superbly thoughtful writer, Chambers was burdened with a single-minded loathing of communism. The antagonists soon came to represent the two sides of the internal cold war that America was fighting with itself. As Americans learned of Chambers's ostensibly patriotic and cathartic allegations to HUAC that he and Hiss had, among other supposed transgressions, participated in a communist youth group in the 1930s, the battle lines were quickly drawn. Depending on one's orientation, Hiss was either a traitor or a persecuted New Deal intellectual, and Chambers was either a heroic rock turner helping other to find the communists underneath or a vicious character assassin who had co-opted fear of communism as a tool.

The only thing that can be said of this complex and infuriating case with any certainty is that both men were liars. Hiss lied to HUAC about his relationship with Chambers (he had originally insisted that he had never known Chambers, a statement that he was soon forced to admit was false), and Chambers lied to HUAC when he said that his cell had not engaged in espionage (if accepted as authentic, classified State Department documents in Chambers's possession—the "Pumpkin Papers"—confirmed the conclusion that both men were traitors). Yet it was Hiss, after one hung jury, who was eventually convicted on two charges of perjury.

Obviously Nixon stood to reap a political windfall from a successful Hiss hunt. To suggest that Nixon had only justice on his mind would be to reconstruct history inaccurately as well as to downplay Nixon's political acumen, which was in an advanced stage of development. If Hiss was kept on the front page during the 1948 presidential election, Harry Truman would be embarrassed. Nixon had correctly charged that Truman systematically and skillfully suppressed the flow of governmental information to HUAC. Although Nixon's protests did not ultimately cost Truman the election, they did lay the groundwork for charges that would plague Truman through his second term.

More important for Nixon was the publicity from the Hiss case that propelled him into the Senate. His rise had been meteoric. After only two terms in the House, the thirty-six-year-old Nixon had a national reputation, instant name and face recognition, and an issue that continued to make headlines. Indeed, Nixon and others who were stumping on the anticommunist issue were turned into prophets by the June 1950 invasion of South Korea by the communists of the North. He was also the unintended beneficiary of a California Democratic Party that had split itself wide open with a divisive primary, producing a candidate, Representative Helen Gahagan Douglas, of impeccable liberal credentials. Douglas was opposed by virtually all factions in the state, except those on the Left. Nixon was perceived to be ahead during the entire campaign, and he won with 59.2 percent of the vote.

Despite being the front-runner, Nixon used a strategy in this campaign that would set the standard for all smear campaigns to come. With the help of public relations specialist Murray Chotiner, Nixon turned Red-baiting into an art form, berating Douglas's congressional voting record and repeating a previously used campaign slur as he labeled her the "Pink Lady" (Douglas retorted with an even more memorable epithet, calling him "Tricky Dick"). In a direct-mail piece that made political history, Nixon directly misrepresented Douglas's voting record so that it appeared to coincide with the record of radical representative Vito Marcantonio of New York. So that the point could not be missed, the mailing was even printed on pink paper. One can salvage little from the 1950 campaign that is of any moral value. It is all the more perplexing because, as in 1946, Nixon would have won the race easily without using smear tactics.

All stratagems aside, Nixon was now a certified Republican superstar. For two years he spent as much time on the road making speeches as he did on the floor of the Senate. It was inevitable that his name should emerge as a leading candidate for the vice presidency in 1952. He was young, articulate, and acceptable to most of the party bosses; most important, he had a positive reputation as a Red-baiter (as compared with Joseph McCarthy, whose attacks were becoming increasingly wild). With Nixon on the ticket, the Republicans would diminish the chances of a flanking attack by McCarthy against a fellow Republican. Nixon would balance the ticket of either of the two Republican front-runners. Senator Robert Taft of Ohio and General Dwight Eisenhower each wanted Nixon on his ticket, and both men offered him the second spot well in advance of the party's convention. After considering both offers, Nixon cast his lot with Eisenhower.

Nixon's role in the fall campaign grew out of his 1946 and 1950 victories: he would again take the offensive. Nixon was quite successful in this role. His campaign speeches slapped at Democrat Adlai E. Stevenson as "Adlai the Appeaser," who had graduated from "Dean Acheson's College of Cowardly Communist Containment." But Nixon's campaign suffered a nearly fatal blow on September 18 when a *New York Post* headline charged: "Secret Rich Men's Trust Fund Keeps Nixon in Style Far Beyond His Salary." The story was, to put it charitably, a gross exaggeration. There *was* a fund, totaling $18,235, set up by Nixon supporters to help him with his senatorial expenses. However, the solicitation of donations to the fund had been a public matter, and the existence of the fund itself was not kept secret (it was kept in a bank account under the name of Nixon's lawyer, Dana Smith, and Nixon did not attempt to hide the fact when first approached about it by reporters). It wasn't very big, even by 1952 standards, and Stevenson had a similar fund. It was also quite legal. An independent Price Waterhouse audit, commissioned by the Republican National Committee, made this point clear.

But the Eisenhower campaign could not afford to just let the matter drop. Since the convention, all Republican hands, including Nixon, had been relentlessly attacking the scandals of the Truman administration. Nixon's fund had jeopardized a campaign that Eisenhower himself had dubbed a "crusade" against bad government. Most of Eisenhower's aides wanted Nixon to resign. For his part, Eisenhower distanced himself from the disaster, waiting for two days after the *Post* broke the story before contacting Nixon to discuss the issue. The press, which had been largely pro-Nixon since his entry into Congress, began to savage him. Literally overnight Nixon went from young superstar to being completely expendable.

It was a devastating experience for Nixon. This was the first time he had experienced this kind of political rejection, and it was in the midst of his first national campaign. Yet his entire career had prepared him for this moment of emergency. Only a man who had run a campaign like that of 1950 could have survived an attack like that of 1952. Though he knew that he had little support on the Eisenhower train, Nixon gambled. It is of critical importance that he gambled on television; to that point he had used it very little, and he knew little about it. But he turned out to be a natural.

What became known as the "Checkers speech" was actually two speeches in one. In the first part Nixon spoke directly to the voters who had supported him since 1946—the voters of the Middle. As he bared his financial past to a public unaccustomed to such real-life video drama, Nixon invoked sympathy for his plight as a homeowner. He reminded viewers that he too had a mortgage, he too had bills, and his wife wore not mink but a "respectable Republican cloth coat." He was just like them, even to the point of being hounded and persecuted by authority. Nixon did not deny the fund, correctly insisting that it was "not secret," not "morally wrong," and that "not one cent of the $18,000 . . . ever went to me for my personal use." He then moaned that his salary was small and that his wife had to work weekends in the office just to make ends meet. But the clincher that equated Nixon with every middle-class family in America was that he owned a dog. No matter that this little black cocker spaniel, Checkers, was a gift to his children from a Texas supporter; "regardless of what they say about it, we are going to keep it."

While the first part of the speech is the most famous, the second part kept Nixon on the ticket. The senator from California directly challenged the hero of World War II to a political showdown. First he demanded that the Democratic candidates release reports on their finances, as Nixon had just done, but certainly Eisenhower could not be left out of the deal. This was not mere spite but a shrewd political judgment, as there had been rumors about the financial arrangements surrounding Eisenhower's wartime memoirs. Next he yanked the decision on his political future out of Eisenhower's hands. Nixon instinctively knew that he was in better shape with the voters than he was with his party's leadership, so he asked his audience to call or write the Republican National Committee. A flood of letters and phone calls somehow found their way there, even though no address had been provided for them (Nixon's paid time ran out before he could finish the last moments of his speech, and the network cut him off). The question of his guilt or innocence was now secondary. He would have to be kept on the ticket—and was.

A casualty of the Checkers speech was any hope that Nixon might have had for a close personal relationship with Eisenhower. Thanks to the challenge issued at the end of the speech, the two men—despite Nixon's earnest hopes—never became close. That is not to say, however, that Nixon was a failure as vice president; quite the contrary. Appalled by Vice President Truman's lack of preparation at the time of President Franklin Roosevelt's death, Eisenhower strengthened both the office and the expectations of the vice presidency. By statute Nixon already sat on the National Security Council; at Eisenhower's request he also sat with the president's cabinet, attended most meetings between the president and legislative leaders, and chaired several influential commissions. This expanded activity eventually gave Nixon his role as political arbitrator of the Eisenhower administration. He acted as broker between the conservative wing of the party and the more centrist administration, deftly handling, for example, negotiations between Joe McCarthy and the administration while the senator from Wisconsin was raking the U.S. Army over the coals. Nixon was also a key player in negotiations that helped to settle the steel strike in 1960, serving as honest broker between David McDonald of the steelworkers' union and Roger Blough, chairman of

U.S. Steel. Nixon was also the administration's designated campaigner, act-ing as a one-man political surrogate in the off-year elections.

During Eisenhower's illnesses Nixon set the standard for the vice presi-dent's role in a time of presidential incapacitation. He acted with calm and restraint, even refusing to sit in the president's chair during a cabinet meeting although it would have been his right by protocol to do so. After Eisenhow-er's stroke in November 1957, Eisenhower and Nixon dealt with the problem of the void in the law of presidential succession. They privately entered into a pact stating that if Eisenhower was incapacitated or for some reason unable to communicate, Nixon could decide on his own if the president was inca-pable of carrying out his duties. Clearly one does not venture into hyperbole by stating that Nixon and Eisenhower created the modern vice presidency.

By 1960 Nixon's star had risen achingly close to its apex. Then it plum-meted into free-fall, until by 1963 Nixon was treated by most observers as a political has-been. The story of Nixon's 1960 campaign against John Ken-nedy has been told here in chapter 2. It bears repeating that the Kennedy—Nixon debates were not only a watershed event in American political history, but they clearly cost Nixon the 1960 election. Nixon had forgotten the big-gest lesson of the Checkers speech: television works for a politician only if the politician controls it. As we have seen in chapter 2, the debates were a draw, but Kennedy had succeeded in looking presidential—it was the deciding fac-tor in his *razor-thin* victory.

Nixon made it clear on several occasions that he felt he was robbed in 1960. Yet after the election Nixon did not retreat into despondency. Nor, in retrospect, was there any need to. Both his party and his career were still intact. He returned to California, joined a law firm, and wrote the first vol-ume of his memoirs, *Six Crises*. But the lure of politics still tugged at him. Because he had no desire for a rematch against Kennedy in 1964 and his old congressional seat had become safely Democratic, Nixon began to think about running for governor of California. Although he sincerely planned on staying in Sacramento for the entirety of his four-year term, Democrats and anti-Nixon Republicans alike attempted to scare him out of running by charging that he was using the state as a "stepping stone" to a 1964 run for the presidency.

The campaign was a disaster. Incumbent governor Edmund G. "Pat" Brown did not lend himself to attacks. Neither was he a political neophyte; during the Cuban Missile Crisis, Brown had flown to Washington to be seen in his role as vice-chairman of the National Civilian Defense Committee. For his part, Nixon seemed incapable of generating the fire-breathing passion that had typified his earlier campaigns. He was hurt by the "stepping stone" issue, the complicated issue of paying for medical care ("socialized medicine") in California, and fallout from a loan given to Nixon's brother Donald by financier Howard Hughes, ostensibly to start a restaurant—a loan for which Hughes did not demand repayment. The deciding factor in Nixon's defeat, however, was Kennedy's successful handling of the missile crisis. The result was the expected resounding defeat.

Two years of exile from power and two political reversals tormented Nixon. The press had been hounding him since the Hiss case, and although reporters had not caused his loss in 1962, they were certainly reveling in it. Nixon would have done well to heed the advice of his press secretary, Herb Klein, and stay away from reporters the morning after his defeat. But despite Klein's urging, Nixon strode downstairs from his hotel suite and committed what most thought at the time to be political hara-kiri. His opening line— "Now that Mr. Klein has made a statement, now that all the members of the press are so delighted that I lost, I would just like to make a statement of my own"—tipped his hand. The long, rambling talk that followed attempted to explain his defeat and discuss his plans for the future, but its crux was an assault on the press. Nixon claimed that he had "never complained to a publisher, to an editor, about the coverage of a reporter." But he held no hopes that he would be treated fairly that day. "I leave you gentlemen now and you will write it. You will interpret it. That's your right. But I leave you what I want you to know—just think how much you're going to be missing—you won't have Nixon to kick around anymore, because, gentlemen, this is my last press conference." It was, of course, never intended to be his last press conference. It was, however, the first time during the campaign of 1962 that Nixon had been on the attack.

It is doubtful that Nixon was thinking about a run for president in 1968 when he packed up his family in early 1963 and moved from California to Manhattan, but his relocation is easily one of the most important events of the 1968 presidential campaign. In light of his distrust, dislike, and awe of the eastern liberal establishment, Nixon's move can be seen as a rare act of personal courage as well as political shrewdness. He was not only going into a state controlled by his nemesis, Nelson Rockefeller; he was even moving into Rockefeller's neighborhood: he rented an apartment in a building where the governor lived. He was moving into a world unlike any he had lived in before. In New York the emphasis was not on political power but on wealth. His new law firm gave him the opportunity not only to increase his own income but also to meet influential bankers, lawyers, and other men of means who might be potential contributors. Thanks to the generosity of benefactors such as DeWitt Wallace of *Reader's Digest,* Nixon was able to travel widely, visiting many foreign countries where he was accorded head-of-state status. All this would help Nixon in his drive to convince the party that he was no longer a political albatross.

Perhaps more important was the fact that Nixon learned to truly love New York. He lived there for almost three years as a political expatriate, using the temperament of the city to prepare him for his reentry into presidential politics. It matured him. Many of those who observed Nixon during this period have since commented on his tendency to read more, to discuss more, to laugh more, and to listen more. He was more accessible to reporters and, within the bounds of their mutual suspicion, more open with them.

Nixon began his 1968 campaign during the 1966 congressional campaign. He used the off-year election to begin mending his public image and dealing with the "he can't win" attitude. Nixon traveled over thirty thousand miles and visited eighty-two congressional districts in a whirlwind campaign for Republican hopefuls. The ideology of the candidates for whom he was speaking meant less than the fact that he was storing up political IOUs. The perfect example of this tactic was Nixon's vocal support of Rockefeller in his uphill but ultimately successful reelection battle. The 1966 election was a victory both for the party—it picked up forty-seven seats in Congress—and for Nixon. He had helped his entire party, not just one wing of it, and he had received valuable political exposure in the process. The exile had come to an end; Nixon was back.

The presidential campaign of 1968 was conducted under a pall of violence. The war dominated the primary campaigns, and assassination once again invaded the political process. Small wonder that by the time of the conventions, the nation was already exhausted by the process.

It had long been clear that the financial cost of Johnson's Great Society programs, as well as his single-minded policy of victory in Vietnam, had lost him the support of voters of the Middle. Yet the search for a Democratic candidate who could carry the center was a particularly frustrating one. The doves flocked to the banner of Senator Eugene McCarthy. The soft-spoken Minnesotan was an enigma in politics. On one hand, he was accompanied on his campaign—for no other reason than his own intellectual stimulation—by poet Robert Lowell, and he continually made it clear that ending the war was more important than his own political fortunes. On the other hand, his drive in New Hampshire and Wisconsin to unseat a sitting president was a thing of political beauty. The organization of his student minions—thousands of clean-cut youngsters (anyone who needed a haircut was firmly asked to leave) pounding on thousands of Democratic doors—gave McCarthy a close runner-up finish in New Hampshire. Polls predicted a clear McCarthy victory over Johnson in Wisconsin. Yet despite these early successes, McCarthy possessed too liberal a reputation to seriously hope to carry the Middle. He had, however, scarred Lyndon Johnson, thus setting the stage for a candidate who had a true chance of carrying the Middle.

Robert F. Kennedy—the epitome of active emotion—entered the race in March because he felt McCarthy was unelectable even if Johnson was toppled. Bobby Kennedy was a human bridge between the doves who supported the antiwar stance that he had been taking since his 1964 election to the Senate and the cold war hawks who had cut their diplomatic teeth with Harry Truman and perfected their craft with Kennedy's brother John. With enough political skill to avoid being terminally tied to either wing, Kennedy had the best chance of winning the nomination. Johnson saw the handwriting on the wall, and after Kennedy's entry into the race, Johnson withdrew. Like his brother before him, Bobby had a true chance of riding the center to victory. His June 1968 assassination, moments after he had claimed victory in the California primary, threw the Democrats into turmoil.

With McCarthy's campaign disintegrating, and Kennedy dead, the situation was made to order for Vice President Hubert Humphrey. During the campaign Nixon would often call Humphrey a "sincere, dedicated radical." Perhaps this description had been true twenty years earlier, but not in 1968. Humphrey, whose virulent pro–civil rights speech to the 1948 Democratic convention had so inflamed the South that its delegates walked out and formed a new party, had mellowed into a man of rather narrow vision. He had been a good party man since 1948 and had been a consistent supporter of Johnson's policies in Vietnam. Throughout the 1968 campaign, Humphrey was perceived, with a great amount of justice, as Lyndon Johnson's candidate. It was the inevitability of his nomination after the Kennedy assassination that played a large part in drawing thousands of disaffected youths to the Chicago convention for a protest, which quickly turned into a bloody street brawl with police. Despite the swirling pace of events around him, Humphrey persisted in calling for an absurd-sounding "politics of joy." The Left despised him. The Right could not forget his past. More than anything in 1968, the Middle wanted to clean house and get rid of any taint of Johnsonism in Washington.

That made disaffected Democrat George Wallace surprisingly appealing to the Middle. As noted in chapter 3, Wallace had built for himself a comparatively progressive record during his two terms as governor of Alabama. However, his refusal to allow two black students to register at the University of Alabama was the cornerstone of a racially demagogic strategy that Wallace knew appealed to most white Alabamians, and he hoped it would be the stepping stone to a presidential run from the right. There was no question that Wallace's 1968 candidacy, running at the head of the renegade American Independent Party, had no hope of outright victory. His best hope was to throw a close race into the House of Representatives. Nevertheless, Wallace's message was undeniably appealing to much of frustrated Middle America. As he grumbled about students on northern campuses, whom he typified as "damn uncultured, ignorant intellectuals," baited those same students into shouting matches during his speeches, and promised that if "some anarchist lies down in front of my automobile, it's going to be the last automobile he lies down in front of," he became a folk hero to blue-collar workers in every part of the nation. Much like Joseph McCarthy in 1950s, Wallace touched the deep resentment that many workers held against the "big shots." As he fought government, he was fighting the good battle for the little guy. But the violent racial overtones of his rhetoric kept even larger numbers of the Middle outside the South from supporting Wallace. Most could not get past the promise in his 1963 inaugural address to defend "Segregation now! Segregation tomorrow! Segregation forever!" It was this fact that kept Wallace from capturing the Middle; while many privately grumbled in agreement with his histrionics, they would never vote for him.

However, simply because the Democrats could not propose a candidate who excited the Middle did not mean that the Republicans would win it by default. The Goldwater debacle of 1964 had left Republicans with a bad taste in their mouth. More than anything else, they were looking for a man who could win the election.

In his superb study *The Making of the President, 1968,* Theodore White refers to the "inevitability" of Richard Nixon. Certainly in one sense that is true. The challenges of Michigan governor George Romney, Nelson Rockefeller, and California governor Ronald Reagan were hardly challenges at all. Yet that should not obscure a key point in Nixon's success in 1968: Nixon was the only candidate, except for Robert Kennedy, who seemed even to care about carrying the Middle. In speech after speech he reassured the Middle that he had heard them and was ready to lead their rebellion against the sixties. The Middle heard and heeded. It was ready to flock to the banner of any leader who promised not total victory, not peace at any price, but peace of mind. Despite Nixon lore, he did not *come* back in 1968; he was *brought* back by a massive segment of America that was plotting to overthrow Johnson's Great Society. Nixon would channel the discontent of this group, which he would soon label the "Silent Majority," and win his party's nomination for the presidency.

The war in Vietnam loomed large as an issue that could easily destroy the candidacy of either Nixon or Humphrey. Polls consistently reported an interesting dichotomy. Most Americans disapproved of the way Johnson was handling the war, but at the same time the majority of Americans did not want to stop the bombing of North Vietnam. By 1968 the safest thing that could be said about the Vietnam issue was that it had become completely unpredictable. It had long since defied traditional political or demographic explanation.

Despite the unstable nature of the issue, both Humphrey and Wallace hit Vietnam hard during the campaign. Wallace *wanted* to talk about the war; a strong hawkish line fit nicely with both his overall strategy and his rhetorical style. Wallace's choice for a running mate, former member of the Joints Chief of Staff General Curtis LeMay, went even further than Wallace when he advocated "bombing North Vietnam back to the Stone Age." Humphrey, however, *had* to talk about the war. He was faced with the dilemma of having to separate himself from Johnson without losing the support of pro-administration war hawks in the process. The result was a compromise strategy on Vietnam that ended up appealing nicely to the Middle. On September 30 in Salt Lake City, Humphrey pledged that he would end the bombing of the North if the communists would restore the demilitarized zone between the North and South. It was not enough war to satisfy the Right and not enough peace to satisfy the Left. It was, however, the light at the end of the tunnel for the Middle. Immediately after the talk, Humphrey soared in the polls.

Nixon did not have an administration to please; nor did he see any political value in calling for immediate victory. As a result, he took no chances. For all intents and purposes Nixon voiced no Vietnam policy throughout the campaign. When he did talk about it, he hinted that he had a way out but claimed that he should not jeopardize any chance for peace by prematurely discussing his plans. In a 1985 televised interview, Nixon admitted that he had no plan, secret or otherwise, to end the war; it had all been a smokescreen. In the long run, however, it didn't matter. The Middle could not reject Nixon for his stand on the war as it had Johnson—it didn't know what Nixon's stand was.

Instead of Vietnam, Nixon chose to center his campaign on an issue that was by his reading the key concern of the Middle—the question of law and order. Actually, given the events of the sixties, the issue was more a *lack* of law and order. The rioting in the streets of Chicago during the Democratic convention there had galvanized the issue. Chicago was, in microcosm, the dilemma of violence the Middle had faced throughout the sixties: blood in the streets, and no one could figure out whom to blame. The Middle had watched both the protesters and the cops run amok for the last time. Eight years of Democratic rule had brought only war and chaos. Wallace was too impulsive to be trusted. The Middle turned to Richard Nixon to be calm but firm.

That he was in 1968, and more. In his acceptance address to the Republican convention, Nixon announced that his attorney general would "open a new front" against crime. Nixon was on the offensive with the issue from the opening week of the fall campaign. No one missed the symbolism of his giving his first major speech in Chicago, and he noted later with some satisfaction that the "contrast with the bitter confrontation that Humphrey was now tied to could not have been greater." As Humphrey struggled with Vietnam, Nixon stepped up his rhetoric on law and order. A key facet of this strategy was a merciless attack on Johnson's attorney general, Ramsey Clark, as being soft on crime to the point of negligence of duty. Another was his subtle slurring of Earl Warren's Supreme Court, which he treated as the ultimate symbol of softness toward alleged criminals.

Nixon's skillful media campaign effectively managed the law-and-order issue. Nixon hated the idea of being a packaged candidate, but the experience of 1960 had taught him the value of controlled television exposure. Harry Treleaven, a New York advertising consultant, developed a television campaign that completely ignored Nixon's stands on the issues and concentrated instead on developing an image of the candidate as calm, confident, and thoughtful. Nixon's political advisors disliked this strategy, preferring to show Nixon as having meaningful stands on the issues. However, Nixon supported Treleaven, and image won out over substance. Two of Treleaven's techniques were particularly fruitful. The first was a new twist on a campaign staple: the question-and-answer session. Nixon stood in the middle of bleachers that completely encircled him; he took questions from an audience that surrounded him. The concept of the "man in the arena" gave the impression that even while surrounded by accusers and questioners, Nixon was calm and thoughtful, the perfect man to deal with chaos. The second method was an imaginative series of television commercials that showed graphic still pictures of horrors in American streets. Nixon narrated the commercial without being seen on screen. The message given was that these scenes were not Nixon's doing, but his deep baritone voice calmly promised to cure these ills.

Humphrey's Salt Lake City speech had cut Nixon's lead in half. On his own, however, Humphrey would never have closed the gap. It took the power of the incumbency to tighten the race into a dead heat. On October 31 Johnson announced that the bombardment of North Vietnam would cease from 8:00 A.M. the next day and that peace talks would begin in Paris on the day after the elections. The gap between Humphrey and Nixon closed overnight, but Nixon stuck to his strategy of staying away from Vietnam. Instead of attacking Johnson for what was most likely pure political opportunism, Nixon presented himself as a statesman. In a speech at Madison Square Garden the day after Johnson's announcement, Nixon proclaimed he would not "say anything that might destroy the chance to have peace." Three days later, after being secretly promised by a Nixon go-between that he would fare better under a Nixon administration than under a Humphrey presidency, South Vietnamese president Nguyen Van Thieu announced that his nation would not participate in Johnson's negotiations. The shift to Humphrey bottomed out, as did the Middle's hopes for an end to the brutality in Vietnam.

In his scathing 1969 essay *Nixon Agonistes,* journalist and historian Garry Wills postulates that the results of the 1968 election were determined by a "nihilist vote" on the part of an exhausted America. According to Wills, the country had ignored its traditional values and beliefs and had voted *against* Humphrey rather than *for* Nixon. Certainly there was a national sigh of relief that Johnson was leaving the White House. Indeed, 28 percent of Democrats who had voted for Johnson in 1964 voted for Nixon in 1968. The election was a hairline decision, with Nixon winning by only 0.7 percent of the popular vote—the smallest percentage of the national vote since Woodrow Wilson's victory in 1912. The final vote count gave Nixon 31,785,148 (43.4 percent), Humphrey 31,274,503 (42.7 percent), and Wallace 9,901,151 (13.5 percent). Nixon received 301 electoral votes, Humphrey 191, and Wallace 46. Not only was there a gain in Democratic governors; Nixon would be the first president in 120 years to begin his administration with the opposition controlling both houses of Congress.

Yet this should not deny Richard Nixon his victory. As Humphrey talked about the war and Wallace made threats, the law-and-order strategy established Nixon as the candidate of the Middle. The Republicans ran well in the suburbs, the first such showing since Eisenhower. Nixon's campaign was strong enough to survive even the last-minute scare of Johnson's bombing announcement, showing a resilience of planning that it had not shown in 1960. The low-key confidence of the candidate was an unexpected asset.

The difference in Nixon's victory was clearly his surprising success in the South. White southerners deserted the Democratic Party in droves. One might add Johnson to this analysis; by 1968 the South detested Johnson's Great Society and Johnson's war with a virulence that was found in a few other areas of the country. It is not surprising that Nixon, whose entire strategy revolved around a promise to reform Johnsonism, did so well in the South, despite the presence of Wallace in the race. Although there was a rise in the number of southern ballots, the Democrats carried only 31.1 percent of the total vote in the South, some two-thirds of which was made up of black voters. In the Deep South Humphrey won only Texas; Wallace captured the rest. Nixon, however, won the border states of Virginia, Tennessee, and Kentucky, as well as North and South Carolina. The stage was set for the Republican Party to adopt what Nixon campaign staffer Kevin Phillips, in his influential 1969 book, *The Emerging Republican Majority*, would call "the Southern Strategy." Once the Wallace phenomenon had spent itself, as analysts such as Phillips were confident that it would, a major realignment was possible in American politics—a permanent Republican majority.

The task that awaited the new president was hammered home to him on Inauguration Day 1969. On the way back from the Capitol after Nixon had delivered his inaugural address, the presidential parade drove through a throng of protestors some three blocks long. They threw stones at Nixon's car, chanted epithets, and hoisted a North Vietnamese flag. Nixon recalled the scene in his memoirs in words that might well describe his plans for reforming Johnsonism: "I was angered that a group of protestors carrying a Vietcong flag had made us captives inside the car. I told the driver to open the sun roof and to let the other agents know that Pat and I were going to stand up so the people could see us."

The sixties were over.

Recommended Reading

The literature on Richard Nixon is vast. The best biography remains Stephen E. Ambrose's multivolume *Nixon* (New York: Simon and Schuster, 1987, 1989, 1991). The opening chapters of Melvin Small's superb *The Presidency of Richard Nixon* (Lawrence: Univ. of Kansas Press, 2003) help to set the stage for his administration. More so than most American presidents, Nixon himself *must* be read: of his nine books *Six Crises* (New York: Doubleday, 1962) and *Memoirs* (New York: Grosset and Dunlap, 1978) most directly address the events of this volume. On the Columbia uprising, see James Simon Kunen, *The Strawberry Statement: Notes of a College Revolutionary* (New York: Random House, 1968). One of the most thoughtful views of 1968 is Garry Wills, *Nixon Agonistes: The Crisis of the Self-Made Man* (New York: New American Library, 1969); Lewis Gould's survey of the election, *1968: The Election That Changed America* (Chicago: Ivan R. Dee, 1993) remains the standard. The reader may also wish to consult the next book in this series, Stephanie Slocum-Shafer, *America in the Seventies* (Syracuse: Syracuse Univ. Press, 2003), which opens with an interpretation of the rise of Nixon, and John Robert Greene, *The Limits of Power: The Nixon and Ford Administrations* (Bloomington: Indiana Univ. Press, 1992).

Index